# 185
# Inspirational Daily Devotions

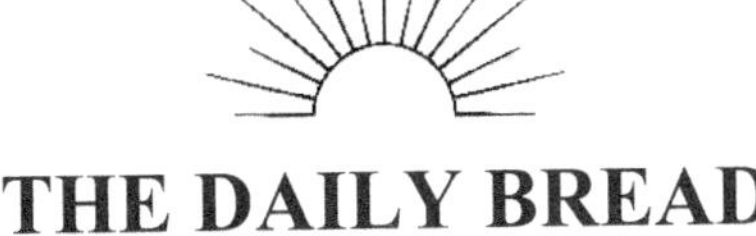

# THE DAILY BREAD

You dodged a bullet. You must praise God that you did not get that job, did not get married to that person, did not get that tender, maybe you lost a job, a broken promise, you did not get that promotion, your business closed down, and your life somehow become stagnant. There is something that you really liked and thought it's the real deal, but it never came your way, or you lost it, God let it happen because it was a weapon which was going to be used by the devil to take you away from your destiny. I also remember I went to interview for at certain company, but I was not considered for that position. The recent news I heard is that the company was closed some time ago. There is no need to mourn over about people who left you, job opportunities and business deals you missed God was protecting you. Tell yourself praise God I dodged a bullet. There is certain lady at church who wanted to be married to this guy. She did everything to make the guy notice her at church but alas he married another girl. 2 years down the line that guy passed on. God did not allow her to be married to this guy because of saving her for the future heart break. We serve a jealous God who does not allow us to go through certain things. "The steps of a good man are ordered by the LORD: and he delights in his way" (Psalms 37:23). Sometimes we make our own plans but at the end of the day, we will get back to God's plans. Your life is not an accident. Those things were not yours; God has the best for you. One day you will thank God for not getting those things when the best things have come to you. Samuel mourned a lot when God rejected Saul as a king, but God had the best replacement in David, a man after God's heart. "And the LORD said unto Samuel, How long will you mourn for Saul, seeing I have rejected him from reigning over Israel? fill your horn with oil, and go, I will send you to Jesse the Bethlehemite: for I have provided me a king among his sons."(1 Samuel 16:1) Do not mourn about the past seek God he will take you to your to destiny. By keeping on holding on to Saul, we are delaying David to come in our lives. God is in control have peace even in a storm. There is a lady who went to a minibus rank to get transport home. It was raining. When she arrived, she was soaking wet. The minibus was full, and she asked the driver if she can fit in. The driver said ask the passengers. The passengers said no. The minibus left her, and she took the next one which quickly filled up. When she was about to get home she saw that minibus that left her was involved in an accident and it's on fire. People were trapped inside. Where you are it's a perfect position, you are neither too late nor too early just be still and know he is Lord. Trust God that he has your back. Don't be disappointed with missed opportunities just know that they were not meant to be for yours. God bless you.

**Prayer**

Thank you Lord for blessing us with a wonderful life. Help us not to compare our lives with other people. Teach us on waiting on you as your word says, "But those who wait on the LORD Shall renew their strength; They shall mount up with wings like eagles, They shall run and not be weary, They shall walk and not faint." As your word says, "Trust in the LORD with all your heart, And lean not on your own understanding;" we shall put all our trust on you. We confess that, all things are working together for good for us because we love you God, and we are called according to your purpose". Amen


**Bible Verses to study**

Psalms 37:23; 1 Samuel 16:1; Isaiah 54:17; 2 Thessalonians 3:3; Psalms 41:1; Deuteronomy 31:6; Isaiah 41:10; Psalms 34:7; Psalms 32:7

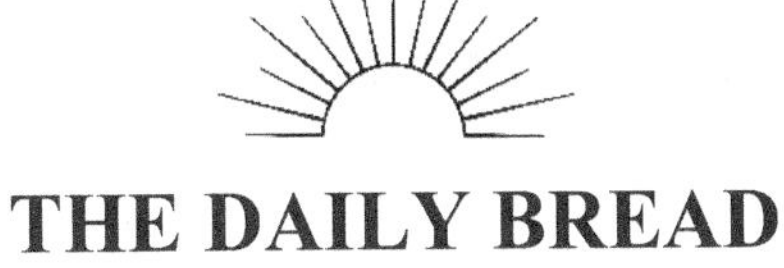

# THE DAILY BREAD

Let God be God in your life. Shadrack, Meshach, and Abed-Nego were taken into captivity. Israel was in captivity. They were living in foreign land. Shadrack, Meshach, and Abed-Nego were taken on King Programme as noble young men to be taught the language and serve before the king. They saw how the army of Israel was defeated, their relatives killed, and property looted. They had a reason to think that God hand abandoned them. Their gift of negotiation made them not to eat king's delicacies but to be fed with fruit and vegetables so that they do not get defiled. Nebuchadnezzar the king made an image of Gold, and the word was sent out to the whole of Babylon that at the sound of the music everyone should fall down and worship the golden calf. Whoever does not fall down and worship, shall be cast immediately into the midst of a burning fiery furnace. Shadrack, Meshach, and Abed-Nego refused to bow down. For example, it's easy for a child to say I do not want to clean the plates when the mother is not around. Just imagine when the mother is around and the child to say I can't clean the plates, there will be consequences. They were given a second chance and called before the king. The Kings were known to keep their word and not go against it. They knew the consequences of refusing the king's orders. Looking at the fire and looking at the king, a rational person would have said I want to worship the golden calf. They had a reason to do so because in their memory, it still lingers on how they were taken into captivity that God had abandoned them. Why they will trust on this God who had abandoned them? Again, the fire took time being made and there was a third chance to change their mind. There was no sign that God will help them. It's difficult these days to find people who will continue with God's will even if they do not see the hand of God in what they are doing. People are now moved by sight than by faith. I love how Shadrack, Meshach, and Abed-Nego the way they answered the king. "If that is the case, our God whom we serve is able to deliver us from the burning fiery furnace, and He will deliver us from hand, O King. But if not, let it be known to you, O King, that we do not serve your gods nor will we worship the golden image which you have set" (Daniel 3:17-18). The king was so angry that fire was heated seven times. Shadrack, Meshach, and Abed-Nego knew what the fire can do that it burns. They did not have history of anyone who survived after being through into the fire and came out with not even smelling the smoke . Yet they believed on God. We must stop thinking on how God should run our lives and put our demands. God is a Sovereign God. Have you ever known of a child who tells his/her father when are you going to buy groceries? A child will always expect a father to buy grocery and their duty is to just open the cabinet. They trust their father. Why do we want to control God and pray in a way that God must follow us. We want to tell God we know better than you. My life should go like this. If God does not want me to drive that car its fine, if he wants to wait for my healing, it's okay and if he wants me to wait for my life partner a little be longer it's okay. We must have faith on God, God is leading us, and he knows what he is doing. "Be anxious for nothing, but in everything by prayer and supplication, with thanksgiving lets your requests be known to God" (Philippians 4:6) Today let God be God in your life. "Then King Nebuchadnezzar leaped to his feet in amazement and asked his advisers, "Weren't there three men that we tied up and threw into the fire?" They replied, "Certainly, Your Majesty." He said, "Look! I see four men walking around in the fire, unbound and unharmed, and the fourth looks like a son of the gods." Nebuchadnezzar then approached the opening of the blazing furnace and shouted, "Shadrach, Meshach and Abednego, servants of the Most High God, come out! Come here!" So Shadrach, Meshach and Abednego came out of the fire, and the satraps, prefects, governors and royal advisers crowded around them. They saw that the fire had not harmed their bodies, nor was a hair of their heads singed; their robes were not scorched, and there was no smell of fire on them. Then Nebuchadnezzar said, "Praise be to the God of Shadrach, Meshach and Abednego, who has sent his angel and rescued his servants! They trusted in him and defied the king's command and were willing to give up their lives rather than serve or worship any god except their own God." (Daniel 3:24-28) If God wants you to go through the fire, it's okay because he promised us that he shall never leave us nor forsaken us. God bless you.

## Prayer

As your word says, "Be anxious for nothing, but in everything by prayer and supplication, with thanksgiving lets your requests be known to God", we still believe in power of prayer and when we pray God you answer our prayers. Your word says, "But those who wait on the LORD Shall renew their strength; They shall mount up with wings like eagles, they shall run and not be weary, they shall walk and not faint." If God, you want us to go through the fire, let it be because you promised us that you shall never live us nor forsaken us. Today we pray to let God be God in our lives by us surrendering our will to him. Your word says, "And we know that all things work together for good to those who love God, to those who are the called according to His purpose." If God is for us who can be against us. His grace is sufficient for us. Amen

## Bible verses to study.

Daniel 3:16-28; Deuteronomy 31:6; Exodus 14:10-31; Philippians 4:6; Daniel 6:10-23; James 1:2; 1 Corinthians 10:13; Romans 8:28; 1 Samuael 17:1-58

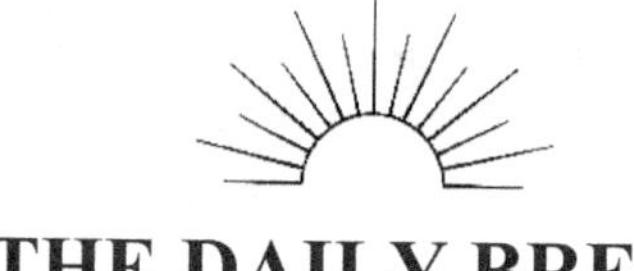

# THE DAILY BREAD

After victory. The enemy wants to attack you in your most vulnerable time. That is after your victory. After our prayers have been answered we rejoice and forget the basics. We lower our guard. Sometimes an accomplishment in life may end up harming you than blessing you. Now you have lot of money, driving a big car and have a great source of income, instead of you seeking God more, that money have given you wings and more muscles to sin more. You can afford things you could not afford before and it makes you blind to forget where you came from. I heard stories where the families were happy when they were just getting by but as soon as more income came people ended up divorcing. This money was meant to bless a family, but it become like a curse. Some people, you may never know who they are, until they get hold of that cheque. Their character comes out and you will wonder if it is that the same person who you always knew. We cannot afford to relax. Now my prayers have been answered, I do not need to pray as I did before. You begin to worship the blessing more than God. You become like untouchable. It feels like you did it yourself and you don't even need God anymore. Excitement can lead you to drawback. No matter how successful you become, prayer should be still important in your life and reading the word. Remain rooted in Jesus Christ. Do not compromise. Seek God more and let the fire keep burning in you. My prayer is after we get blessed, let us live a life that will not cause God to regret why he gave us that car, that money, house, that business, that company, promotion and that job. Amen. The blessings should draw you closer to God than drive you to hell. That's why some people always experience problems in life it's because if they do not have those problems, they do not seek God. "Bless the LORD, O my soul, and all that is within me, bless his holy name! Bless the LORD, O my soul, and forget not all his benefits, who forgives all your iniquity, who heals all your diseases, who redeems your life from the pit, who crowns you with steadfast love and mercy, who satisfies you with good so that your youth is renewed like the eagle's. The LORD works righteousness and justice for all who are oppressed. He made known his ways to Moses, his acts to the people of Israel. The LORD is compassionate and merciful, slow to get angry and filled with unfailing love." (Psalms 103:1-8) God bless you.


## Prayer

We pray that after we get blessed, we should live a life that will not cause God to regret why he gave me that job, that car, that money, house, that business, that company, promotion and that job. We will never worship a blessing but you God. Help us O Lord to keep the fire burning both during the times of lack and abundance. We pray that the blessings you give us should drive us closer to you not driving us to hell. Your word says "Bless the LORD, O my soul, and all that is within me, bless his holy name! Bless the LORD, O my soul, and forget not all his benefits, who forgives all your iniquity, who heals all your diseases, who redeems your life from the pit, who crowns you with steadfast love and mercy, who satisfies you with good so that your youth is renewed like the eagle's. The LORD works righteousness and justice for all who are oppressed. He made known his ways to Moses, his acts to the people of Israel. The LORD is compassionate and merciful, slow to get angry and filled with unfailing love." Amen


## Bible verses to study.

Psalms 103:1-8; Revelations 3:15-16; Mathew 26:41; 1 Peter 5:8; Proverbs 4:23

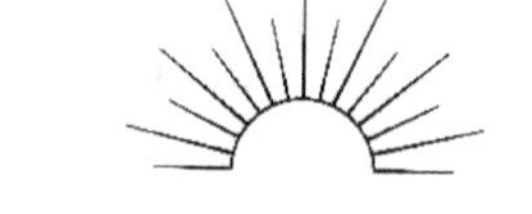

# THE DAILY BREAD

Bangle. There is man who loved bangles. He saw a small snake and put it as a bangle on his hand. It was very beautiful. He knew that snakes are dangerous, but he loved bangles. He kept the snake. He loved the snake and kept on feeding it. It was very beautiful. It looked very innocent. It grew until he made a belt of it. One day it was hungry, and its nature took over it and it bite him. The man died because of the snake bite. Sin maybe small at the moment. If you entertain it in life one day, it will grow. The nature of sin is death. "For the wages of sin is death, but the gift of God is eternal life in Christ Jesus our Lord" (Romans 6:23) It might be nice, sweet and fun but stay away from sinful life, it will destroy you. It will start to control you. The sin which we entertain in our lives it start so small, so beautiful, so sweat and so innocent. Everyone is doing it; I am not robbing anyone and one day I will stop. Let me warn you one day is one day. The nature of sin is death. Sin will grow that you become a prisoner and you are under bondage. Before you know you are no longer coming to church, you lost your family and everything in your life. The devil is a liar our bodies are temples of the Holy Spirit. The devil makes us believe it's the only way for us. We lose self-esteem. We are dead whilst we are living. We give up on life. We settle for the second best. Obedience is better than sacrifice. If we leave, we should not go back to ways of darkness. Please let's spend time reading the word and praying. We need to have a disciplined prayer life. Never give a place to the Devil. Do not forsake the gathering of the saints. When you take a piece of wood out of the fire the fire on it gradually fades away. Let's come to all the meetings of the church and keep the fire burning. We know about our family members and people in the world at large who lived life of glorifying their sinful nature and where are there now. Their lives were ruined and ruined other people's lives. No one deserves to die because of a drunk driver, and no one deserves to be in prison, but their crimes put them there. "For the love of money is a root of all kinds of evil. Some people, eager for money, have wandered from the faith and pierced themselves with many griefs." (1 Timothy 6:10). Just know that "For there is nothing hidden that will not be disclosed, and nothing concealed that will not be made known and brought to light." (Luke 8:17). The devil lies to you that you can jump into the swimming pool and never get wet. Crime does not pay. The consequences of sinful life outweighs the benefits of sin itself. "And what do you benefit if you gain the whole world but lose your own soul?" (Mark 8:36). God bless you.

.

**Prayer**

Your word says, "Therefore we also, since we are surrounded by so great a cloud of witnesses, let us lay aside every weight, and the sin which so easily ensnares *us,* and let us run with endurance the race that is set before us," The wages of sin is death, we pray that we shall never live a sinful life. Your word teaches us that, "If we say that we have fellowship with Him, and walk in darkness, we lie and do not practice the truth." You word says, "My grace is sufficient for you, for My strength is made perfect in weakness." Therefore, most gladly I will rather boast in my infirmities, that the power of Christ may rest upon me. Your word teaches us that, "What will it benefit me to gain this world and lose my soul." Amen

**Bible verses to study**

Romans 6:23; 1 Timothy 6:10; Luke 8:17; Mark 8:36; 1 Peter 5:8; John 10:10; 2 Corinthians 6:14; 1 Corinthians 15:33; Romans 16:17; Deuteronomy 7:2-4; Psalms 1:1; Psalms 26:4; Proverbs 1:10

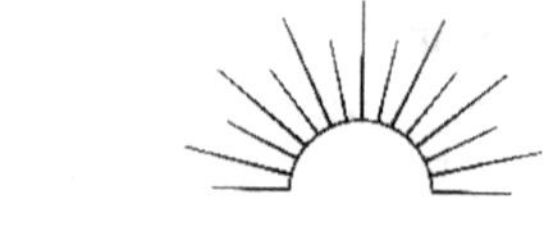

# THE DAILY BREAD

Aspire to grow. You were of this world but now you are in the world and not of this world. The worldly life needs to go. God said through Apostle Paul "I fed you with milk and not with solid food; for until now you were not able to receive it, and even now you are still not able; "(1 Corinthians 3:2). Salvation is freely given but for your faith, you need to work on it. "Therefore, my beloved, as you have always obeyed, not as in my presence only, but now much more in my absence, work out your own salvation with fear and trembling" (Philippians 2:12) For a fruit tree to grow, it needs to be watered, add manure and cultivated. The work must be done otherwise it may fail to grow. When was last time you fasted? When was last time you read your bible? When was last time you attended cell and church. When was the last time you praised and worshipped God? We cannot rely on yesterday's glory or anointing, we need to seek God daily. "Do not be conformed to this world but be transformed by the renewing of your mind. Then you will be able to test and approve what is the good, pleasing, and perfect will of God". (Romans 12:2) God want to show you great and mighty things, but you need to change your lifestyle. You must look ahead not back again. You cannot keep the yesterday manna, its spoilt let go daily get the fresh one. You have tasted manna, it's great but God have so much better waiting for you in the Promised Land. My prayer for you is God to open your eyes and see how the devil is robbing you by living an ungodly life. God has the best for you; do not let the devil rob you. Never settle for less than what God has promised you. The devil is giving you a soup in exchange of your birthright. You will never gain by living a sinful life but it's a loss. "But seek you first the kingdom of God, and his righteousness; and all these things shall be added unto you" (Matthew 6:33). We need to live for God first and everything will be added to us. How many times you have put trust on money, and it disappointed you, people and they changed their minds and even you, but you failed yourself. Today put all your trust in God, live a life worthy the calling you received. Spiritual growth needs you be deliberate about things of God. You need to plan about your prayer time, time to the read word, budget for offering and tithes. You need give yourself targets and stick to them. It's a sowing and reaping principle, if you sow nothing, you will reap nothing and if you sow bountifully, you will reap bountifully. God bless you.

**Prayer**

We pray that Lord we grow spiritual so that we do not live a worldly life and be able to experience the life that God has set before us. Salvation is freely given but for our faith, we need to work on it. As your word says, "Therefore, my beloved, as you have always obeyed, not as in my presence only, but now much more in my absence, work out your own salvation with fear and trembling", we shall work on our faith with fear and trembling. Help us O Lord to work on our faith daily as your word says "Do not be conformed to this world but be transformed by the renewing of your mind. Then you will be able to test and approve what is the good, pleasing, and perfect will of God". We pray that we shall seek you God in our lives first as you say, "But seek you first the kingdom of God, and his righteousness; and all these things shall be added unto you". We shall never rely on yesterday anointing, we shall seek you God daily. Amen.

**Bible verses to study**

1 Corinthians 3:2; Philippians 2:12; Romans 12:2; Matthew 6:33; Ephesians 4:11-16; 2 Peter 3:18; 1 Corinthians 3:1-3; 2 Thessalonians 2:13; Hebrews 4:12

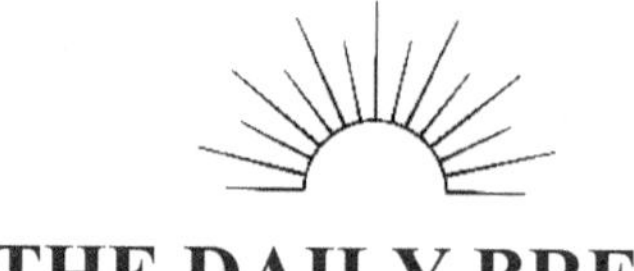

# THE DAILY BREAD

Living in the past. Have you heard people tell you these wonderful stories but when you look at them now it's no longer believable? If you live a sinful life your glory days will be in the past. People will tell you that I used to have a lot of money, own lot of cars, to be a manager and own businesses. They blossomed for a while and their glory faded away. Their future was robbed by devil through ill-gotten gains. The word of God says "The thief does not come except to steal, and to kill, and to destroy. I have come that they have life, and that they have it more abundantly" (John 10:10). Whatever you compromise for, you will lose it. Easy come, easy go. Life of crime does not pay. Samson compromised and married Delilah a philistine and he lost his power. He also lost his sight, and his glory was now in the past. The devil is in your life to steal, kill and destroy you. When we look at the story of prodigal son it shows us the effects on living a sinful life. He thought it was fun but in fact it was death. He ended up eating the pig's food. People it's not worth it. Sin it's not cheap but in fact it's very expensive, some pay with their lives, so it a daylight robbery by the devil. "There is a way which seems right to a man, but it's end is the way of death" (Proverbs 12:14). Let's not live like the world does because it will bring destruction in our lives. "Then the LORD said, "The outcry against Sodom and Gomorrah is so great and their sin so grievous." (Genesis 18:20). The lifestyle of people in Sodom and Gomorrah brought destruction upon their lives. "Do not be deceived: "Evil company corrupts good habits." (1 Corinthians 15:33). Are your friends driving you to hell or to heaven. The reason why you cannot prosper in your life maybe its attached to the company you keep. If you spend more time with criminals you may end up involved in crime, if you spend more time with who like swearing, you will end up swearing yourself and if you spend more time with people who are prayerful, you may end up being prayerful. Sinful life is a way of the devil to rob us the blessed life God prepared for us. Anytime you think about going back to your sinful life just remember you about to get robbed. God bless you.

**Prayer**

You called us from darkness into marvellous light and we shall never dwell in darkness again. As your word says, " Do not be yoked together with unbelievers. For what do righteousness and wickedness have in common? Or what fellowship can light have with darkness?", we shall never have fellowship with darkness. Your word says "The thief does not come except to steal, and to kill, and to destroy. I have come that they have life, and that they have it more abundantly". Your word says, "Be sober, be vigilant; because your adversary the devil walks about like a roaring lion, seeking whom he may devour". Lead us O Lord as your word says, "There is a way which seems right to a man, but it's end is the way of death". Amen

**Bible verses to study.**

John 10:10; Proverbs 12:14; Genesis 18:20; 1 Corinthians 15:33; Proverbs 14:12; Judges 16:1-31; Proverbs 3:7; Galatians 6:7; Genesis 25-29-34

# THE DAILY BREAD

The old man. "You were taught, with regard to your former way of life, to put off your old self, which is being corrupted by its deceitful desires; to be made new in the attitude of your minds; and to put on the new self, created to be like God in true righteousness and holiness. "(Ephesians 4:22-24). It was easy for God to take the Israelites out of Egypt but very difficult to take Egypt out of them. The time for them to move out of Egypt was very short but changing their way of thinking took so many years. God has called us from darkness into marvellous light. We are used to our former life. Our reference and experiences are linked to our past life. Darkness is all what we knew before we were saved. It does not work automatic like a switch that when you press it, up comes the light. We are naturally conditioned and programmed to sinful life by the world we are living in. Sin it's not something you are holding that you can drop it but something that is in you. When we got saved, our Spirit got saved but our body was not. My beloved in Christ the day you got saved was not the end of the road but the beginning of journey of moving away from what we are used to; moving to where God has promised us. The problem with us Christians is that when we come to Christ, we forget that the body is not saved. We forget that we need to work on our body. The putting off the old man is not easy and it takes time. Many Christians have come to Christ but even after so many years, they are still putting on the old man. Now false Christianity is promoting mediocrity life that if you come to church is all that you need and fail to teach people how it is important to work on their faith. The devil is comfortable with us if we come to church and after that we commit adultery, steal, go clubbing, drink alcohol, watch pornography and fail to the read the bible and pray. I know my identity, so I am no longer living anyhow. I am working on my faith with fear and trembling. Its lie that's living a sinful life its normal brother and sister repent. You cannot serve two masters. My fellow Christians are finding it difficult to change because they are fighting this fight in the flesh. The word of God says, "For we wrestle not against flesh and blood, but against principalities, against powers, against the rulers of the darkness of this world, against spiritual wickedness in heavenly places" (Ephesians 6:12) Children of light, let's take this fight into spiritual realm through prayer and fasting. Finally, "Do not conform to the pattern of this world but be transformed by the renewing of your mind. Then you will be able to test and approve what God's will is--his good, pleasing and perfect will" (Romans 12:2). God bless you.

**Prayer**

We pray that we do not treat the day we got saved as our final destination, we keep the fire burning in our lives to know more about you God and growing spiritual. Your word says, "work on your faith with fear and trembling". As your word says, "You were taught, with regard to your former way of life, to put off your old self, which is being corrupted by its deceitful desires; to be made new in the attitude of your minds; and to put on the new self, created to be like God in true righteousness and holiness", help us O Lord not to keep holding on our sinful past life so that we can move into the life you have promised us. Our faith shall never fail. As your word says "Do not conform to the pattern of this world but be transformed by the renewing of your mind. Then you will be able to test and approve what God's will is— his good, pleasing and perfect will", we will keep on studying your word so that our faith can grow. Amen

**Bible verses**

Ephesians 4:22-24; Ephesians 6:12; Romans 12:2; 2 Corinthians 5:17; Galatians 2:20; Galatians 5:16; Jeremiah 17:19; 2 Peter 1:4; Romans 7:18

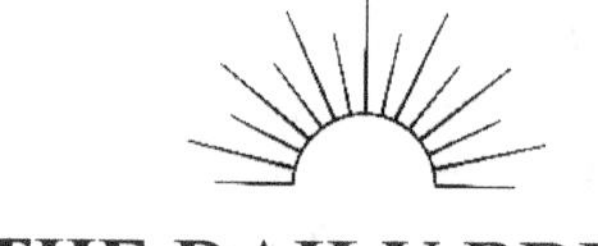

# THE DAILY BREAD

And no one puts new wine into old wineskins; or else the new wine will burst the wineskins and be spilled, and the wineskin will be ruined" (Mathew 9:17). When Jesus started his ministry here on earth, he faced a lot of challenges but not from unbelievers but from the people who said they knew God. The people had been accustomed to certain of way of living life. The Pharisees could not handle a change. The Pharisees they thought they knew everything thereby depriving themselves opportunities to learn. How many times do people value traditions more than the word of God? God want to move and do greater things in our lives but because as long as we remain religious, we limit God's power over our lives. The woman at the well told Jesus "Our fathers worshiped on this mountain, and you Jews say that in Jerusalem in the place where one ought to worship". Jesus said to her "Woman believe me, the hour is coming when you will neither on this mountain, Jerusalem, worship the Father. "You worship what you do not know; we know what we worship, for salvation is for the Jews. But the hour is coming and now is when true worshipers will worship the Father in spirit and the truth, for the Father is seeking such to worship Him" (John 4:20-23) . Lots of traditions, human created boundaries and old systems are hindering the spread of the gospel. The old wineskins need to be changed; we really need the new ones to preserve the new wine. We should yearn for the presence of God than fulfilling our traditions. Our level of worship should not be tailor made to suite the usual. Something has no to change, they should be a great shift in the Spirit, the old wineskins need to be replaced by new wineskins. We need to move with God than religious way of doing things. God bless you.

**Prayer**

As your word says "Do not conform to the pattern of this world but be transformed by the renewing of your mind. Then you will be able to test and approve what God's will is—his good, pleasing and perfect will," we pray that we shall never be religious, but we will worship God in the Spirit and the truth. Teach us your ways O Lord. Your word says, "I will give you a new heart and put a new spirit in you; I will remove from you your heart of stone and give you a heart of flesh". We are more than convinced that, the Spirit of him who raised Jesus from the dead is living in us, he who raised Christ from the dead will also give life to our mortal bodies because of his Spirit who lives in us. Amen

**Bible verses to study.**

Isaiah 43:19; Mathew 9:17; John 4:20-23; Mark 2:21

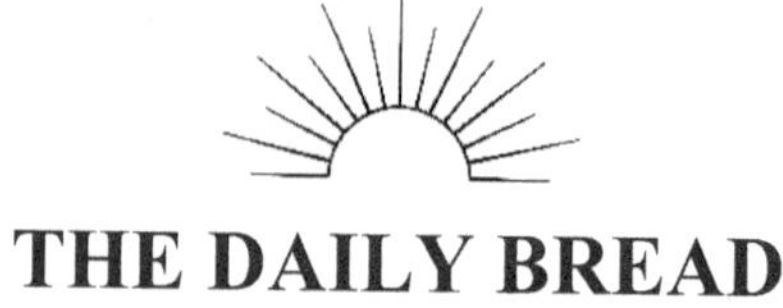

# THE DAILY BREAD

The River Flowing Out of Eden. Have you ever looked at the size of the human head and considered how much information it could keep? How about the size of the foot and the agility of the human body? What about those dancers who seem to execute their fancy moves with amazing precision. Indeed, we are all created with astounding capabilities. However, it is unfortunate when we focus on the things that we DON'T HAVE and then conclude on the quality of our lives and everything associated with it, based on what we DON'T have. You were created with more sophistication than the Garden of Eden which was watered by a river flowing FROM it. As the Bible says, "Now a river went out of Eden to water the garden, and from there it parted and became four riverheads." (Genesis 2:10 NKJV) In other words, the Garden of Eden was more of a SOURCE of water than a place needing water. As you look at yourself in the mirror, think about the astounding blessings that you have been given by God. Look at all the miracles around your life; count your blessings, naming them one by one. Find time to appreciate God then you will see the river of life flowing out of your belly. You are amazing! God bless you.

**Prayer of the day**

We thank you God for the abilities you have given us. We are wonderfully and fearfully made in the image of God. The grace of God is sufficient for us. We acknowledge that those who are with us are more than against us. Christ in us is the hope of Glory. We are more than a conquerors through him who gives us strength. Amen

**The bible verses to Study**

Genesis 2:1; Genesis 1:27; Psalms 139:14; Ephesians 2:10

19

# THE DAILY BREAD

Airtime. When we make phone calls, we rely on the airtime in our phones. When the airtime is too much in our phones, we can call anyone, we do not mind. But when the units are very little, we phone people who we value most. Because the airtime is limited, it limits us on who to call. The 24 hrs we have in a day is our airtime. The 24 hrs look like much, but they are limited. The way we spend our day and who we spend with, it shows how we value them and how we value an activity. When you value God and on your 24 hours day you do not sacrifice at least one hour of your airtime on things of God it's cheating. Which means there is someone who you value more than God? When you love someone, you need spend time with them, how do you say you love God if you cannot spend time with Him? Your time is limited but you need to sacrifice. Some people they go to work and when they come back, they watch soapies and sleep. They are too busy for God. Where your treasure is that's where your heart is. If your treasure is in world, you will not have time things of God. People who always give excuses are not yet ready for the kingdom. I challenge you to use your airtime on things of God. Do not just feed your flesh but your spirit too. Some people are just working for their flesh but what about your soul. Your flesh we remain here on earth and your soul go to God or hell. Most of the things which eat our airtime, they corrupt our lives, they stunt our growth, and they stop us to reach what's God wants with our lives. I challenge you once again to value your airtime. Life is too short. There is not time to waste. When you eat the right food amen the result will show. Jesus said I am the bread of life. The devil robbed my airtime in past, I loved the world too much. That was shown by the channels I watched on TV but now I know my airtime belongs to God and I value it. Also, you must watch out who is eating your time. Some people are not worth your airtime. There is no relationship between darkness and light. The devil can use people to steal your airtime. If Jonah was not thrown in the water, the boat was going to sink. Take the Jonahs out of your boat. You shall stay in the presence of God and produce much fruit. God bless you.

**Prayer**

We thank you God for the grace of our Lord Jesus Christ. You called us from darkness into marvellous light for a reason to shine the light to those who are still sitting in the darkness. Your word says, "Delight yourself also in the LORD, And He shall give you the desires of your heart." Jesus, you spared our souls, whilst we were a sinners Jesus Christ you died for us. Help us live for you Lord and forsake our evil our ways. We pray that we shall serve you Lord alone for all the days of our lives and dwell in the house of the Lord forever. As your word says, "Do not love the world or the things in the world. If anyone loves the world, the love of the Father is not in him," we shall count the lifestyle of the world as loss so that we can gain Christ.

**The bible verses to study.**

1 John 2:15; Mathew 4:8: Romans 12:2; James 1:27; Mathew 6:24; James 4:4

# THE DAILY BREAD

Dark side. Whitney Houston had a dark side. She was one on the best sellers and sold million copies of albums, but she was drug addict. She always thought, she is in control. Even if someone would have told her that drugs will kill you one day, she would have laughed it off. There was an interview she did with Oprah and said she is clean for one year. She said the drug problem is over but in the near future drugs killed her. The pollution caused by drugs destroyed her life. My dear family evil is still around, and its purpose is to kill destroy and steal. Her child also later died because of drugs. The world has darkness and Jesus is the true light. Jesus is the way; Jesus is life and Jesus is our saviour. Neither give a place to the devil. Families are destroyed, lives lost, and people are in jails because of substance abuse. Let's bring light to those still sitting in the darkness. Most of the people come to church but are still battling with the dark side. The devil is holding you back because of the dark side. You need to understand that the wages of sin is death. "There is a way that seems right to a man, but its end is the way of death." (Proverbs 14:12). That sin you entertain in your life may lead you to your demise. Its looks too insignificant but it will grow one day and control you. The word of God says, "Then Jesus said to His disciples, "If anyone desires to come after Me, let him deny himself, and take up his cross, and follow Me" (Mathew 16:24). You can't be discipled if you can't deny yourself. Your old self need to die. The word of God says, "I have been crucified with Christ and I no longer live, but Christ lives in me. The life I now live in the body, I live by faith in the Son of God, who loved me and gave himself for me." (Galatians 2:20). You can never be fruitful if you have a dark side. You can blossom for a while but because of sin in your life, you get choked and bear no fruit. It's not the talent that will keep you on top but the character. If you live ungodly life you will live in the past. I used to be married, I used to have money and I used to be manager, then what happened, the devil robbed you because of your sinful life. The word of God teaches us to never give a place to the devil. God bless you.

## Prayer

As your word says, "The thief comes only to steal and kill and destroy; I have come that they may have life and have it to the full," we shall never entertain sin in our lives. We were robbed by devil now it's enough as your word teaches us that, "neither give a place to the devil. Like Paul, "I have been crucified with Christ and I no longer live, but Christ lives in me. The life I now live in the body, I live by faith in the Son of God, who loved me and gave himself for me." Your word says, "If anyone desires to come after Me, let him deny himself, and take up his cross, and follow Me". There is nothing good about our past and our hope is in Lord Jesus who gave us a new life. Amen.

## Bible verses to study.

Proverbs 14:12; Mathew 16:24; Galatians 2:20; Romans 5:12; Mark 9:13; Romans 6:23; Galatians 6:7-8; Isaiah 59:2; Ezekial 18:20; 1 Peters 2:1-25

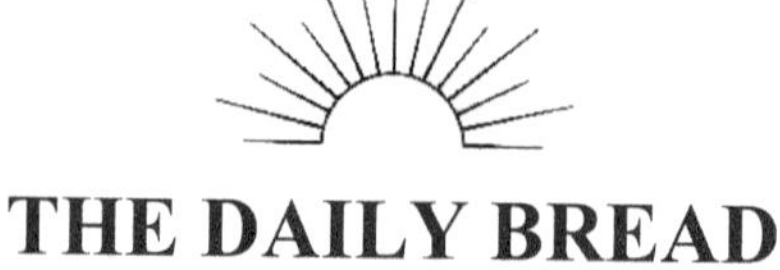

# THE DAILY BREAD

'Wait patiently for the Lord. Be brave and courageous...' (Psalms 27:14). It's in looking back that we realise: (1) God had something better in mind for us. (2) We weren't mature enough at that point to handle what we were asking Him for. We think we're ready, but God knows when we are. Scripture often commands us to 'wait on the Lord'. Learning to wait is a test of maturity. People find it difficult with life if they can't instantly gratify every desire. They want to eliminate every discomfort, difficulty, injustice, or deprivation instantly. Scripture responds with two revolutionary concepts: heavenly mindedness and delayed gratification.' Waiting forces, us to accept that we're not in control. It humbles us in ways we need to be humbled. Consider the trapeze artist: for a split second, which must feel like an eternity, he or she is suspended in nothingness. They can't go back, and it's too soon to feel the grasp of the one who'll catch them. They must wait in absolute trust. You may be at that same point in your life right now. You've let go of what God called you to let go of, but you can't feel His hand catching you yet. Moses waited eighty years for a ministry that lasted forty years: two–thirds of his life was spent getting ready! Jesus spent thirty years preparing for a ministry that would last three–and–a–half years. From God's perspective, your life isn't measured by its length, but by its effectiveness and its impact for His Kingdom. So, wait, and keep a good attitude while you're doing it. God won't disappoint you. God bless you.

**Prayer**

As your word says, "Trust in the LORD with all thine heart; and lean not unto thine own understanding", we pray that Lord we have faith and trust that you will answer my prayers. Give us wisdom and courage and to keep holding on to the word of the truth. Let us not depart from your word neither left nor right and believe you are the one who rewards those who seek you diligently. For we are your workmanship, created in Christ Jesus unto good works, which God has before ordained that we should walk in them. Thank you, Lord Jesus, for answering our prayers, you have turned our mourning in dancing. Amen.


**Bible Verses to study.**

Romans 12:12; Isaiah 40:31; Lamentations 3:25; Psalms 27:14; Habakkuk 3:2; Romans 12:12; Luke 24:49; Genesis 8:10-12

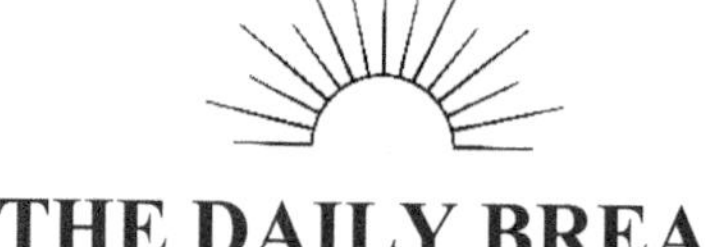

# THE DAILY BREAD

Stop running away from your problems but start solving them. Problems are part of life so we must learn to deal with them. Jesus did not promise us that our lives will be smooth sailing without problems. Have you noticed people who move from one relationship to another, from one job to another, from one marriage to another and from one country to another, they keep on moving. Some people can be married 5 times in their lifetime. Hey no one is perfect, and you too are not perfect too. The problems you ran away from, you will meet them again and then you ran away again until it becomes a pattern in your life. If left not checked, you will spend the rest of life running away. Then you will form a career of running away. They say that the grass is always greener the other side. Things will not remain the same, sometimes we will go through wonderful times and other times we will go through the suffering times. We can't rely on what we feel. You cannot wake up in the morning to those who are married and tell your wife that I feel that I do not love you or I do not feel married. I encourage you to have the character that I will be there in both in good times and in bad times. If you want to live life when things are going the way you like always, you may have to change the planet maybe. I pray for you to withstand every temptation to run away from your problems, the Holy Spirit to give you the power of endurance, God to give you strength to stay and reap the fruit of your faithfulness. If you plant today and tomorrow you change your mind and uproot the plant and plant it again somewhere and again and again, I promise you that harvest time will never come. Learn to wait and put faith on God even if nothing is happening, God is faithfully he will make your dreams to come forth. God will restore you. Qualities needed in trials "So then, my beloved brethren, let every man be swift to hear, slow to speak, slow to wrath; for the wrath of man does not produce the righteousness of God" (James 1:19-20). I will be fine just trust in the Lord. God bless you.


**Prayer**

As your word says, "For God has not given us a spirit of fear, but of power and of love and of a sound mind," we are not afraid of what the devil is going to do because of our faith in God. Weeping may endure over night, but joy comes in the morning. Your word says "Cast your burden on the LORD, And He shall sustain you; He shall never permit the righteous to be moved. As your word says, "The steps of a good man are ordered by the LORD, And He delights in his way", order our footsteps Almighty God. Holy Spirit lead us as those who are led by the Spirt are the sons of God. We pray that God you can grow our fruit of patience and be able to wait upon you. We will stand on your word O Lord that says "And let us not grow weary while doing good, for in due season we shall reap if we do not lose heart" Amen.


**Bible verses to study.**

James 1:19-20; 2 Timothy 2:22; Psalms 139:7; Psalms 46:1-2; John 3:16; 1 Corinthians 6:9-11; 2 Tomothy 1:17

# THE DAILY BREAD

You are part of the Problem. Have you noticed that people move from one marriage to another and always blame the other partner. They move from one Church to another, one job to another, one relationship to another. If you ask someone after he/she break up with a partner, most of the times they will blame the other partner. So, you are a saint and perfect. No one is perfect. Its high time for you to realise that you are not perfect and start to accept other people who are imperfect. If you don't accept that you are imperfect, you will always run away from problems. Accept that you are part of the problem. Adam after sinning, he blamed Eve for eating the fruit. Let's us be accountable. If you blame others, you will not fix your problems. Are you still looking for a perfect person to marry, perfect job, perfect marriage and perfect Church? My advice is that there nothing like that. You will always be on the move until Jesus Christ comes back or you die. The person who told you that you are perfect was sugar coating you. Next time if someone tell you so much bad things about their previous Partner, Church, Job and nothing good, just know they will be on the move again very soon. Today learn to fix your problems, running away won't solve the issue. If you see that they was a problem, why did you resolve it? The grass is always greener on the other side. The word of God says, "Why do you look at the speck that is in your brother's eye, but do not notice the log that is in your own eye?" (Mathew 7:3). If you want to see change in life, it must start with you. You are part of the problem, allow God to fix you so that he can open your eyes to see your shortfalls. If you think you are a saint, get married, your wife or husband with show you your shortfalls. We are all not perfect that's why we need a perfect God in our lives. Let's take life as a learning curve, we accept where are wrong, we learn, move on and do not repeat the same mistakes. God bless you.

**Prayer**

God grant me the serenity to accept the things I cannot change; courage to change the things I can; and wisdom to know the difference. Living one day at a time; enjoying one moment at a time; accepting hardships as the pathway to peace; taking, as He did, this sinful world as it is, not as I would have it; trusting that He will make all things right if I surrender to His Will; that I may be reasonably happy in this life and supremely happy with Him forever in the next. Amen.

**Bible verses to study.**

Mathew 7:3; Mathew 6:34; John 16:33; Psalms 71:20; Proverbs 4:23; Job 5:8; Job 14:1; 1 Corinthians 13:1-13; Isaiah 40:31

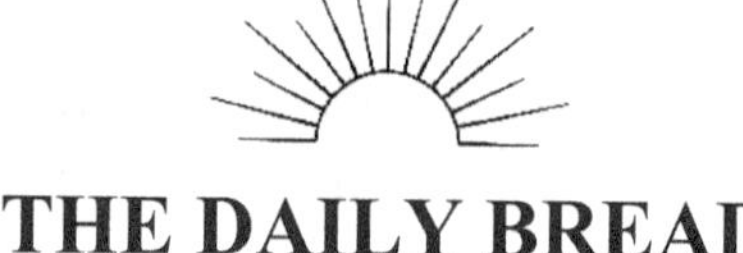

# THE DAILY BREAD

Nothing can satisfy you except Jesus. Well, we live life of chasing; jobs; cars; houses; women; men, and all the fine things in life. Have you prayed to God for a car, house, job, husband and wife but you find yourself with those things but still so much unhappy? You thought Lord if I can be married my life will be complete, if I can get a job all my problems will be gone and if I can win lotto my life will be super. But the word of God says seek first the kingdom of God and his righteousness all the things shall be added unto you. (Mathew 6:33) We are chasing after the wrong things and now we will never be satisfied. The world has blinded us and corrupted us and set value on material things. What are we chasing after today? "The word of God says" "Do not store up for yourselves treasures on earth, where moths and vermin destroy, and where thieves break in and steal. But store up for yourselves treasures in heaven, where moths and vermin do not destroy, and where thieves do not break in and steal for where your treasure is, there your heart will be also." (Mathew 6:19-21). Are you living an empty life? Are you moving from relationship after relationship, job after job, marriage after marriage and career after career? You do not have peace and joy in life because you do not have Jesus in your life. Jesus said the Samaritan woman at the well the water I give you will make you never thirsty again. The devil has robbed your time, money and people in your life by make you a prisoner of material things. The word says that there is way that seen right to men but at the end it leads to death. Its high time we should pray and let God save us from all the evil of the world. The word of God says, "For the love of money is a root of all sorts of evil, and some by longing for it have wandered away from the faith and pierced themselves with many griefs." (1 Timothy 6:10) The devil traps us with materials things. Instead of chasing God, we chase after money. There is a void which only God can fill in our lives but without God we fill with other things like drugs, alcohol, love of money, gambling, pornography and unhealthy relationships. Only God who should fill this void. It's either filled with God or other things.

**Prayer**

As your word says, "But seek first the kingdom of God and His righteousness, and all these things shall be added to you," we pray that we should not seek after material things and seek after God first. Your word says, do not store up for yourselves treasures on earth, where moths and vermin destroy, and where thieves break in and steal. But store up for yourselves treasures in heaven, where moths and vermin do not destroy, and where thieves do not break in and steal for where your treasure is, there your heart will be also." Your word teach us that, "Above all else, guard your heart, for everything you do flows from it." Your word says, "Delight yourself also in the LORD, And He shall give you the desires of your heart. Your word says, "Do not love the world nor the things in the world. If anyone loves the world, the love of the Father is not in him." Amen

**Bible verses to study.**

Mathew 6:33; Mathew 6:19-21; John 4:1-42; Mathew 4:4; Isaiah 58:11; Psalms 16:11; Psalms 17:15; Psalms 37:4; Philippians 4:11-12; Romans 15:13

# THE DAILY BREAD

Sharing. There are those who live life for themselves and others they live life for other people. People like Mother Theresa and Nelson Mandela lived life not for themselves only, even now their legacy continues. If you can live life for yourself only, it's good to have the best of life but when you die who will remember that this man had a house in Sandton and driving a Ferrari. Please I am not against people making it in life and enjoying their success, but I am Illustrating a fact that when you invest in yourself its only good for you. Being rich is a blessing from God. People who really invested in other people's lives and lived a selfless life left a great legacy here on earth. People will still remember you for your good works, the lives you touched and changed. Those people who help others live a fulfilled life. If you want God to intervene in your situation, start by helping other people. By helping others to overcome their problems, God will also help you to overcome your problems. I would personally not be impressed with myself to go and give a testimony to say God blessed with a jet whilst people in the Ministry I am involved with are so poor that they can even afford to pay school fees or buy food. God will bless me one day amen. I do not want to live life for myself only, I want to live for other people. Even people who are not from my family when I die, they must feel a great loss in their lives. It hurts me when we have platforms to make other people's dreams to come true and fail to do so. Let's us triumph not only in our dreams coming true but seeing other people's dreams come true too. Let us be an answer to other people's prayers. God to use us to express His love upon His people. There is too much self in this world, I pray that I die to myself so that the power of God can be revealed through my life. "But mark this: There will be terrible times in the last days, People will be lovers of themselves, lovers of money, boastful, proud, abusive, disobedient to their parents, ungrateful, unholy, without love, unforgiving, slanderous, without self-control, brutal, not lovers of the good, treacherous, rash, conceited, lovers of pleasure rather than lovers of God—having a form of godliness but denying its power. Have nothing to do with such people." (2 Tomothy 3:1-5) God bless you.


## Prayer

We pray that we die to ourselves so that the power of God can be revealed through our lives. Let us prioritise in helping others so that we can live a fulfilled life. We pray that we have passion to empower and open platforms to help others to fulfil their dreams. Let's us triumph not only in our dreams coming true but seeing other people's dreams come true too. Let us be an answered prayer to someone else. Amen.


## Bible verses to study

2 Tomothy 3:1-5; Mathew 7:15; 2 Thessalonians 3:6; 1 Timothy 4:7; 1 Timothy 5:8; Ephesians 4:14

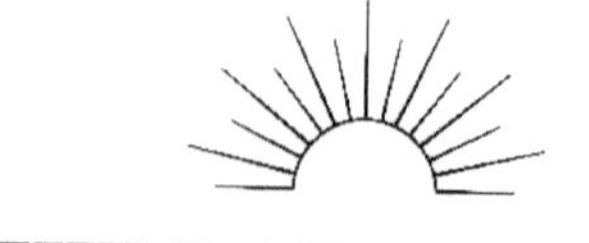

# THE DAILY BREAD

The presence of God. "Then Moses said to him, "If your Presence does not go with us, do not send us up from here" (Exodus 33:15). Moses did not want to reach the Promised Land without the presence of God. Moses was content to stay in the Wilderness with the presence of God than to get to the Promised Land without God's presence. The children of Israel only wanted to be in the Promised Land and did not mind about the presence of God thus why they complained too much and rebelled against God along the way. Moses through his experience in the presence of God, he knew that if he arrived in the promised land (the land flowing with milk and honey) without the presence of God; he was going to be worse off than to be in the wilderness with the presence of God. May God grow us that we do not live life of wanting? Some people their faith is attached to money, houses, cars and jobs. They do not realise they are worshiping money. Their prayer life is always God I need a house, God I need money, God I need car and God I need promotion. God told us to ask from him through his word, but we are to seek him first. We cannot put the material things ahead of our love of God. What happens if you do not get that job; that car; that tender and that house, will you still worship God. The problem is when we come to Christ, we still use the worldly standards to value our lives that if I do not drive this car I am not blessed and if I do not earn this money, I am not blessed. I advise you that if you buy that car without that presence of God, you are worse off than you were before, if you buy that house without the presence of God, you are worse off than you were before and if you earn that money without the presence of God, you are worse off than you were before. The presence of God is our top priority and without it we are doomed. The word of God says, "But seek you first the kingdom of God, and his righteousness; and all these things shall be added unto you" (Matthew 6:33). The problem is that in our natural, we do not know what will happen in future, we look at our current situation and then conclude our life but if the Holy Spirit can reveal to us our future it will never bother us where we are now. Let's crave for the presence of God in our lives. Do not let your present predicament drive you from the presence of God. Maybe you have trusted God for something, and it did not materialise, I urge not go back to your previous life. God has not forgotten about you; He is the same God who raised Lazarus from the dead on the fourth day. Do not compare your life with other people, you may look at them and see how well dressed they are and admire their lives but outside they may look glamorous but inside its unstable like they are volcanoes erupting in them. If you can only know what they are going through, you will never swap your life with them. David after he had sinned, he asked God not to take away his presence from Him "Do not cast me from your presence or take your Holy Spirit from me" (Psalms 51:11). Today I urge you to do everything to seek the presence of God and stay in the presence of God. God bless you.


**Prayer**

There is the presence of God in our health, in our marriages, in our finances, in our homes, in my businesses, at our workplaces, in my families and in our children's lives. Everything that we do in our lives like Moses, "Then Moses said to him, "If your Presence does not go with us, do not send us up from here", may your presence go with us everywhere. As your word says, "But seek you first the kingdom of God, and his righteousness; and all these things shall be added unto you", we pray that we shall seek you first almighty God. Whatever happens, like David, "Do not cast me from your presence or take your Holy Spirit from me". "The steps of a good man are ordered by the LORD, And He delights in his way." Amen.

**Bible verses to study.**

Exodus 33:14-15; Matthew 6:33; Psalms 51:11; Psalms 97:5; Psalms 95:2; Isaiah 41:10; Psalms 23:4

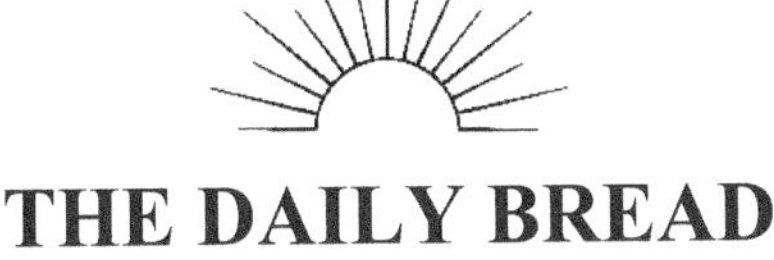

# THE DAILY BREAD

They may take away everything from you but if they haven't taken your ability to pray, then they have done nothing, because you shall rise again! They took away Samson's eyes, they took away his hair and strength, but they forgot to also take away his ability to pray, when he cried out to God his power was restored. Jonah in the belly of the fish also cried out to God and the Lord restored his ministry. Peninah laughed at the bareness of Hanah until she prayed!!!! Prayer changes things no wonder David says I look up to the mountains, from where does my help come from, it comes from God the maker of heaven and earth. I encourage you today to engage God in prayer...You shall rise again, you shall also testify, your vision will also speak, you shall also be celebrated... if there is a man to pray, there is a God to answer!!! God bless you.

**Prayer**

Your word says, "Do not rejoice over me, my enemy; When I fall, I will arise; When I sit in darkness, The LORD will be a light to me." Weeping may endure over night, but joy comes in the morning. Your word says, "He raises the poor from the dust and lifts the beggar from the ash heap, to set them among princes and make them inherit the throne of glory. "For the pillars of the earth are the LORD's, And He has set the world upon them". Your word says, "Confess your trespasses to one another, and pray for one another, that you may be healed. The effective, fervent prayer of a righteous man avails much." Your word says, "Be anxious for nothing, but in everything by prayer and supplication, with thanksgiving, let your requests be made known to God;" Amen.

**Bible verses to study.**

Mark 11:24; Philippians 4:6-7; James 5:16; Mathews 6:6; Jeremiah 33:3; Psalms 145:18; Mathew 6:9-13; 2 Chronicles 7:14; James 5:13

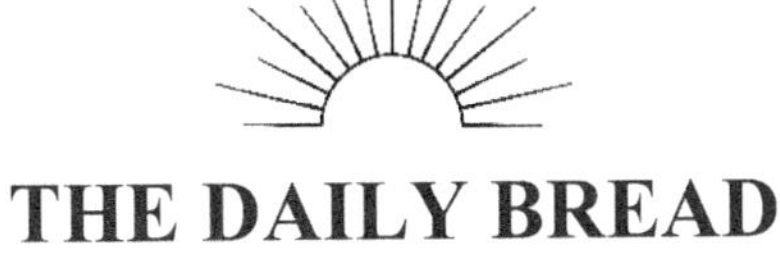

# THE DAILY BREAD

Just for a bowl of soup. Esau sold his birth right to Jacob just for a bowl of soup. The excuse he gave was I am hungry and about to die so what is the birth right to me. The word of God says "...... Thus, Esau despised his birth right" (Genesis 25:34). People sometimes they do not want to wait so they choose instant gratification. They want something now but do not care what it would cost them. We are asking you today that what is your value system. People ruined their lives because of short cuts. It's better to suffer now and have a bright future than enjoy your life now without a future. Ask yourself that is God in it or not. "So, I say, walk by the Spirit, and you will not gratify the desires of the flesh" (Galatians 5:16). You cannot stop birds to fly over your head, but you can stop them to lay eggs on your head. I encourage you to value your life as a believer in Christ Jesus. Whatever you have if you do not value it, you will lose it. Do not make decisions because it pleases your flesh and ignore the consequences. Just that sinful desire entertained and acted upon, may cause a person to regret for the rest of their lives. People are paying with their lives in prisons, stuck in debt, involved in bitter divorces and have lost everything. The reason being that they lacked self-control. Today do you value your freedom, do you value your marriage, do you value your life and do you value your salvation. May you be led by the Holy Spirit and do not be partakers of the works of flesh. The word of God says my people are destroyed for lack of wisdom. The reason why we live an unrighteous life is because we do not understand the consequences. Our flesh urges distract us to see the full picture. You can't live in a moment. We need to understand the principles of sowing and reaping. "Do not be deceived, God is not mocked; for whatever a man sows, that he will also reap". (Galatians 6:7). People who live ungodly life live in the past, I used to have cars, houses, money, career and family. Evil life does not last and in the world, they say crime does not pay. God bless you.

## Prayer

Help us O Lord to make rightful decisions. We pray against the spirit of instant gratification but let us have patience to wait upon the Lord. We shall work on our success and not take short cuts because easy come, easy goes. We shall not compare our lives with others and not convert what others have because we know that God you have the best life for us. Your word says "So, I say, walk by the Spirit, and you will not gratify the desires of the flesh". We shall be led by the Holy Spirit and do not be partaker of the works of darkness. Your word says, "Do not be deceived, God is not mocked; for whatever a man sows, that he will also reap". Your word says" I call heaven and earth as witnesses against you today that I have set before you life and death, blessing and cursing. Therefore, choose life, so that you and your descendants may live," Amen.

## Bible verses to study.

Genesis 25:34; Galatians 5:16; John 14:15; Hebrews 10:26; James 4:17; Romans 14: 1-23; Mathew 6:33; 1 Chronicles 10:13; Mathew 6:24

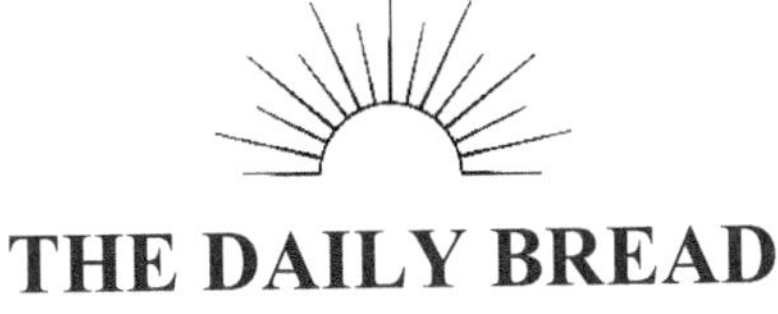

# THE DAILY BREAD

Your enemy is usually not the one far away, but the real one is the one close to you, that knows your dreams and vision and blocks the way, that knows you are about to enter a certain door and closes and hides the key from you. At times you need to learn to be quiet with your plans and let people be surprised when executing them because you don't know who might work against you. This will avoid you saying, I was almost.... no more almost syndromes but you must get where God has purposed you to be. Joseph's brothers thought that they were killing his dreams when they sold him but instead, they were helping to fulfil them. When they tormented Christ on the way to the cross, the devil had no idea that he was unwrapping the power Jesus had inside Him. If Jesus didn't die and rose up, we would not have the Holy Spirit. The enemy paved the way. Give thanks to God for your enemies for each time they tear your heart apart, they are unwrapping the power and the potential bestowed. God bless you.

**Prayer**

We pray that we must not worry about what our enemies will do but to focus on you God as your word says, "You prepare a table before me in the presence of my enemies." We pray that we must not reveal our plans prematurely so that we do not let the enemy know what we are planning to do. If God is for us who can be against us. Greater is he that is in us than he that is in the world. Like Job you have put a hedge around us. All things are working together for the good for us. Yet in all these things we are more than conquerors through Him who loved us. "Not by might nor by power, but by My Spirit,' says the LORD of hosts." Your grace is sufficient for us, for your strength is made perfect in weakness." Therefore, most gladly we will rather boast in your infirmities, that the power of Christ may rest upon us. Amen

**Bible verses to study.**

Genesis 37:1-44; Isaiah 54:17; Jeremiah 29:11; Philippians 1:6; Isaiah 55:11; Romans 8:28; 1 Peter 2:9; Proverbs 19:21; Isaiah 46:10

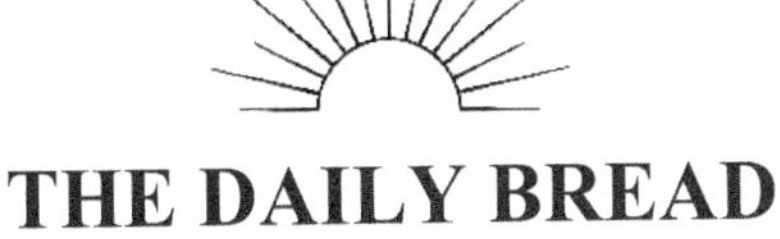

# THE DAILY BREAD

Stability. "Therefore, my dear brothers and sisters, stand firm. Let nothing move you. Always give yourselves fully to the work of the Lord, because you know that your labour in the Lord is not in vain" (1 Corinthians 15:58). Today we need to be stable in our Christian walk. You can't be planted here, planted there and tomorrow you are planted at another place and expect to bear fruit. If you plant a crop and keep on removing it from the sand and plant again on a different place, I promise you, harvest time will never come. God put you where you are for a purpose. If we allow our feeling to lead us, we will become unstable people that is church hoppers. People stop serving in Church for petty reasons and even leave a Church because they think they were not treated fairly. It's high time where we should not be controlled by our feelings but let our purpose aligned our feelings to our destiny. Things are not going to be as you expected but you need to have a character. You need to understand that things will not remain like that always. When you sow a seed, you can't harvest tomorrow. Do not compare your life with other people. God is faithful. He said that in His word "Let us not become weary in doing well, for at the proper time we will reap a harvest if we do not give up." (Galatians 6:9). I pray that we shall be still in our lives and know that He is the Lord. Today I urge you to fight the temptation of leaving, remain where you are, it's just your faith being tested, and you shall bear much fruit. The devil is not happy to see us maturing in Church, to see you as a leader in Church and only what he wants is to take you out of Church. God is perfect and He did not make a mistake to plant you in that Church. God bless you.

**Prayer**

As your word says, "Therefore, my dear brothers and sisters, stand firm. Let nothing move you. Always give yourselves fully to the work of the Lord, because you know that your labour in the Lord is not in vain", we shall be planted at a local Church. Your word says, "Let us not become weary in doing well, for at the proper time we will reap a harvest if we do not give up." We pray that we shall be still in our lives and know that He is Lord. Help us O Lord to keep trusting the process and grow in the local Church, which you planted us. When we face challenges, let us not move but remain faithful to our purpose. Amen.


**Bible verses to study**

1 Corinthians 15:58; Galatians 6:9; Psalms 1:1-3; Jeremiah 17:18; Mathew 6:24; James 5:7; 1 Timothy 4:16; Galatians 6:9; John 14:1

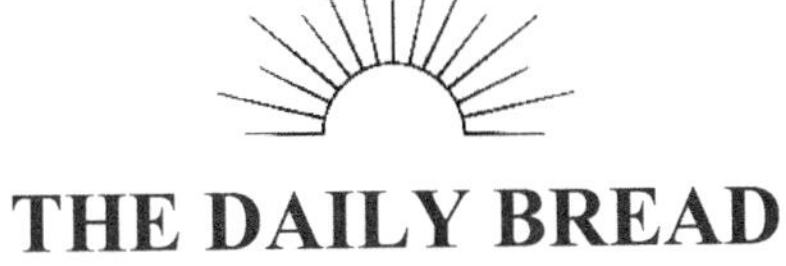

# THE DAILY BREAD

Negative talking of other people. Four years ago, I was told by the Holy not to talk negatively about other people. Most of the people say we have not killed anyone, but we have killed by speaking negatively about other people. When you read the newspapers, magazines and listen to news most of their content is to speak negative about other people. The world love negative news. The motive of the devil to kill, steal and destroy us. If you are not careful you fall into his plans and you destroy people. You will be doing the devil's work by destroying people's lives through your negative talking. When God spoke about Job being a righteous man, the devil attacked his character by saying does Job worship God for nothing. When you meet your friends or your friend what do you speak about. Negative speaking about other people may stunt your growth. You may wonder why you are not getting promoted in life. Negative talking creates a delay. The children of Israel spent so many years in the wilderness because of their negative talking about God. It's now a norm to talk negative about other people and even pastors, be careful to bring a curse in your life. Mirriam and Aaron, they spoke negative about Moses the Man of God and the anger of God arose they were smitten with diseases. Please change, if you are asked about someone do not judge them, be careful of what you say and if do not have control do not comment. Negative talking can be like cancer, it has destructive effects to church, cells and families. The word of God says, "Death and life are in the power of the tongue: and they that love it shall eat the fruit thereof." (Proverbs 18:21). The word of God says, "And I heard a loud voice saying in heaven, Now is come salvation, and strength, and the kingdom of our God, and the power of his Christ: for the accuser of our brethren is cast down, which accused them before our God, day and night." (Revelation 12:10). The devil is accuser of men not you. God bless you.

**Prayer**

We pray that we should not speak negatively about other people. Help us Lord to keep our mouths shut if we do not have something positive to speak about other people. We shall use our mouth to bless other people instead of cursing them. We pray that we will not do the devil's job as your word says, "And I heard a loud voice saying in heaven, Now is come salvation, and strength, and the kingdom of our God, and the power of his Christ: for the accuser of our brethren is cast down, which accused them before our God, day and night." Your word says, "Death and life are in the power of the tongue: and they that love it shall eat the fruit thereof." Amen

**Bible verses to study.**

Proverbs 16:28; Proverbs 20:19; Proverbs 11:13; Ephesians 4:29; Proverbs 26:20; Psalms 34:13; 1 Timothy 5:13; Ephesians 5:4; Titus 3:2; Proverbs 18:21; Revelation 12:10

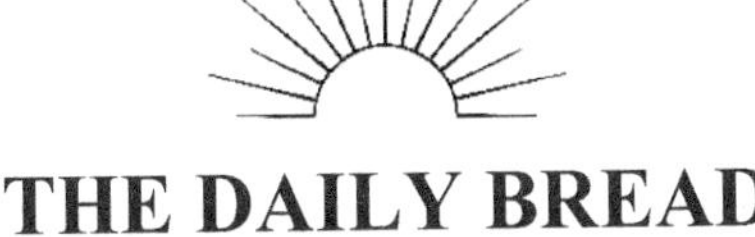

# THE DAILY BREAD

Faith grows. I encourage you this morning not to have a drowning faith. Jonah waited until they threw him in the sea to have faith in God. We cannot use God like crutches; always have faith on him when we are in need. When a child is born, he/she cries for everything and feeds on milk. The child thinks it's only about me. They have not developed so they are still helpless. There comes a time when the child grows, now he/she can eat solid food. They now know how to talk but still they have not developed. There comes when a child becomes man or a woman. Praise God for that because he/she is full wisdom and can work for themselves. Paul said, "When I was child, I spoke as a child, I understood as a child, I thought as a child; but when I became a man, I put away childish things" (1 Corinthians 13:11). Your faith must grow, you cannot remain a child. The growth of your faith can be tasted by the fruit of your mouth. I hear people cursing themselves every time, "hey this flue is killing me", "I am suffering in this house" because the computer it's taking time to come on someone will say "I am going to have a bad day today". It's sad because some even curse their children "this one will amount to nothing in life", and to their husband "he is a useless man". We need to grow to the level where no curses should proceed from our mouths. We need call on things which are not seen as they are there. Faith comes by hearing and by hearing the word of God. Living a wordless life leads to faithless life. The life you live is the picture of your faith in God. Just like growing tomatoes, our faith needs to be watered, cultivated and add manure. Faith needs right condition to grow that is to stay in the presence of God. Whatever you feed yourself, is what you will become. This morning be hungrier for Jesus. God bless you.

**Prayer**

We pray that we should never have a drowning faith. We shall live a life full of faith as your word says, "Now the just shall live by faith; But if anyone draws back, my soul has no pleasure in him." As your word says, "But without faith it is impossible to please Him, for he who comes to God must believe that He is, and that He is a rewarder of those who diligently seek Him", we shall seek you Lord diligently. Your word says, "So then faith comes by hearing, and hearing by the word of God.". As we know that confession bring possession, we shall confess positive things in our lives. Amen


**Bible verses to study.**

1 Corinthians 13:11; Hebrews 11:1; Hebrews 11:6; Proverbs 3:5-6; Mathew 17:20; Romans 12:1-2

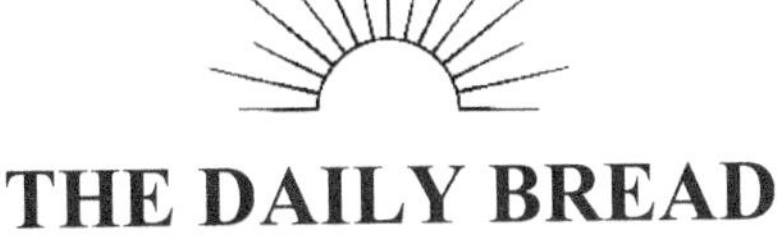

# THE DAILY BREAD

Complete package. I just wonder if David had asked to date a woman when he was still looking after the sheep what would be her response. She might have thought he is a joke. Not all women will think like that. David became a king and his status changed. Sometimes we miss our blessings because we are looking at the packaging. The packaging might not be attractive and thereby people they miss their best. Sometimes you need to pick your rough diamond and polish it. A worldly standard to measure a man is what kind of a car does he drives, does he have a house, the job and income he is earning and other things they think, they will compromise. As children of God, we need to outgrow those things. If God bless you with something, it will not add sorrow into your life. A man without a vision is dangerous. A man is the head, and a woman is the neck so a man without a vision will cause the body to have a dysfunctional head. A woman needs to support the vision of her husband. Look for Jesus in someone who you will spend the rest of life with and then all those things shall be added unto you. Water the Camels. Rebecca watered the camels. A woman needs to be humble; you are a helper show a man that you can help and go an extra mile. Sometimes in life you need to sow before you can reap. People look at all these things the world is chasing after but at the end they realize there is no love. Some of these wonders of the world people are chasing are temporary. The finished products people are looking for are few and some are not genuine. Dig your own well, those wells you are looking at some people dug them. Do not blame God for not answering your prayer because He may have answered it already. Are you matured enough in the Spirit to be able to see God's reply when he answers you but because of expectations people may miss it? God bless you.

**Prayer**

Help us O Lord to find a life partner and when you bless us with one open our eyes so that we can see he/she is the right one made for me. Remove the scales from our eyes that the world system has put so that I do not miss our David. We know "its Not by might nor by power, but by my Spirit,' says the LORD Almighty." Your word says, "Now unto him that is able to do exceedingly abundantly above all that we ask or think, according to the power that works in us." We will put our trust on you Lord. Amen.

**Bible verses to study**

1 Corinthians 11:3; Mark 11:24; Psalms 37:4; Ecclesiastes 4:9-11; 2 Corinthians 6:14; Genesis 13:10-11; 1 Samuael 16:7

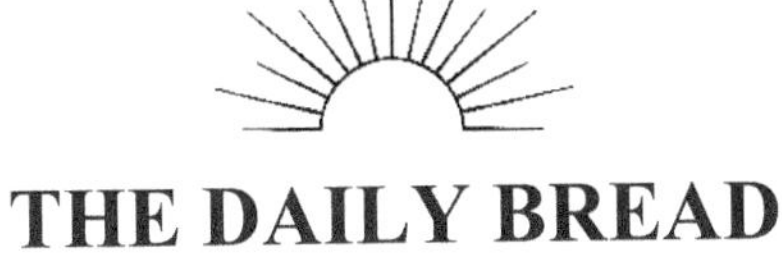

# THE DAILY BREAD

A delay is not a denial. God had inspired a dream of the Promise Land in the heart of the Israelite people. They dreamed of a land that flowed with milk and honey. A land of freedom; A land where they could be free from the whips of the evil taskmasters of Egypt. Scholars say that the journey to the promise land was only a one-two week journey. However, it took the children of Israel 40 years to get there. This delay was designed by God for a particular reason. Let's look at three ways God uses delays in our lives. (1) God uses delays to prepare us. The Israelites were a slave people, and they weren't prepared for war, and God knew if they went to war, they wouldn't be able to handle it. Every dream has its difficulties. God uses delays to get us ready for those difficult times that we are going to face while in our journey. These delays are designed to strengthen our faith and make us stronger. (2). God uses delays to test us. "God led you through the wilderness for forty years... testing you to find out how you would respond and if you would obey Him." (Deut. 8:2,) God uses delays to test how we will respond under pressure and to test our loyalty and obedience to Him. (3) God uses delays to train us because sometimes it takes longer to get Egypt out of us than it does to get us out of Egypt. The culture and habits of Egypt was engrained in the hearts and minds of the Israelite people. God could bring them out of Egypt in one night, but it would take years to get Egypt out of them. When you and I got saved we had habits and thought patterns that were of this world. When we got saved those thought patterns and habits came with us. God uses the delays to break those habits and thought patterns and train you in His way of thinking and doing things. The best thing to do when you are in God's waiting room is patient and let God do His work in your life. I want you to notice that it was God that was leading them to where they were going. Sometimes God will lead you through the wilderness. But I believe that your response determines how long you stay in the wilderness. Your test of maturity is how well you handle the delays in your life. Sadly, the children of Israel flunked this test. They never made it through the delay. Only two Israelites who left Egypt got to go into the Promised Land. A whole generation had to die in the desert. The next generation got to go in. Only two of the first-generation Joshua and Caleb got to go in. Why? Because they trusted God to take them. God bless you.

**Prayer**

Give us understanding Lord that delay is not a denial. Your word says, "being confident of this very thing, that He who has begun a good work in me will complete *it* until the day of Jesus Christ". You said in your word "The thief comes only to steal and kill and destroy; I have come that they may have life and have it to the full." Thank you, Lord Jesus, for giving us life abundantly. Help us O Lord to develop the confidence of understating that all things are working for good for me. Let us be patient and wait on the Lord as your word says, "but they that wait upon the LORD shall renew their strength; they shall mount up with wings as eagles; they shall run, and not be weary; and they shall walk, and not faint". We will keep holding of your faith because we know that your word says, "But as it is written, Eye hath not seen, nor ear heard, neither have entered into the heart of man, the things which God hath prepared for them that love him". Amen

**Bible Verses to Study**

Isaiah 40:31; Luke 18:1; 2 Corinthians 4:8; 2 Corinthians 4:16; Galatians 6:9; Isaiah 8:17; Isaiah 25:9; Psalms 84:7; Mathew 25:1-12

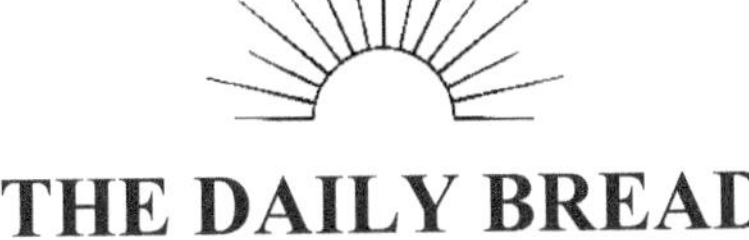

# THE DAILY BREAD

If you have a relationship with God, your life is not shapeless. People who know about the clothes they can tell for example if you are wearing dolce and gabbana. The brand has a designer, and their designs are well known all over the world. But someone does his own design and calls it dolce and gabbana; it may look like the original but it's not the same. Although it has a same name on the tag, but the design will be different. If you design your own thing and call it dolce and gabbana people will call it fake. God told Jeremiah "Before I formed you in the womb, I knew you, before you were born, I set you apart; I appointed you as a prophet to the nations." (Jeremiah 1:5). God had plans for Jeremiah so as for you too. Your life has a shape. God has shaped your life and gave you a purpose. But the moment when you are going to shape your life, make your design, it might be good looking, sweet, like the originally but if it's not of God its fake. Those who have denied that God is there , those who does not have the relationship with our father the creator their life is shapeless . "All things were made by him; and without him was not anything made that was made." (John 1:3). God gave you the life you are living. "The steps of a good man are ordered by the LORD: and he delights in his way." (Psalms 37:23) .The parable of the prodigal son is the one that highlight the danger of moving away from our father and design our own lives. The pain he suffered was because of the separation (fake design). Fake might be good for a while, but it does not last. But the devil is busy selling to us a fake. Many are buying because it looks easy and cheap, but the consequences have far reaching effects. In fact, fake is too expensive although advertised as cheap. Life without God is the worst life a person can live that is shapeless and fake. It's your choice. "For I know the plans I have for you," declares the LORD, "plans to prosper you and not to harm you, plans to give you hope and a future." (Jeremiah 29:11) God bless you.


**Prayer**

We cannot seize to thank you Lord because our lives are not shapeless. Jesus died for us so that we can have a future and hope. Jesus is the Alpha and the Omega, the author and finisher of our faith. Jesus you are the light of the world; we cannot walk in darkness. Jesus has done it all for us, if we are willing and obedient, we shall eat the good of the land. Your grace is sufficient for us. Your word says, "For I know the plans I have for you," declares the LORD, "plans to prosper you and not to harm you, plans to give you hope and a future." Our future is blessed like Jeremiah as your word says, "Before I formed you in the womb, I knew you, before you were born, I set you apart; I appointed you as a prophet to the nations." Amen


**The bible verses to study.**

Jeremiah 1:5; John 1:3; Psalms 37:23; Jeremiah 29:11; Genesis 1:2-3; Ephesians 2:10; Isaiah 64:8

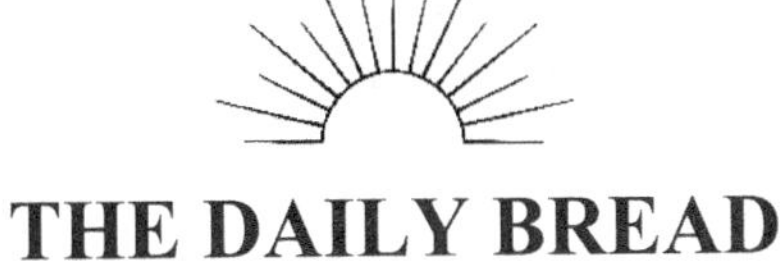

# THE DAILY BREAD

3 Meters. We put it in that 3 meters is the ideal life for everyone. For us to call it 3 meters it means that it was measured by a tape measure. But most of the people have heard about 3 meters, seen it somewhere, they have a picture of it in their minds and they know who have 3 meters. In this life we are living there are so many sizes. How will you know its 3 meters, the careers you desire is 3 meters, your wife or husband to be is 3 meters and your plans are 3 meters. Yes, you can know. You need a tape measure. Without that you may be having 5 meters whilst you think and tell people I have 3 meters. Don't you know your eyes sight may deceive you, so many thought it was 3 meters no, our friends also add their input together with our families they can also say its 3 meters. But they do not have a tape measure. The tape measure is the word of God. The word of God can show us whether its 3 meters. Satan is deceiving people and some they have lost everything including their lives. "There is a way that appears to be right, but in the end, it leads to death" (Proverbs 14:12) If you can get of the hold of the word, you will never miss the 3 meters. So today as the word of God says man shall not live by bread alone but from every word that proceeds from the mouth of God, mediate on word of God daily, it shall tell you who you are and lead you to your 3 meters. God bless you.

**Prayer**

As your word says, "The steps of a good man are ordered by the LORD, And He delights in his way, "order our footsteps O Lord. We pray that Lord you let your word be thy light upon thy path; be thy lamp upon thy feet. Let us not lean on our understanding and put our trust in you Lord with all our hearts, with all our souls. Let us meditate on your word day and night and neither depart from it neither right nor left. Your word says, "I will give you a new heart and put a new spirit in you; I will remove from you your heart of stone and give you a heart of flesh." Amen

**The bible verses to study.**

Proverbs 14:12; Romans 7:13; Isaiah 35;8; Isaiah 40:9; Isaiah 55:12; Psalms 37:23; Psalms 23:1

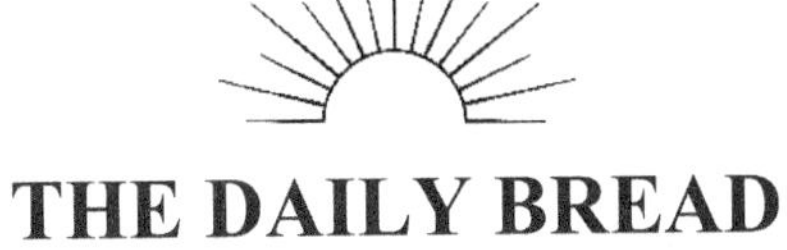

# THE DAILY BREAD

The prayer of a righteous person is powerful and effective. (James 5: 16) Elijah was a human being even as we are, He prayed earnestly that it would not rain, and it did not rain for 3 and a half years. Again, he prayed, and the heavens opened and gave rain, and the earth produced its crops. My brothers and sisters our prayers are powerful and effective because we are the righteous of Christ! Jesus said whatsoever you ask in my name I will do so that my Father may be glorified (John 14:13) The condition is this: We must stay connected to Jesus who is the vine, and we are the branches who will bear fruit because of the vine! the branch cannot bear fruit on its own, our prayers are powerful and effective because we are connected to Jesus, who is the middleman between us and God! Somebody help me? The bible tries to bring to our understanding that even though Elijah done great things, he was an ordinary man like you and I, he was no different. Elijah earnestly prayed, which means he sincerely, intently and seriously prayed and the heavens opened Halleluiah...the heavens is about to open in your life, staying connected to Jesus the doorway to victory! Remember we are in a spiritual battle...Don't give up praying, keep praying until you see Gods Glory manifest, remember the more you pray the more your angels excel in strength! God does not come down from his throne; he has angels assigned to us! That's what Jesus meant in Luke12:8 "I will acknowledge you before the angels of God "The rain is coming! Rain speaks about the blessing, God wants us to be fruitful, productive and our lands to produce crops and live abundantly, dry land speaks about a famine or curse, that's why when Adam sinned and disobeyed God cursed the ground! (Genesis 3:17) Let it rain Lord! Let it rain! In Jesus name. God bless you.

**Prayer**

As your word says, "Confess your trespasses to one another, and pray for one another, that you may be healed. The effective, fervent prayer of a righteous man avails much," we shall confess our sins to one another and pray in all seasons. Your word teaches us that, "Be anxious for nothing, but in everything by prayer and supplication, with thanksgiving, let your requests be made known to God;" We shall live a life of prayer. We shall never live a prayerless life because it leads to faithless life. Thank you, Lord Jesus, for answering our prayers. Amen

**The bible verses to study.**

James 5: 16; John 14:13; Philippians 4:6; 1 Kings 8:28; Proverbs 3:6; Daniel 6:10; 1 Samuel 1:15; 1 Samuel 30:6

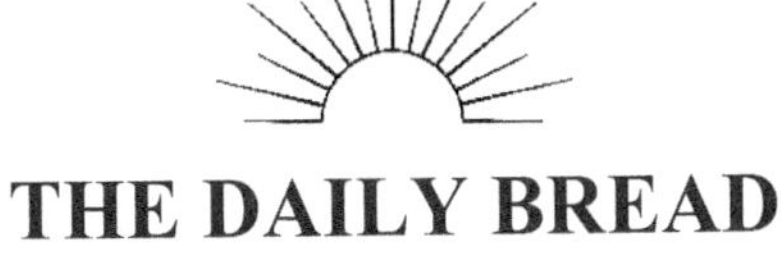

# THE DAILY BREAD

The saying, "CLOTHES MAKES A MAN" may seem simple, but it has touched something within me. I enjoyed and have always talked about Nelson Mandela's comment regarding clothes when he said, "In prison I saw lawyers, doctors, pastors and teachers being stripped naked and I said to myself, 'Indeed, clothes makes a man'." Clothes give you dignity. They make you respectable. But the first thing the enemy does to you is to take away your covering, your clothes and your dignity. Your challenges want you to be naked and vulnerable. Your problems are meant to shame you before the whole world so that you can never recover. Your poverty, stagnation, strife, sickness and failure are all shameful and the enemy wants to immobilise you with that shame. Peter was kept naked in prison, but God is interested in covering your shame. As the Bible says, "the angel said to him, 'Put on YOUR CLOTHES and SANDALS." And Peter did so. "Wrap your cloak around you and follow me," the angel told him." (Acts 12:8) The trouble you have faced may be so serious that your dignity is in tatters. But your end is nowhere near. See the angel of the Lord has come to break every chain and allow you to wear your clothes and cover your shame. You are about to conquer your financial, spiritual, relational, social, academic and professional challenges. The angel of God is here to help you cover your shame and restore your dignity. Hold on to your faith. Don't give up now because the angel of God is here. God bless you.


**Prayer**

Thank you, Lord, because you will never leave us nor forsaken us. When we were sick and you healed us, when we were thirsty, and you gave us water to drink, when we were hungry, and you fed us. Your word says, "But God demonstrates

His own love toward us, in that while we were still sinners, Christ died for us. We were naked and God, you clothed us. Because of you Lord Jesus our lives, we shall never be ashamed. Your grace is sufficient for us. Thank you, Lord, for our jobs, a place to stay, for the gift of life and for our businesses. You have covered our shame. We do not lack any good thing in our lives. God you are faithful. Amen


**The bible verses to study.**

Acts 12:8; Genesis 27:16: Exodus 28:42: John 11:44; Ezekial 16:8; Genesis 9:23

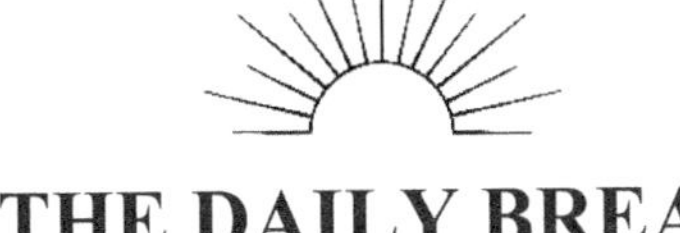

# THE DAILY BREAD

Help is coming. The parable of the good Samaritan. There was a man moving away from Jerusalem to Jericho and fell among thieves. They stripped him his belongings, beat him up and leave him half dead. This man was moving away from Jerusalem the city of God going to Jericho the world. He may have done it several times and successful. He was now accustomed to moving away from light to darkness. The sinful life, that is the pleasures of flesh, it was now the order of the day. He became accustomed to the ways of darkness. Jericho may be attractive but one day is one day. Some of you have already pitched your tents in Jericho, and you are now part of their lifestyle. The devil have strapped you to believe that it's all rosy. The ungodly life will make you pay a heavy price. Sin is too expensive, some paid with their lives. The devil want to rob you, destroy you and kill you. The man was stripped naked and left half dead. He could not help himself. The priest came by and maybe was too religious to help saying he brought this to himself because of sinful life he was living. As children of God, we need to pay our tithes and offering so that there is no lack in the house of God. Maybe the priest did not have enough resources to cater for this hurt man. Are there any good Samaritans in the house amen. Praise God for the good Samaritan. It will cost you money and time to minister help to someone. May God raise more good Samaritans. The good Samaritan carried him on his transport and took him to the hospital to get help. He paid the bill, and he said the extras must be put on his account. You might be half dead, stripped naked but help is coming. The mistake that the devil made was to live you half dead. As long as you are breathing, you will get a second chance. I warn you choose life today and stay away from Jericho. God is saying today I will never leave you nor forsake you. Let's be faithful with our tithes so that the Church's hands are not tied to play the role of a good Samaritan.

We are God's hands here on earth. Let's love our neighbour. This man helped a stranger not even his own blood. The hand of God is not shortened, may he send a good Samaritan to minister to your needs. God bless you.

**Prayer**

Your hand Lord is not shortened in our lives. As your word says, "He who dwells in the secret place of the Most High Shall abide under the shadow of the Almighty", we shall stay in your presence. Your word teaches us that, "Love your neighbour as yourself". Teach us how to love because God you are love. Your word says, "A man who has friends must himself be friendly, but there is a friend who sticks closer than a brother". Your word says, "Anyone who believes in him will never be put to shame." Your word says, "Surely God is my help; the Lord is the one who sustains me." Amen

**Bible verses to study**

Psalms 121:1-8; Isaiah 41:10; Psalms 55:22; Philippian 4:6-7; Mathew 11:28-30; Isaiah 40:31; Psalms 54:4; 1 Peter 5:7; Luke 1:37

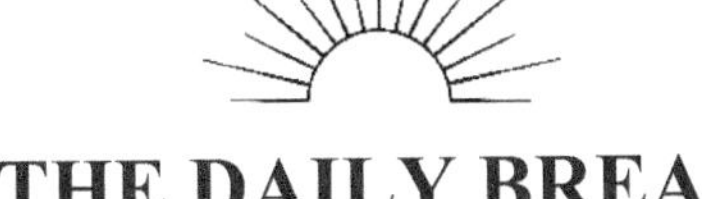

# THE DAILY BREAD

Focus. Let us not lose focus and forget the reason why men fell in the first place. Man, disobeyed God and then sin entered the world. The word of God says if anyone says that there is no sin their life, he is a liar. Everyone has feet made of clay, but it does not mean we just ignore sin in our lives. It's not right for us to receive Jesus Christ as our saviour and continue live like heathens. Paul literally begged us "I beseech you therefore, brethren, by the mercies of God, that you present your bodies a living sacrifice, holy, acceptable unto God, which is your reasonable service" (Romans 12:1). The word of God also says we need to work on our faith with fear and trembling. The fear of the Lord is the beginning of wisdom. If we entertain sinful life, we lack wisdom. I have gone to prison Ministry seeing young people whose future have been robed; I have ministered in the park where I saw the effects of drugs and, I have seen people in hospitals dying because of sinful way of life. A fire is a fire it burns. We need to be bold and let the young generation not to stray away. We don't need people to second guess, they really need to know what the right way is. Another Man of God said, if something looks like a devil, talks like a devil, dresses like a devil, smells like a devil, it is a devil. Let's us remember that whatever we sow, we shall reap. God will forgive us but remember they are consequences. Today I am focused; I know who my enemy is, and his ways lead me to destruction. There is way the seems right to men but at the end it leads to death. I urge you today not be an example of living ungodly life but rather be an example of living life of pursuing righteousness. "Be sober, be vigilant; because your adversary the devil walks about like a roaring lion, seeking whom he may devour". (1 Peter 5:8). Don't let your guard down. You may entertain sin in your life, but the consequences may have far reaching to you and your future generation. The wages of sin are death. The devil may lie to you showing you the good part but not the consequences. Just know that sin is very expensive, and some pay with their lives. Don't waste your time following ungodly life it's a weapon by the devil to rob you your youth and your time. God bless you.

**Prayer**

As your word say, "I beseech you therefore, brethren, by the mercies of God, that you present your bodies a living sacrifice, holy, acceptable unto God, which is your reasonable service" we shall forsake our evil ways and live a righteous life. Your word says, "*There is* therefore now no condemnation to those who are in Christ Jesus, who do not walk according to the flesh, but according to the Spirit." Today we are focused; we know who is our enemy and his ways lead us to destruction. Your word says, "Be sober, be vigilant; because your adversary the devil walks about like a roaring lion, seeking whom he may devour". Amen.

**Bible verses to study.**

Romans 12:1-2; Romans 6:23; James 4:17; James 1:15; Mathew 10:28; 1 John 1:9; John 8:44; Galatians 5:19-21; Proverbs 14:12; 1 Peter 5:8

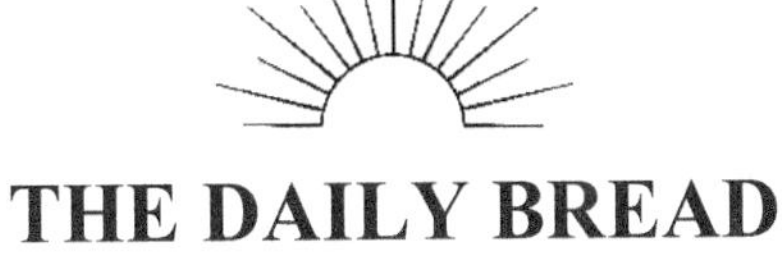

# THE DAILY BREAD

We are coming back. When our father spoke that we must come back, I realised that some bones have become dry because of staying in an open valley. He is our Moses, our prophet, the one who is carrying the rod. When the word God was spoken, I could see the dry bones coming together, the breath entering them and becoming a great army. Whatever dead in us becoming alive. When Jesus called Lazarus from the dead, death did not hold him back. People are returning to the heart of worship. God is raising his great army. I want to have a shouting faith like Bartimaeus. A blind faith that I do not care attitude. Faith that irritates the world. People may not understand the way you worship God because they have not been in your position. Paul understood grace. If you can see how drugs, alcohol, promiscuous life and criminal life, affecting the youth, you can never be lukewarm. We need to rise, take our position in Christ and save this generation. "You are the salt of the earth. But if the salt loses its saltiness, how can it be made salty again? It is no longer good for anything, except to be thrown out and trampled underfoot" (Mathew 5:13). We need people with a different Spirit like Caleb who can say let's go and take the land right now. They are no secret under cover James Bond 007 Christians. Let's be hungrier for the things of God. The word of God says "if my people, who are called by my name, will humble themselves and pray and seek my face and turn from their wicked ways, then I will hear from heaven, and I will forgive their sin and will heal their land. We should return our heart to God by paying our tithes and offering. "For I am the LORD, I do not change; Therefore, you are not consumed, O sons of Jacob. Yet from the days of your fathers, you have gone away from My ordinances and have not kept them. Return to Me, and I will return to you," says the LORD of hosts. "But you said, 'In what way shall we return?' "Will a man rob God? Yet you have robbed Me! But you say, 'In what way have we robbed You?' In tithes and offerings. You are cursed with a curse, for you have robbed Me, even this whole nation. Bring all the tithes into the storehouse, that there may be food in My house, and try Me now in this," Says the LORD of hosts, "If I will not open for you the windows of heaven and pour out for you such blessing That there will not be  room enough to  receive  it". Malachi  3:6-10). God bless you.


**Prayer**

As your word says "Do not store up for yourselves treasures on earth, where moths and vermin destroy, and where thieves break in and steal. But store up for yourselves treasures in heaven, where moths and vermin do not destroy, and where thieves do not break in and steal. For where your treasure is, there your heart will be also", we shall bring the offering and tithes to the house of God so that you can rebuke the devourer in our lives and open the windows of heaven and pour out a blessing we cannot contain. We are the salt of the earth, the light of the world and a city that is built on a hill that cannot be hidden. Amen


**Bible verses to study.**

Mathew  5:13;  Malachi  3:6-10;  1  Peter  5:7;  Isaiah  45:22; Psalms 119:59; Joel 2:13; Lamentations 3:40; Isaiah 55:7

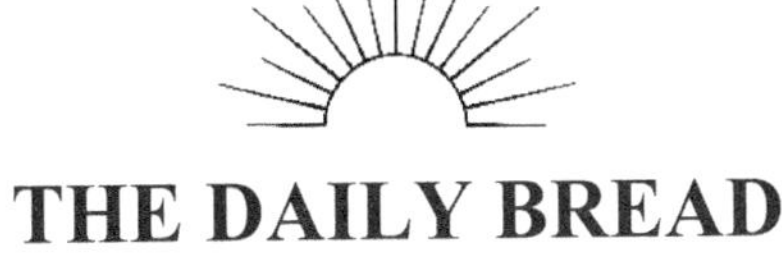

# THE DAILY BREAD

Secret "Now Naaman, captain of the army of the king of Syria, was a great man with his master, and honourable, because by him the LORD had given deliverance unto Syria: he was also a mighty man in valour, but he was a leper" (2 Kings 5:1). Being an army commander, it meant that Naaman was second in charge from the king. Naaman because of his position, he was a rich man, an honourable man and a man of valour but he was a leper. Just imagine having all those riches but looking in the mirror every day and see leprosy all over your body. Everyone has a problem so do not think you are alone. Naaman had a secret which he could not hide for long. During those days when someone had leprosy, they were separated from the community, forced to wear torn clothes and when they meet people, they were to shout unclean. The king new that Naaman had leprosy, his wife and family and yet the word of God said he was an honourable man and a great man of valour. Your gift will make a room for you, although he was a leper, he made them to win a war. Who you are and where you come from will not limit your destiny. The slave girl is the one who told her mistress that "if only my master were with a prophet who is in Samaria! For he would heal him of his leprosy". God will place people in your life to change your destiny. The slave girl did not look at her present situation but instead she saw that her master needed healing. She had a right to be angry with her master and she did not but saw a moment to preach about the God of Israel. The king of Syria sent Naaman to the king of Israel with ten talents of silver, six thousands of shekels of gold and ten changes of clothing. The king sends him to the wrong person instead of the prophet. When the king of Israel read the letter, he tore his clothes. When Elisha heard that the king has torn his clothes, he said let him come to me. "Elisha sent a messenger to say to him, "Go, wash yourself seven times in the Jordan, and your flesh will be restored, and you will be cleansed. But Naaman went away angry and said, "I thought that he would surely come out to me and stand and call on the name of the LORD his God, wave his hand over the spot and cure me of my leprosy" (2 Kings 5:10-11) . The things of God do not work the way people want. If Naaman knew how to heal himself why did he need the prophet? "Then he went down, and dipped himself seven times in the Jordan, according to the saying of the man of God: and his flesh was restored again like unto the flesh of a little child, and he was clean" (2 Kings 5:14). God gave him a new skin which was far better to those of his age. God will restore you. God bless you.

**Prayer**

Due to our relationship with you Almighty God, we are more than a conquerors and we are a mighty men of valour. Greater is he that is in us than he who is in the world. If God is for us, who can be against us. Your grace is sufficient for us. Your word says, "A thousand shall fall on myside and a 10 thousand on my right hand, But it shall not come near me. No evil shall befall me, Nor shall any plague come near my dwelling; For He shall give His angels charge over me, to keep me in all his ways". Your grace is sufficient for us. We shall tread upon the lion and the cobra, The young lion and the serpent shall we trample under our feet. We are a head not a tail and always above not beneath. We are more than conquerors through Him who loved us. Amen

**Bible verses to study**

2 Kings 5:1; 2 Kings 5:10-11; 2 Kings 5:14; Isaiah 41:10; Isaiah 43:19; Psalms 27:13; Hebrews 10:35; Philippians 4:19

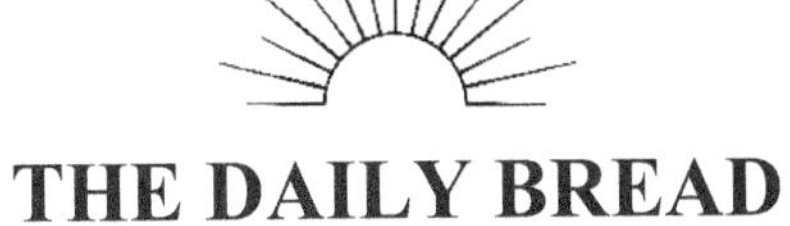

# THE DAILY BREAD

Healing. May God heal you today. Some of you were wounded by family, friends, strangers, yourself and those in authority. Wounded people also hurt other people that why we need healing. Sometimes our soul becomes wounded. The word of God says, "He restore my soul" (Psalms 23:3) Only God can restore your soul. There is an old lady whose cat died. Every time you meet her, she will tell you my cat died. Yes, but after 3 years you still talking about your cat died. The enemy wants you to be victim. To some, the enemy wants you to hide your wound and to others to talk about it and fail to move with their future. You might be struggling with a certain addiction; the enemy has wounded your life. Covered wounds won't heal. You need let the people know what you are struggling with so that you can get help. Other people they fail to progress in life because of what happened in past. Maybe you grew up in an abusive environment. You can't be looking back and fail to head on with your life. Some people blame their parents for not affording them a proper education, but now you are 40 years old and you still a victim of your parents, grow up. Every time you give an excuse of being abused. We need to cast our burdens unto Jesus for he cares for us. Don't be a victim be a victor. You are an overcomer. If we keep on mourning about our painful past, we will miss God's next big thing in our lives. Let not your abusers have joy by seeing you going down the drain, show them that they can't break you. I pray for healing for those who have wounded yourself and are failing to forgive themselves. May God heal you today. Your future is ahead of you. Don't linger around your past. Now take a giant leap of faith and open up to new possibilities in life. You are no longer a slave of fear, you are a child of God. The best way of fighting against the people who hurt you is to keep winning. God bless you.

**Prayer**

Your word says, "if My people who are called by My name will humble themselves, and pray and seek My face, and turn from their wicked ways, then I will hear from heaven, and will forgive their sin and heal their land." As your word says, "He restore my soul", heal us O Lord from the hurts of our lives. We pray that we cast all our burden unto you for you care for us. We are a overcomers and winners through the blood of the lamb. We are no longer a slave to fear, We are children of God. Amen

**Bible verses to study.**

Psalms 23:3; Psalms 43:5; Proverbs 17:22; Psalms 147:3; Jeremiah 17:14; Psalms 51:10; Psalms 41:4; Romans 16:17; 2 Chronicles 7:14

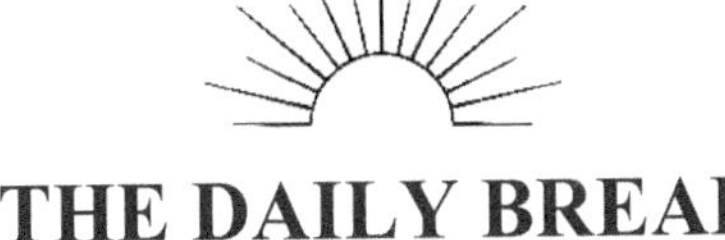

# THE DAILY BREAD

Available. Are you available? The devil always calls you; do you answer the call? The devil always invites you; do you accept the invitation? Have you told yourself, I will never answer his calls or accept his invitations. The question is availability. The devil does not give up on calling us and inviting us. You may ignore his calls or not reply to his invitations, but he will not give up. He knows your weakness. You may resist for a while but one day, you will answer the call. "Be sober, be vigilant; because your adversary the devil walks about like a roaring lion, seeking whom he may devour. (1 Peter 5:8) The devil will come to you and question word of God. Eve fall because she answered the call. She did find this call irresistible. She went against the word of God and ate the fruit. Are you being tempted? If its fornication, Paul said flee away from fornication. We get into uncompromising positions and end up answering calls we said we will never answer. Be filled with the Holy Spirit amen. Don't just live life anyhow. We are in a spiritual warfare. The devil will make a party of you. The problem is, we have not said goodbye to the life of the world completely. The devil knows those grey areas. Some of you are always available because you are wordless. Jesus was tempted too. The devil wanted him to answer the call. Listen, Jesus was full of the Holy Spirit. He was more in the Spirit than in flesh. If you walk in the flesh, you will fulfil its desires. Do not just be hearers of the word only but be the doers too. Some of you now you are too relaxed amen, you no longer pray and fast, always watching Soapies, listening to worldly songs, and hanging around evil people. I tell you now, you are available. You can't resist anymore. On Sundays at church, you act up holy but during the week you live like a devil. You see some people crying in church sometimes thinking it's the anointing whilst its sinful life that is tormenting them. The word of God says, "Therefore submit to God. Resist the devil and he will flee from you." (James 4:7) God bless you.

## Prayer

We are sold out for you Lord Jesus, like Paul we can say, "I have been crucified with Christ; it is no longer I who live, but Christ lives in me; and the life which I now live in the flesh I live by faith in the Son of God, who loved me and gave Himself for me". Your word says, "See then that you walk circumspectly, not as fools but as wise, redeeming the time, because the days are evil. Therefore, do not be unwise, but understand what the will of the Lord is. And do not be drunk with wine, in which is dissipation; but be filled with the Spirit, speaking to one another in psalms and hymns and spiritual songs, singing and making melody in your heart to the Lord, giving thanks always for all things to God the Father in the name of our Lord Jesus Christ." We pray that we shall never be hearers of the word only but be doers too. We shall walk in the spirit so that we not become a prisoners of urges of the flesh. Amen

## Bible verses to study

1 Peter 5:8; Galatians 2:20; Ephesians 5:15-17; James 1:22-25; James 4:7; Ephesians 6:11-12; Mathew 6:33; 1 John 2:15-17; Romans 12:1-2

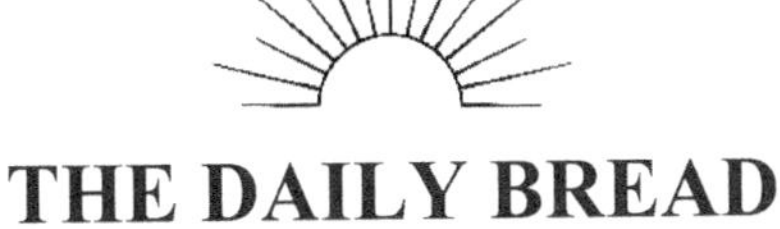

# THE DAILY BREAD

Faithful. We were born not saved. They maybe people who fasted for us to be saved. People who went down on their knees and cried to God for our souls. Although we were deep living a sinful life and glorifying our flesh, they never gave up on us. They saw us in heaven with them. They are Holy Spirit filled people who put their resources, time and even travelled distance for us to be saved. It must not end there, now it's our time to cry for our family members and those who we know are not saved. We need to pray for them and sow our finances too. Who are you praying for this year? Do not give up on anyone. It may be at work, in your community, if you know anyone who is not saved, let it be a burden for you to pray for them and share the word of God. God wants every sinner to be saved "Do I take any pleasure in the death of the wicked? declares the Sovereign LORD. Rather, am I not pleased when they turn from their ways and live? (Ezekiel 18:23). In the story of the rich man and Lazarus, the rich man only realised that his family needed to be saved when he was dead and in Hades. Then it was too late. Now is the time, lets praise God, our families, friends and the nations shall be saved. "The woman then left her waterpot, went her way into the city, and said to the men, "Come, see a Man who told me all things that I ever did. Could this be the Christ?" Then they went out of the city and came to Him." (John 4:28-30). The Samaritan woman who met Jesus at the well went to the city and told her story. The people of that city were drawn to Jesus because of her story. Your story can cause people to be saved. You need to go out there and tell the people what Jesus did in your life. The goodness of God in your story will draw people to Jesus. The word of God says "And how shall they preach unless they are sent? As it is written: "How beautiful are the feet of those who preach the gospel of peace, who bring glad tidings of good things!" (Romans 10:15). God bless you.

**Prayer**

As your word says, "For I am not ashamed of the gospel of Christ, for it is the power of God to salvation for everyone who believes" we shall tell our story to the rest of the world and help to save souls. Help us O Lord to keep the fire burning for saving souls in our lives as your word says "Then I said, I will not make mention of him, nor speak any more in his name. But his word was in mine heart as a burning fire shut up in my bones, and I was weary with forbearing, and I could not stay." Your word says, "The fruit of the righteous is a tree of life, and the one who is wise saves lives." Amen


**Bible verses to study.**

Romans 10:15; Romans 1:16; Ezekiah 37:1-28; Psalms 23:1-3; Deuteronomy 4:29; Mathew 16:26

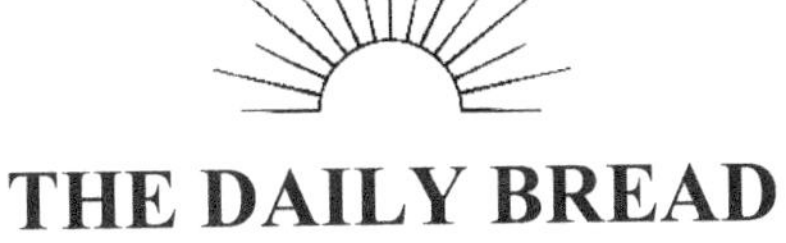

# THE DAILY BREAD

God is not silent. God is still speaking into our lives in various ways. The Holy Spirit who guides and teaches us speak to us regularly. "But the Helper, the Holy Spirit, whom the Father will send in My name, He will teach you all things, and bring to your remembrance all things that I said to you" (John 14:26). It's your choice to be obedient after hearing from God. They are many times when I made wrong decisions in my life and God spoke to me before. Sometimes I will feel down and pain inside me. By continuing with my decision, it always brings sorrow in my life. The devil can rob me because I will have ignored warning from God. Today are you doing something which you feel uneasy inside and everyone is telling you don't do it. God can use people inside your circle to advise you. Young people often want to be rebellious and say they are jealous of me, and I know everything attitude. When God put Adam in the garden of Garden of Eden, He spoke to Adam and even after he sinned, He still spoke to Adam again. In Deuteronomy 31:6 God said that I will never leave you nor forsake you. God will never want you to fall into a pit or drown. His plans are to prosper you not to harm you. We pray about an investment decision, choosing a life partner, God to bring good people in our lives and for jobs. God always speaks because God is faithful. Don't be like a prophet who was so stubborn and kept ignoring God, until God spoke to a donkey. I have learnt from the past that not everyone means good to your life; the world is corrupt, and the devil may even use people close to you to rob you. It's high time we need to put our trust on God not on people. Don't say in future if I only listened to the voice of Spirit. What are you trusting God for today? Pray for the perfect will of God upon your life. Let God reveal his will upon your life. You may spend more time praying for something which is not in God's will upon your life. Not everyone is going to be a millionaire, but God will provide you differently. God bless you.

**Prayer**

When you speak your word to me O Lord let me not harden my heart. I pray that I have a teachable Spirit so that the Holy Spirit can guide me and teach me many things. As your word says, "obey is better than sacrifice, I shall be obedient to your word. "So, then faith comes by hearing, and hearing by the word of God." Order my footsteps O Lord as your word says, "The steps of a good man are ordered by the LORD, And He delights in his way." "Teach me to do Your will, For You are my God; Your Spirit is good. Lead me in the land of uprightness." Amen

**Bible verses to study.**

John 14:26; Psalms 37:23; Genesis 3:8; John 10:27; Romans 10:17; Jeremiah 33:3; 1 John 5:14; Isaiah 30:21

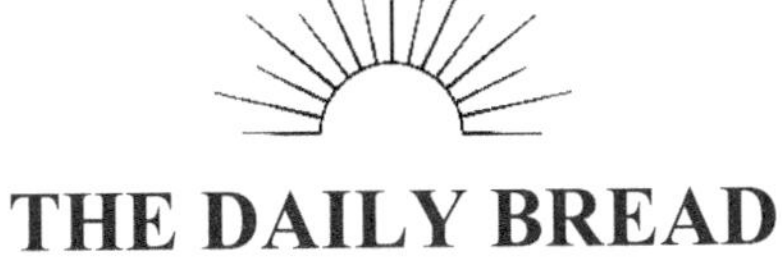

# THE DAILY BREAD

God is love. If you kill for your god, carry bombs for your god and kidnap people for your god, please I do not want to know your god. People must see the fruits in your life (the love) and say we want to know your God. The life we are living now it's too demanding and most of the people have a busy schedule. This does not give an excuse for us not to show love. One of our Pastors said that I would not want people to say when I die, he was a great man but only for my children to say we wish we could have known him. When you love your family it's not about showering them with the gifts only, you need to be there personally and have quality time with them. It's sad that people put their businesses, jobs and careers ahead of their families. One day when you are old, you will realise you do not even know your children. Your children will not be able to relate to you. We must see really is it worth it to invest our time on materials things at the expense of our loved ones. When was the last time you told your wife or husband that you love them, your children, your father, your mother, your sisters and your brothers. Your vision as a ministry may include, connect, care and grow. As a coach, cell leader, small group leader, when was the last time you called one person in your group not inviting them to come serve or to cell but just to show them how much you appreciate them, to strengthen them and pray for them. We are the light of the world but do our lights still shining, I wonder. Faith without works is dead. I know personally they are some people; I need to call, visit and spend time with them. My prayer most of the times is God you are love, show me how to love. Paul said, "that Christ may dwell in your hearts through faith; that you; being rooted and grounded in love" (Ephesians 3:17). "Though I speak with the tongues of a men and angels but have no love, I have become sounding brass or a clanging cymbal." (1 Corinthians

13:1). Love is a fruit of the Spirit it needs to be developed so let practice it every day in our lives. God bless you.

**Prayer**

God you are love, teach us how to love. As your word says, "Though I speak with the tongues of a men and angels but have no love, I have become sounding brass or a clanging cymbal." And though I have the gift of prophecy, and understand all mysteries and all knowledge, and though I have all faith, so that I could remove mountains, but have not love, I am nothing. And though I bestow all my goods to feed the poor, and though I give my body to be burned, but have not love, it profits me nothing. Love suffers long and is kind; love does not envy; love does not parade itself, is not puffed up; does not behave rudely, does not seek its own, is not provoked, thinks no evil; does not rejoice in iniquity, but rejoices in the truth; bears all things, believes all things, hopes all things, endures all things", help us O Lord to grow our fruit of love. Amen

**Bible verses to study**

1 Corinthians 13:1-13; Ephesians 3:17; 1 John 4:19; 1 John 4:8; John 15:12-13; 1 Peter4:8; 1 Corinthians 16:14; Ephesians 4:2

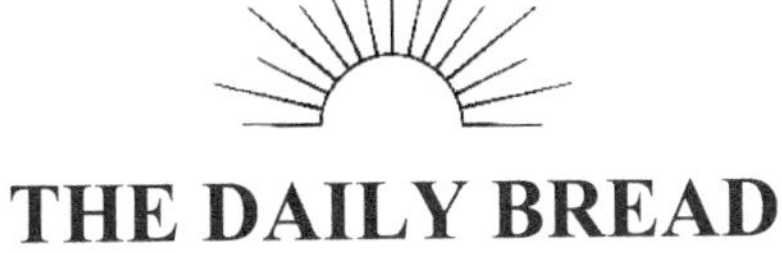

# THE DAILY BREAD

Decisions. The decisions you are making every day have an impact on your life. We all make decisions every day - what to eat, who to spend time with, and which tasks to prioritise. Good decisions lead to contentment and fulfilled lives. Bad decisions lead to disappointment, pain, and inner turmoil. As the Bible says, you reap what you sow. He guides the humble in what is right and teaches them his way " (Psalms 25:9) and "I will instruct you and teach you in the way you should go; I will counsel you and watch over you" (Psalms 32:8) .As the Holy Spirit is the one who both gives us the desire to do God's will and enables us to do it, then one of the chief evidences that we have indeed received the Holy Spirit, and been reconciled to God, is that we really want to do his will. God expects us to use our intelligence. God says, "I will instruct you and teach you in the way you should go; I will counsel you and watch over you. Do not be like the horse or the mule, which have no understanding but must be controlled by bit and bridle" (Psalms 32:8, 9). A young man who wanted to get married asked a Pastor's opinion whether to date a particular girl. The pastor said to him I will pray about it. After 2 days he came back again and said Pastor did you get the answer from God, but the Pastor said he is still praying. The young man was impatient and kept on asking the Pastor, but he said wait. Every time he was told to wait, he became sad. After 3 months, the young man came to the Pastor and he was so happy and said to the pastor I will never marry that girl even in 1000 times, because God had showed to him the things he could not see with his eyes. The Pastor had prayed to God to show the young man if he was making a right a decision. We are all capable of making bad decisions either born again or not. We need to pray to God and ask other people to pray for us to help us to make important decisions in life. You need to live a prayerful life and listen to the voice of the Holy

Spirit. God will show you, but your obedience will save you from making a bad decision permanent. The spirit of rebellion causes people not to accept correction and thereby suffer the consequences of bad decisions. No matter what decisions you are making today, God is thinking about you. "For I know the thoughts that I think toward you, said the LORD, thoughts of peace, and not of evil, to give you an expected end" (Jeremiah 29:11). God bless you.


**Prayer**

We pray that we live a prayerful life and being able to listen to the voice of the Holy Spirit. As your word says, "I will instruct you and teach you in the way you should go; I will counsel you and watch over you", Let us "Trust in the LORD with all your heart and lean not on your own understanding;" Help us O Lord to make good decisions as your word says" The steps of a good man are ordered by the LORD, And He delights in his way". May we not depart from your word neither right nor left so we can live a blessed life like Joshua. Teach us your ways O Lord. May the Holy Spirit lead us and guide us to everything we need. Amen


**Bible verses**

Philippians 4:6-7; Proverbs 3:5-6; James 1:5; Psalms 19:8; 2 John 1:8; Proverbs 16:10; Deuteronomy 1:17; Exodus 28:15; Proverbs 16:1; Proverbs 15:22; Proverbs 19:21

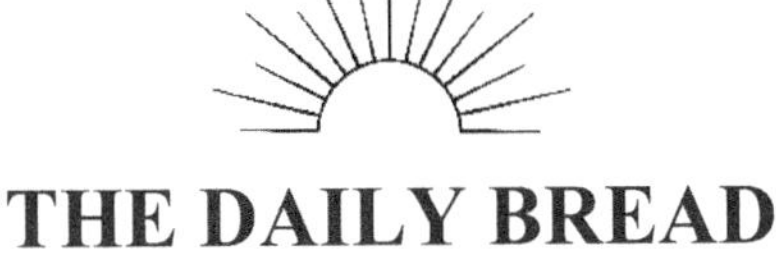

# THE DAILY BREAD

Opportunity. "Jesus entered Jericho and was passing through" (Luke 19:1). This speaks volumes that Jesus entered into Jericho. The story of Zacchaeus started with Jesus entering Jericho. Zacchaeus was a rich man, a chief tax collector. When he heard that Jesus was passing by, he went personally to meet him. He was least of people who would have wanted to see Jesus. Zacchaeus did not procrastinate but he went at once. The relationship we have with Jesus it's personally that's why each one must work on their faith. Zacchaeus could have said Jesus must send me an invitation to come and missed the salvation. Zacchaeus could have sent his servants, but he took it personally. When he arrived where Jesus was, he could not see him for he was a short man. In everything we seek to achieve in life, there is something always in our way; there is an opposition that is the limitation factor. But what is important is not what is outside but what is inside of you. Thank you, God, for the opposition because it makes our faith stronger. The word of God says that the one who is inside of us is greater than he who is in the world. In life you need humble yourself, Zacchaeus climbed on a tree so that he can see Jesus. What is limiting you to see Jesus in your life today? There were a lot of people who were following Jesus but a person who did not know Jesus took the opportunity. You maybe have been coming to Church for many years but someone new comes and grabs the opportunity and gets blessed. We serve a God of suddenly. Jesus asked Zacchaeus to come down for he wanted to have dinner at his house. Jesus is moved by faith. Zacchaeus had a mean Spirit and no peace because his God was money. When he met Jesus, his life changed. There is Zacchaeus before Jesus and Zacchaeus after the encounter with Jesus. The two can never be the same. Everyone who encountered Jesus their life would be drastically changed. Jesus brought salvation, peace and Joy in Zacchaeus's life and money was no longer his God. What he lived for suddenly became insignificant in his life. He even gave back four times to those whom he cheated before and started to have compassion to the poor because the word says he gave to the poor. If Jesus is in your life, you will have his love for the people. This is the time to seek God. Take this opportunity and seek God diligently. God loves you. Why are you holding back, surrender your life to Jesus today." But seek you first the kingdom of God, and his righteousness; and all these things shall be added unto you" (Mathew 6:33). God bless you.

**Prayer**

We pray that when Jesus you pass by our lives, we should not miss the opportunity to be blessed by you. When you call us Lord Jesus, we will answer because we will be somewhere waiting for our names. We thank you God for our opposition, because they make us stronger. Your word says, "For many are called, but few *are* chosen." We pray that we should have an encounter with you Lord Jesus. Your word says "But seek you first the kingdom of God, and his righteousness; and all these things shall be added unto you" Amen.

**Bible verses to study.**

Luke 19:1-10; Mathew 6:33; John 3:1-21; John 4:17-26; Acts 9:17-18

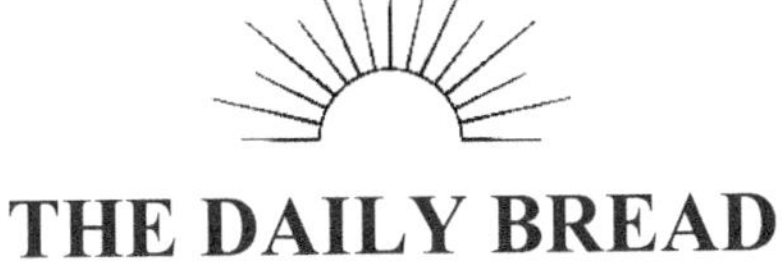

# THE DAILY BREAD

Preach your way throughout the day. I preach indirectly during the day. Most of the people I meet in my daily routines, I will always say a word to bring a smile on their faces. It starts by you having joy and peace in life. By having a good relationship with God, peace and joy follows. You cannot give something you do not have. The word of God says, we are the salt of the earth and the light of the world. I encourage you to make your life preach to others. Someone who I once worked with, she used to see me taking a protein supplement for mass gain for gym, she said I want to know what your drink is. She was wondering why I am always full of joy. She did not know the secret. The secret was being filled with the Holy Spirit. The Holy Spirit made me to be full of joy every time. We cannot love God and fail to love our brothers and sisters. Let the life you live be a testimony. People will respect you and they will say really you are a child of God. When you wake up every morning choose to live positive and rub this on all other people. We take this for a granted; we do not know what other people are going through. That smile maybe is all they need to change their mood. If you make them laugh maybe its preaching, they needed to cast away negative thoughts. Your comment and energy may change someone's day. Be like choir master and carry other people during the day and be blessing to other people. God bless you.

**Prayer**

Create in us O Lord the Joy, that can help us to preach our way throughout the day. Fill us with the Holy Spirt until we overflow. We are the salt of the earth and light of the world. A city that is built on the Hill that cannot be hidden. Let us be able to spread the gospel of Jesus in the way of interacting, talking, singing , and giving. May the light of God be illuminated through us. God you are love, teach us how to love. We pray that we become more of you and less of us. The joy of the Lord is our strength. Amen


**Bible Verses**

Romans 1:16; 2 Corinthians 3:2-3; Marck 16:15; Johah 1:1-2; Mathew 10:5-7; Ephesians3:7-9

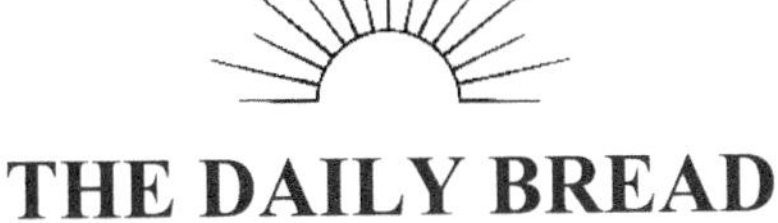

# THE DAILY BREAD

Materialistic. This is a major difference between early Church and ministries of today is materialistic. In early church they passed materialistic test. "And all the believers met together in one place and shared everything they had. They sold their property and possessions and shared the money with those in need. They worshiped together at the Temple each day, met in homes for the Lord's Supper, and shared their meals with great joy and generosity— all the while praising God and enjoying the goodwill of all the people. And each day the Lord added to their fellowship those who were being saved. (Acts 2:44-47) The early church were not putting high value on materials. They shared and were content. Nowadays people have faith on materials. They judge you according to materials. The more materials you have it means that you are too blessed. That's wrong. People compete now, chase money to be valued. Jesus showed that money is not everything to the rich young ruler. He told him to give everything he had to the poor and follow me. He was shocked because he thought God is materials. People were shocked when Jesus said it is difficult for the rich men to enter into the Kingdom of God because they thought the rich are the ones close to God. Our faith is too low if we are moved by material things. If we value material things more, we end up greedy. We fail to total be obedient to God and fail to minister to the needy. If we are too materialistic, we are not different to the world. We say we love with the mouth and fail in works then our faith is dead. "For what will it profit a man if he gains the whole world, and loses his own soul?" (Mark 8:36). The word of God has warned us, "Then he said to them, "Watch out! Be on your guard against all kinds of greed; life does not consist in an abundance of possessions." (Luke 12:15). "So, we fix our eyes not on what is seen, but on what is unseen, since what is seen is temporary, but what is unseen is eternal." (2 Corinthians 4:18). God bless you.

**Prayer**

As your word says, "No one can serve two masters. Either you will hate the one and love the other, or you will be devoted to the one and despise the other. You cannot serve both God and money", we shall never serve money but God. We pray that we shall never be materialistic as your word says, "So, we fix our eyes not on what is seen, but on what is unseen, since what is seen is temporary, but what is unseen is eternal." You word says, "For what will it profit a man if he gains the whole world and loses his own soul?". Amen

**Bible verses to study.**

Luke 18:18-30; Acts 2:44-47; Mark 8:36; Luke 12:15; 2 Corinthians 4:18; Mathew 6:33; Romans 12:1-2; Mathew 6:24; 1 Timothy 6:10; Galatians 2:20

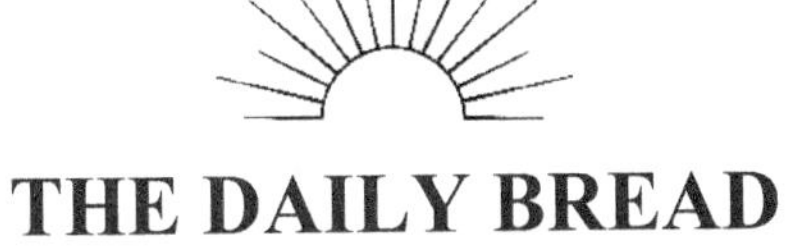

# THE DAILY BREAD

Never give up. It's easy to quit and say it does not work. Everyone can quit but it takes character and faith to stay on when there is no glimpse to show that it would work. Why do people quit? We rely too much on ourselves and do not have faith in God. We always believe it's all about us. Who do you believe on today, yourself or God? When the children of Israel heard about giants, they melted like butter "That night all the members of the community raised their voices and wept aloud. And all the children of Israel murmured against Moses and against Aaron: and the whole congregation said unto them, Would God that we had died in the land of Egypt! Or would God we had died in this wilderness! Why is the LORD bringing us to this land only to let us fall by the sword? Our wives and children will be taken as plunder. Wouldn't it be better for us to go back to Egypt?" (Numbers 14:1-3). The devil wants you to give up. In our daily life not everyone who starts a course will finish it. When they registered, they were excited, but something happened, and they quitted. Some of the people are still coming to church physically but they have quitted on their faith. Others are no longer coming to church because when they faced the challenges, they gave up and returned to their previous life. They have met challenges and stopped their faith journey. Their enthusiasm about the things of God has died. People like Paul were shipwrecked, stoned, jailed and faced death but their faith on God did not waiver. As a child of God, you will meet disappointments, suffer loss and even be prosecuted for the word of God. What do you do when you suffer disappointment, will these bring you closer to God or rebel against God. Today let's watch our attitude because it will determine our altitude. "And let us not be weary in well doing for in due season we shall reap, if we faint not" (Galatians 6:9). Today let the giants you are facing bring you closer to God than make you quit. God bless you.

**Prayer**

Lord help us to have the zeal to finish our races like Paul, as your word says "But none of these things move me; nor do I count my life dear to myself, so that I may finish my race with joy, and the ministry which I received from the Lord Jesus, to testify to the gospel of the grace of God. Your word says, "Not that I have already obtained all this, or have already been made perfect, but I press on to take hold of that for which Christ Jesus took hold of me. Your word says, "And let us not be weary in well doing for in due season we shall reap, if we faint not". As your word says, "And He said to me, "My grace suffices you, for the power is perfected in weakness." Therefore, will I boast rather most gladly in my weaknesses, so that the power of Christ may rest upon me". Our faith shall never fail. Being confident of this, that he who began a good work in us will carry it on to completion until the day of Christ Jesus. Amen

**Bible verses to study.**

Numbers 14:1-3; 2 Corinthians 11:25; Psalms 30:5; Philippians 1:6; Acts 20.24; Philippians 4:13; 2 Chronicles 15:7; Galatians 6:9; Isaiah 40:10

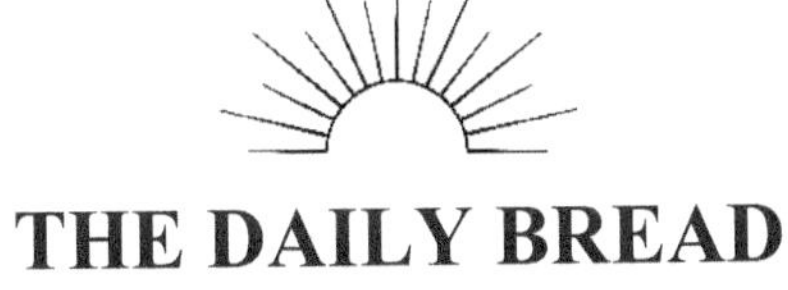

# THE DAILY BREAD

Locker. A locker is a small compartment usually mental but lockable. The owner of the locker keeps the keys unless he/she gives them to someone else. It is very private in a way that if the owner does not open it, you won't see what is inside. People can hide stuff inside the locker. Everyone have their private life that if we are not told about it, we may never know what is inside the locker. When we got born again, we had locker full things of the world. These things are not good for us but not easy not let them go. These are habits, things which were acceptable to world but not with God. Today has your locker been emptied. I had also things in my locker. I said God I want to follow you, but I want to keep these things in my locker. Later, through my spiritual walk with God I realised that keeping ungodly stuff in my locker, it robs me my relationship with God and delays the plans God has for my life. When I got victory, it will be short lived because of stuff of the world I was keeping in my life. The devil can tell you, just a glass of wine, it would not harm anyone. By honouring one request by the devil, you will end up getting drunk and opening a gap to drawback. I have emptied my locker. I am not saying I am perfect, but I have cut ties with everything I knew were contrary to the word of God. We must be totally depended on God. David said the Lord is my Shepherd, I shall not want. You can fool the people but not God. The word of God says, "For there is nothing hidden that will not be disclosed, and nothing concealed that will not be known or brought out into the open" (Luke 8:17). Whatever you do in your private life, let it be something that when your pastor walks in, you will say amen. God bless you.

**Prayer**

As your word says, "You were taught, with regard to your former way of life, to put off your old self, which is being corrupted by its deceitful desires;" we shall never admire our past and go back to it. There is nothing good about our past, we are now focused on the life which Christ has laid before us. Your word says, "And do not be conformed to this world, but be transformed by the renewing of your mind, that you may prove what *is* that good and acceptable and perfect will of God". Your word says, "Take no part in the unfruitful works of darkness, but instead expose them." Your word teaches us that "If we say that we have fellowship with Him, and walk in darkness, we lie and do not practice the truth. Amen.

**Bible verses to study.**

Luke 8:17; Romans 8:1-2; Ephesians 4:22; Mathew 6:24; Ephesians 5:11-14; Mathew 11:28; 1 John 1:6-7

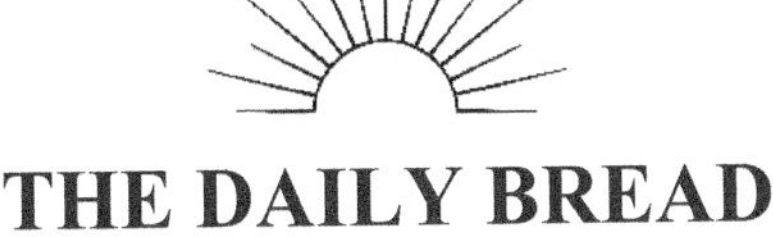

# THE DAILY BREAD

Waiting. It's not easy to wait but it's necessary. How many times have we not waited on the Lord and found ourselves wanting. Waiting is not easy. This generation now want to behave like microwave Christians. Everything is I want it now. No one is prepared to wait. Waiting is not actually a bad thing; it trains us before we receive a blessing. Receiving the blessing too early may harm you than empower you. We need to pray and wait on the Lord. "And whatever things you ask in prayer, believing, you will receive." (Mathew 21:22) People usually pray and do not wait for God to answer. God answers our prayers. It might be a business venture, another job, investment, life partner and decision on a particular subject. When we pray, we need to have faith. "But without faith it is impossible to please him: for he that comes to God must believe that he is, and that he is a rewarder of them that diligently seek him. (Hebrew 11:6) God does not delay. It may look like a long time, but God will answer our prayers. God' timing is the best for us. He knows everything and who are we to question God. "But those who wait on the LORD Shall renew their strength; They shall mount up with wings like eagles, they shall run and not be weary, they shall walk and not faint. (Isaiah 40:31) The other reason why people can't wait on the Lord is when we pray, we are just doing it as a routine since we presume to know everything. We need to let God be God in our lives. Let's stop telling God what He must do with our lives and start asking Him to show us the way. The word of God says we must ask, and it shall be given to us, but we ask amiss. The reason why is that we do not know the perfect will upon our lives, and we also ask with wrong motives. In most of the cases Christians find themselves in whole lot of problems because they just pray and do not wait on the Lord. God is still speaking in our lives. We need to pray and wait on the Lord. "Surely none who wait for You will be put to shame; but those who are faithless without cause will be disgraced". (Psalms 25:3) God is faithful. Waiting on the Lord does not mean that you become idle. If you are waiting on God for a job, you need to apply, if you are waiting on God for marriage for men, you need to save money and find the woman and as for women you need to serve in Church and be available. May the Holy Spirit teach you to be humble so that when God answers your prayers, you do not miss the blessing. We should not use worldly standard for the things of God, otherwise we will wait forever. The word of God teaches us that, "Trust in the LORD with all your heart and lean not on your own understanding;" (Proverbs 3:5). God bless you.


**Prayer**

As your word says, "Surely none who wait for You will be put to shame; but those who are faithless without cause will be disgraced", we shall wait on you. Your word says, "But those who wait on the LORD Shall renew their strength; They shall mount up with wings like eagles, they shall run and not be weary, they shall walk and not faint." Your word says, "And whatever things you ask in prayer, believing, you will receive." We pray that we should have faith to wait on you as your word says, ""But without faith it is impossible to please him: for he that comes to God must believe that he is, and that he is a rewarder of them that diligently seek him". Amen


**Bible verses to study**

Mathew 21:22; Hebrew 11:6; Isaiah 40:31; Psalms 25:3; Proverbs 3:5; Psalms 27:14; Psalms 37:7; Psalms 37:9; Psalms 130:5; Psalms 25:4-5; Habakkuk 2:3

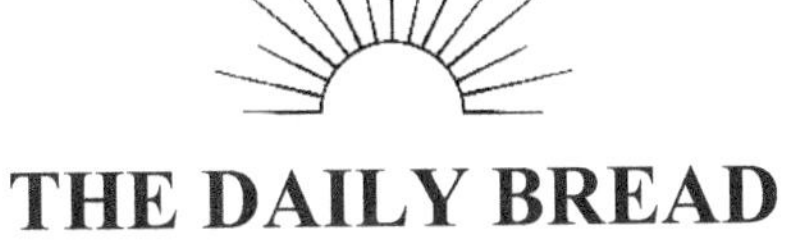

# THE DAILY BREAD

Don't go back to Egypt. When people receive Jesus Christ as their Lord and saviour, they are so excited. They know now there have been set free. But there is a journey ahead waiting for you. The children of Israel cried to the Lord because of bondage in Egypt. The Lord delivered them from Egyptians in one day. When they left Egypt, they were so excited. But their excitement died quickly because of the Journey ahead. First it was the red sea, the bitter water, the food got finished and the wars they had to fight to continue with the journey. It may be tough child of God but don't go back to Egypt. Yes, they were pots of meat, the garlic and spices. But remember you were under bondage. You did not have the freedom. You were tormented, beaten up and robbed of your time and resources. Yet you still believe that maybe this time things will change. Maybe I will love Pharaoh more, maybe he will treat me right. Maybe Pharaoh is a changed man, he has learnt a lesson and things will change. Insanity is keeping on doing the same thing expecting a different result. If you use a cow dung to make a cake no matter how beautiful it looks, it still stinks. Let me tell you, don't look back. Your old self was corrupt. You cannot be like a dog that returns to its vomit. That lifestyle that is ungodly will kill you. Just this extra fix, I can cheat with this guy, I can gamble for the last time and just one more drink. It's the call of the flesh that is weighing you down. Who said it was going to be easy. Jesus said if you want to be my disciple, you must deny yourself and carry your cross daily. Your peers may look like successful with the worldly life and you look like a fool because you have not attained those things. God is faithful. You are in the right direction just have faith. But without faith it is impossible to please Him, for he who comes to God must believe that He is, and that He is a rewarder of those who diligently seek Him". (Hebrews 11:6) By going back to Egypt, you are telling God that I trusted you and it has failed me, now I trust myself. "For I know that good itself does not dwell in me, that is, in my sinful nature. For I have the desire to do what is good, but I cannot carry it out." (Romans 7: 18). We need to deny ourselves and carry our crosses daily so that we don't go back to our past lives. God bless you.


**Prayer**

We pray that we will never go back to my past life. We have decided to follow Jesus no turning back. The devil robbed us in the past but now not anymore. Your word says, "Therefore do not let sin reign in your mortal body, that you should obey it in its lusts." Your word teaches us that, "Be sober, be vigilant; because your adversary the devil walks about like a roaring lion, seeking whom he may devour." We pray that we have faith in you God as your word says the just shall live by faith. Your word says, "But without faith it is impossible to please Him, for he who comes to God must believe that He is, and that He is a rewarder of those who diligently seek Him". Amen.


**Bible verses to study**

Hebrews 11:6; Romans 7: 18; Jeremiah 6:16; Isaiah 43:18-19; Romans 12:2; Luke 9:62; Hebrews 6:4-6; Philippians 3:13; Hebrews 12:1; James 4:8; Ezekial 36:26

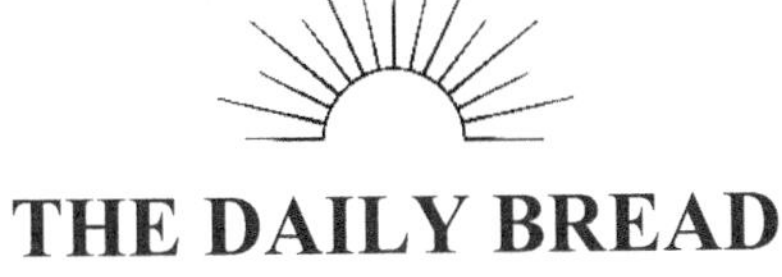

# THE DAILY BREAD

Threatened. Do you feel threatened today. Are you seeing yourself perishing, your job on the line, your marriage in turmoil, your business closing down, your health turning worse, losing your car or house and in financial doldrums. It's not true. The devil wants you to believe that you are going down, no one can save you and he will destroy you. There is a letter written by the devil threatening your life. Hezekiah received a letter from the king of Assyria, that he will destroy him and his people. Some of you, you received letters that there will never be peace in your life, you will never get married, you will amount to nothing, you will stay poor, you will die, and you are not qualified. Hezekiah took the letter to the house of God and presented it before God and prayed. God said to Hezekiah, "Therefore thus says the Lord concerning the King of Assyria: He shall not come into the city or shoot an arrow there or come before it with a shield or cast up a siege mound against it " (Isaiah 37:33). Today trust God with your situation and circumstances. Pray and praise God. Whatever negative words said in your life shall not come to pass. God will fight for you and defend you. Have faith. His plans are not to harm you but to prosper you. You shall never have a drowning faith like Jonah to start calling on God in the belly of fish. You must seek God in good times and bad times not to use God as crutches and seek God in trouble only. Fear is the opposite to faith, its believing what the enemy is going to do than God. The word of God says, "For God has not given us a spirit of fear, but of power and of love and of a sound mind". (2 Timothy 1:7). Just remember that our weapons are not carnal but mighty to pull down the strongholds. The word of God says, "A thousand may fall at your side, And ten thousand at your right hand; But it shall not come near you." (Psalms 91:7). Blessed is the name of the Lord because when the enemy comes in like a flood, The Spirit of the LORD will lift up a standard against him. God bless you.

**Prayer**

We pray that we should not tell you God how big are our problems but tell our problems how big our God is. Your word says, "For God has not given us a spirit of fear, but of power and of love and of a sound mind". Your word says, "Do not gloat over me, my enemy! Though I have fallen, I will rise. Though I sit in darkness, the LORD will be my light." Like David, your word says, "Yea, though I walk through the valley of the shadow of death, I will fear no evil; For You are with me; Your rod and Your staff, they comfort me. You prepare a table before me in the presence of my enemies; You anoint my head with oil; My cup runs over." Your word says, "I will lift up my eyes to the hills— From whence comes my help? My help comes from the LORD, who made heaven and earth. He will not allow my foot to be moved; He who keeps me will not slumber". Amen

**Bible verses to study**

Isaiah 37:33; Isaiah 37:33; Isaiah 54:7; Micah 7:8; Psalms 23:1-6; Psalms 91:1-16; Psalms 127:1; Jeremiah 29:11; Proverbs 3:5; Psalms 37:4-6

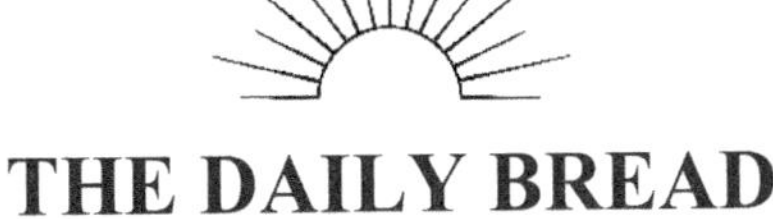

# THE DAILY BREAD

Budget. Personal financial advisers will advise you to draw a budget every month on how to spend your money. Unfortunately, most people live without a budget. They wonder why I am broke in the middle of the month. It does not help to create a budget and you do not follow it. When you have a budget and go to the mall for example when you see those fancy shoes, you will say this is not my budget. You will have guidelines on your spending and thereby create discipline. I was inspired by Bishop TD Jakes when he said we need to have a budget for our life. Because you were living in the world now you are born again amen your life has changed. You cannot walk the way you used to without God. So, you need to draw a life budget that if your friends invite you to go and braai at the place where they sale alcohol, you must say this is not in my budget and say my budget does not allow me to go and braai at place that sales alcohol. If you get tempted with drinking, lying, invited to go to a club, adultery and fighting, you must look into your budget. Without life budget you will end up in areas where you do not want to go and allowing stuff which will end up corrupting you. There is no one who is bullet proof, David a man after God's heart committed adultery and murder because of lack of self-control. A city without walls is weak; the enemy will walk all over it. Have a budget of your life to do and not to do. Have discipline in your life. Your budget must be drawn from the word of God. Therefore, the bible is your master budget. The Psalmist said, "Your word is a lamp for my feet, a light on my path." (Psalms 119:105). Implement your life budget and reclaim those other territories the devil has robed you. David said, "I have hidden your word in my heart that I might not sin against you". (Psalms 119:11). God bless you.

**Prayer**

Thank you, Lord, for the life you have given us. We will not trade it for anything. It is a glorious life, a blessed life and peaceful life. Your word says, What does it benefits man to gain this world and lose his soul? Cover us, Lord. Deliver us from the evil one. We are separated for you Lord. Use us, Lord. Your word says, I beseech you brethren by the mercies of the Lord that you present your bodies as a living sacrifice, holy and acceptable to God that is a reasonable service. Let us say no to sinful life and our souls to say yes to you Lord. Amen


**The bible verses to study**

Luke 12:42; Mathew 25:14-30; Genesis 39:2-6; Genesis 41:39-41; Proverbs 21:20; Luke 16:19; Galatians 5:22

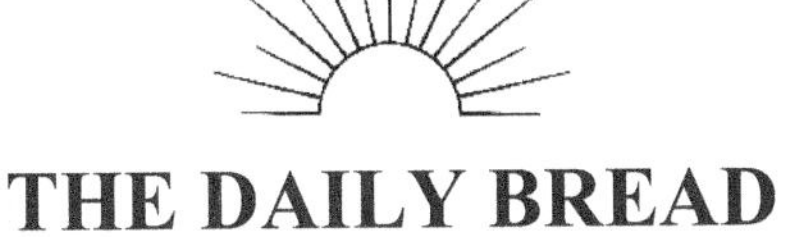

# THE DAILY BREAD

Let there be light. The reason why there is so much darkness in the world is because of lights which are not shinning. It does not matter the magnitude of darkness, when the light comes the darkness flees. The word of God is saying this morning, "Arise, shine, for your light has come, and the glory of the LORD rises upon you". (Isaiah 60:1) "See, darkness covers the earth and thick darkness is over the peoples, but the LORD rises upon you and his glory appears over you. Nations will come to your light, and kings to the brightness of your dawn". (Isaiah 60:2-3). Jesus is the true light. We have the true light when we abide in Him. We have power over darkness because of the light in us. We are the ones giving the power to the darkness. Its high time we must stand up and say let there be light. Speak that light to the lost in the world. Let them see the light. I got the power, and you got the power. We have lost so much by keeping quiet now it's the high time to proclaim the good news to the people. They need to know about the light. The question you must ask yourself today is, does your light still shinning? I can't accept how this world looks like; I will never accept that people will not change but I will persevere. Paul said, "For I am not ashamed of the gospel, because it is the power of God that brings salvation to everyone who believes: first to the Jew, then to the Gentile" (Romans 1:16). The word has been preached to me, I have experienced its power, I have seen that it works and saw people being set free. Today you should never grow weary in proclaiming the Light to the rest of the world. The word of God teaches us that, "You are the light of the world. A city that is set on a hill cannot be hidden. Nor do they light a lamp and put it under a basket, but on a lampstand, and it gives light to all who are in the house. Let your light so shine before men, that they may see your good works, and glorify your Father which is in heaven." (Mathew 5:14-16). Lights that are hidden under the bed are a waste of oil.

We are anointed by God for a purpose. We need to work through the anointing and win souls for the kingdom of God. The reason why our lights are no longer bright is because they are hidden and the supply of oil has been cut off, you are just a dry Christian. God bless you.


**Prayer**

As your word says, "You are the light of the world. A city that is set on a hill cannot be hidden. Nor do they light a lamp and put it under a basket, but on a lampstand, and it gives light to all who are in the house. Let your light so shine before men, that they may see your good works, and glorify your Father which is in heaven", we shall bring the light to those sitting in the darkness. You promised us in your word that, "See, darkness covers the earth and thick darkness is over the peoples, but the LORD rises upon you and his glory appears over you. Nations will come to your light, and kings to the brightness of your dawn". Your word says, "Arise, shine, for your light has come, and the glory of the LORD rises upon you". Amen.


**Bible verses to study.**

Isaiah 60:1-3; Romans 1:16; Mathew 5:14-16; 1 Peter 2:9; John 8:12; John 1:5; Psalms 27:1; 2 Corinthians 4:6; Genesis 1:3; Acts 13:47; Daniel 2:22

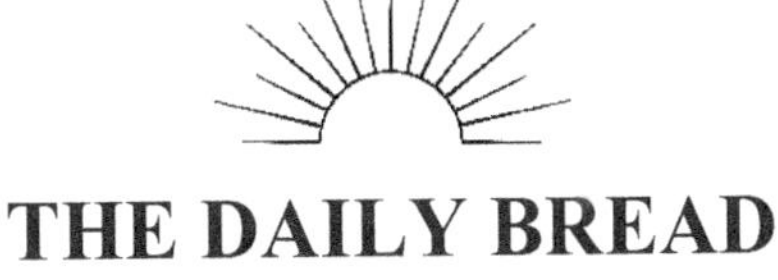

# THE DAILY BREAD

Foolish Galatians. Spiritual, Paul gave birth to these people. He saw them crawling, taking one step and learning to talk. He rejoiced seeing them growing but like a dog, they returned to their vomit. The Galatians when they started, they were spiritual but later they become carnal. Paul wrote to them "You ran so well. Who hindered you from obeying truth" (Galatians 5:7). Jesus had delivered them from bondage, but they returned to a life of being salves. At first, they were zealous about things of God but later on they become zealous of the things of the world. The world had corrupted them. Paul really suffered because of their situation, and he wrote "O foolish Galatians! Who has bewitched you that you should not obey the truth, before whose eyes Jesus Christ was clearly portrayed among you as crucified" (Galatians 3:1). The Galatians were no longer living by faith but by flesh. Like some Christians, when they started the journey of faith, they were very passionate about things of God and very excited. Slowly they started to grow cold, bit by bit they returned to their old ways. The things of the world killed the fire. I pray that your fire shall never stop burning for the things of God, you shall not faint, you shall not depart from the word of the truth which you were saved with, you shall not return to your old self and your faith shall never fail. Let's not make a mistake and think we are something whilst we are nothing and deceive ourselves. We have not attained it yet, but we will keep pushing until we get hold of it what God had laid for our lives. It's painful for a shepherd to lose a sheep because they dearly love the sheep. As we have tasted the goodness of God let's stay put no matter what may come. I have decided to follow Jesus no turning back – no turning back. God bless you.

**Prayer**

We pray that our fire shall never stop burning for the things of God, we shall not faint, we shall not depart from the word of the truth which we were saved with, we shall not return to our old self and our faith shall never fail. As your word says "You ran so well. Who hindered you from obeying truth" nothing shall hinder us from the obeying the truth. As your word says "I know your works, that you are neither cold nor hot. I wish you would be cold or hot. So, because you are lukewarm—neither hot nor cold—I am about to vomit you out of My mouth!", we shall always be hot for your Lord. Amen


**Bible verses to study**

Galatians 5:7; Galatians 3:1; Proverbs 14:14; 1 Joh 1:9; Hebrews 6:4-6; Proverbs 24:16; Hosea 14:1; Proverbs 14:14

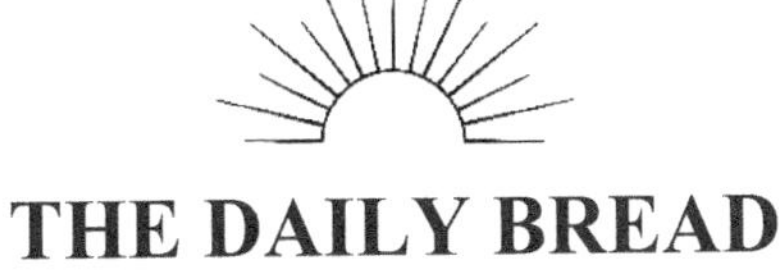

# THE DAILY BREAD

How many things have you failed to accomplish simply because you are AFRAID. The spirit of FEAR can paralyse you and make you feel useless. You may be afraid of starting a new project and leaving your comfort zone. You may be afraid of being hurt again, so you now shun investing your emotions into a relationship or your marriage. You may have been traumatised in ministry, so you are now afraid of being abused! Indeed, there may be people who are plotting against you. It doesn't matter how anointed you are, they will still plot against you. But God has reserved a group of people who love you and will do anything to protect you. The Apostle Paul faced such hatred when he started preaching the gospel. "After many days had gone by, the Jews conspired to kill him, but Paul learned of their plan. Day and night they kept close watch on the city gates in order to kill him. BUT his followers TOOK him by night and LOWERED him in a basket through an opening in the wall..." (Acts 9:23-25) Be assured that there will always be people who hate you, whether you are silent or vocal. Trouble has a way of looking for you even if you are a good person. As the preacher said, "I have seen a righteous man perishing in his righteousness and a wicked man living long in his wickedness...." (Ecclesiastes 7:15) but God did not CALL you so that He could abandon you to the hyenas. Fear Not! For God has created a security system for your situation, that cannot be breached. You are protected. God bless you.


**Prayer**

As your word says," For God has not given us a spirit of fear, but of power and of love and of a sound mind," we shall never live a life in fear. We have hope and expectation because if God you are for us who can be against us. No weapons formed and fashioned against us shall prosper. We pray that God, you put a hedge around us like Job. "For the weapons of our warfare are not carnal but mighty in God for pulling down strongholds," Your word says that goodness and mercy shall follow us all the days of lives. As your word says the just shall live by faith, we shall never bow down to fear. "Yet in all these things we are more than conquerors through Him who loved us." Amen


**The bible verses to study.**

Acts 9:23-25; Luke 10:25-37; 2 Kings 19:14-37; Ecclesiastes 7:15; Psalms 91; 2 Timothy 1:7

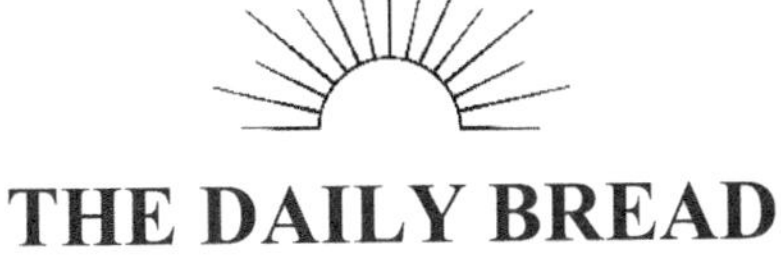

# THE DAILY BREAD

Once upon a time. My wish is for you to say once upon I was single, once upon a time I was unemployed, once upon time I was poor and once upon a time I was sick. All those things must be in your history. There is a part of your life which looked fine yet not so good, when you struggled for answers. But because of Jesus, your story has changed. The word of God says, "But seek first the kingdom of God and His righteousness, and all these things shall be added to you". (Mathew 6:33). People must wonder is that you. The same water that which was killing the people; it was the same water that lifting Noah's ark. In the time of a drought, there was an Isaac who reaped a hundred-fold. So, there is no excuse in life for you not to be successfully. May God make you a burning bush, that there is fire burning on you but not burning you? May the light of Jesus shine on you so that the unbelievers can say that the hand of God. You cannot just live life without a purpose. If your life has not pointed out to you that there is God in heaven, its either you are ignorant or a fool. Do not live life like a trailer, where the car going it goes too. Defy the odds." I will lift up my eyes to the hills - From whence comes my help? My help come from the Lord, who made heaven and earth" (Psalms 121:1-2). Jesus turned water into wine; He will change your story. We serve a mighty God as your word says, "He raises the poor from the dust and lifts the needy from the ash heap; he seats them with princes and has them inherit a throne of honour. "For the foundations of the earth are the LORD's; on them he has set the world." (1 Samuel 2:8) Everyone Jesus met in the bible; He changed their story. There is a resurrection power in your life. If Jesus raise Lazarus from the dead, he will raise you up in every situation. The grave cannot keep hold over you." But if the Spirit of Him who raised Jesus from the dead dwells in you, He who raised Christ from the dead will also give life to your mortal bodies through His Spirit who dwells in you." (Romans 8:11) God bless you.


**Prayer**

Thank you, Lord, we were lost and now we are found. The life we are living now is in hope of who called us. We are moving from glory to glory. And we know that all things work together for good to them that love God, to them who are the called according to his purpose. You have turned our water into wine. There is a resurrection power in our lives. If Jesus you raised Lazarus from the dead, you will raise us up from every situation. We shall never remain the grave and the grave cannot get hold us down. Your word says, "But if the Spirit of Him who raised Jesus from the dead dwells in you, He who raised Christ from the dead will also give life to your mortal bodies through His Spirit who dwells in you." Amen.


**The bible verses to study.**

Mathew 6:33; Isaiah 61:3; Psalms 121:1-2; 1 Samuel 2:8; Romans 8:11; John 3:3; 2 Corinthians 5:17; Ezekiah 36:26; Romans 12:2; Psalms 51:10

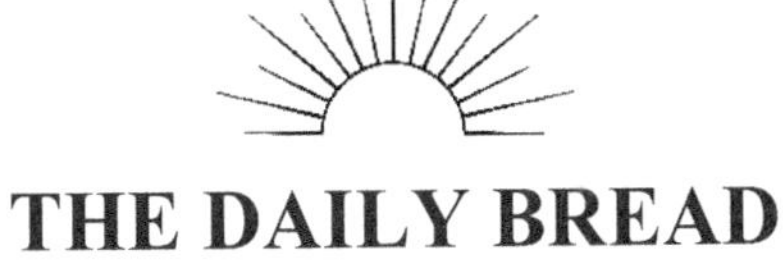

# THE DAILY BREAD

Comfortable. Being comfortable sometimes can make you live a mediocre life. God may allow that comfort to be taken away so that you draw more closely to Him. I thank God for taking away that comfort in my life. Now I have been taught to rely on God. God knows the best for you. There might be things which did not materialise in your life and taken away from you. Your plans were far away from what God has planned for you that's why things did not turn the way you anticipated. Do not think a bit that God does not love you. God wants to bless you with a blessing that's does not add sorrow into your life. It is in the valley where we learn most than being on top of the mountain. Those distractions are gone, look now how you have matured in Christ. We serve a jealous God, anything that we exalt high above God, it shall come down. Joseph was sold into slavery by his brothers. Joseph was thrown into prison although he was innocent. When the comfort was taken away from his life, Joseph remained faithful to God, and he became a ruler in Egypt. You shall be tried and tested. May you remain faithfully in the Lord. Job lost everything including his health, but he remained faithful. Your joy for the Lord should not be related to the materials things. "Being confident of this very thing, that he who has begun a good work in you will perform it until the day of Jesus Christ" (Philippians 1:6). There is life called most, almost and uttermost. Most people remain in most because they do love comfortable life. They do not want to step out of the boat like Peter. If you are an employee, why don't you study further or one day start your business. If you own business, why don't grow your business or add more businesses. The next stage is for the almost. They try to leave the most but when the conditions become tough, they are quick quit. At this stage people say I almost finished my degree, I also got married, I almost started a business. You always remain as almost. Then comes the last stage on uttermost. Uttermost, is a stage where only a few can reach it. How many people have doctorates, how many people who are running their own business and how many people who are billionaires. They are only a few who can withstand the disappointments and never give up. Those who have a vision to say the sky is the limit. You never be satisfied as the most or almost, but you should be uttermost. God bless you.

**Prayer**

We pray that we shall never be comfortable but move out of the boat and walk on top of the water like Peter. As your word say, "And the Angel of the LORD appeared to him, and said to him, "The LORD is with you, you mighty man of valour!", I am a Mighty man of Valour. Mediocre life is not our portion, we shall have life in full as promised by Jesus Christ. Your word says, "Being confident of this very thing, that he who has begun a good work in you will perform it until the day of Jesus Christ". "We can do all things through Christ who gives me strength". Amen.

**Bible verses to study.**

Philippians 1:6; Joshua 1:9; 2 Timothy 1:7; Philippians 4:13; John 15:16; James 1:22; Jeremiah 29:11-14; Proverbs 3:5-6; Mathew 14:29-31

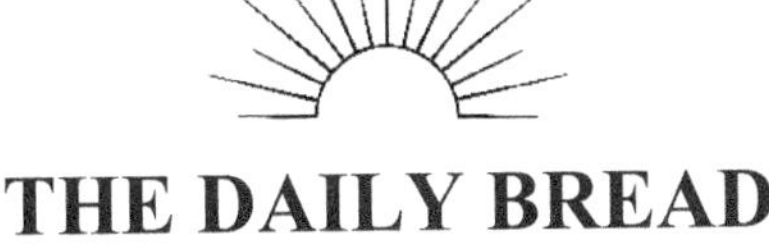

# THE DAILY BREAD

Building a house. When you drive or walk around, you will see that people are building and they are at different stages. On some stands the grass has grown because no activities are happening and on others there is a slab only. All these people when they bought the land, they had intention of building a house. This can be compared to our race of faith. When people got born again, they intended to complete their race, but something happened in between, and they stopped. Some of the Christian just got born again and stopped coming to church. They did not work on their faith, so they are like a land bought but nothing was built on it. Others when they got born again, they were really involved with things of God for a little while but because of continuing living a worldly life, they got corrupted again and were drawn back. You cannot serve two masters. At the end they also stopped coming church. These are the ones who stopped building like at a slab level. Most of the Christians are in this group where they are also still building but their houses are not yet completed. Paul said "Brothers and sisters, I do not consider myself yet to have taken hold of it. But one thing I do: Forgetting what is behind and straining toward what is ahead. I press on toward the goal to win the prize for which God has called me heavenward in Christ Jesus" (Philippians 3:13-14). Brothers and sisters, we cannot afford to build this house without God. "Unless the Lord builds the house, they labour in vain who build it;" (Psalms 127:1). Build your house on the rock not on the sand so that when the storm comes, it will remain standing. Let Jesus be the foundation of our houses therefore we must not be the hearers of the word only but the doers too. One day my house shall be completed like Paul. "I have fought the good fight, I have finished the race, I have kept the faith" (2 Timothy 4:7). God bless you.

**Prayer**

As your word says, "Unless the LORD builds the house, they labour in vain who build it; Unless the LORD guards the city, The watchman keeps awake in vain", we pray that we shall start the race with you God so that you can help us to complete it. We shall not grow weary in doing good because in due season, we shall be rewarded if we faint not. "Being confident of this, that he who began a good work in you will carry it on to completion until the day of Christ Jesus". Our faith shall never fail. We shall dwell in the house of the Lord forever. Amen.

**Bible verses to study**

Psalms 127:1; Philippians 3:13-14; Hebrews 12:1; 1 Corinthians 9: 24-25; Philippians 3:14; 2 Timothy 4:7

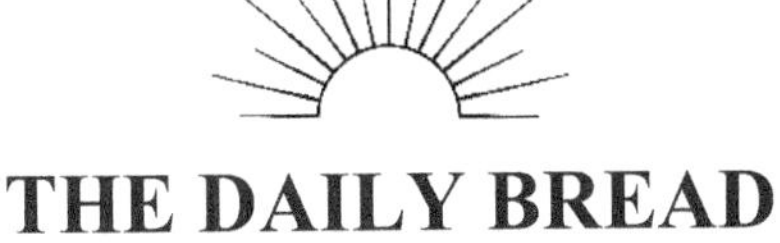

# THE DAILY BREAD

Negative talking takes away the blessing. Its already yours but through your mouth, talking negatively, you talked yourself out of it. The children of Israel spoke bad about the promised land after receiving a bad report by the spies. "And there we saw the giants, the sons of Anak, which come of the giants: and we were in our own sight as grasshoppers, and so we were in their sight. So, all the congregation lifted up their voices and cried, and the people wept that night." (Numbers 13:33 - 14:1) The land was theirs, but they failed to enter into it. It might be a Pastor Shepherding you if you speak negative about him, you will lose all the blessings God wanted to give you through him. You cannot be blessed with something you curse. The people Jesus healed had faith. If you speak negatively, it means you have lost your faith. There might be someone whom God put in your life, your father, brother, sister and a leader. Do not devour them through negative talking. You will lose all the blessings. They will no longer able to bless you. Miriam and Aaron went against Moses and spoke negative things and instead of being blessed through Moses, they brought a curse. The Holy Spirit once told me not to speak negative about people. It's really important for you to live a blessed life. Why we always speak negative about other people? It's the works of the devil wanting us to destroy other people. "And why do you look at the speck in your brother's eye, but do not consider the plank in your own eye?" (Mathew 7:3) Even Psalms chapter one teaches us that, blessed are those who do not sit in the seat of the scornful. Be a blessing, do not judge, there is no one is without a sin. Love and love and love again. "Death and life are in the power of the tongue, and those who love it will eat its fruit". (Proverbs 18:21).

**Prayer**

We pray that we choose to speak positively towards our blessings because negative talking takes away our blessings. Words of life should proceed from our mouths, not curses and death. We shall never use our mouth to gossip and curse people. We choose to see the milk and honey in the land than the giants. Help us O Holy Spirit not to speak negative words against the people. Your word teaches us that, "Death and life are in the power of the tongue, and those who love it will eat its fruit". Amen

**Bible verses to study.**

Numbers 13:33 - 14:1; Mathew 7:3; Proverbs 18:21; Ephesians 4:29; Proverbs 21:23; Proverbs 17:22; Philippians 4:8; Romans 12:2

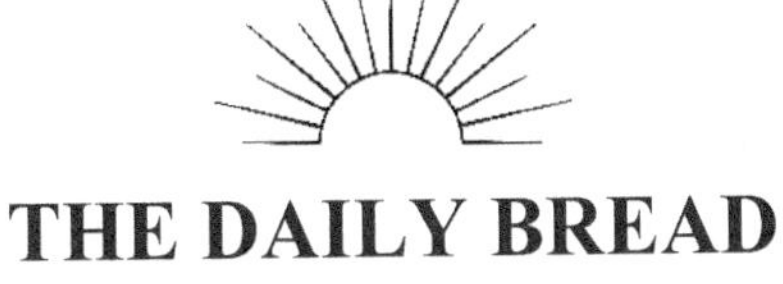

# THE DAILY BREAD

Consistency – It is of paramount importance that we become consistent. Our prayer life should be consistent. When I look into the word of God, I see Daniel had his own prayer time. The people knew at this hour Daniel is praying. People are inconsistent with their prayer life. They don't seem to get it right. For you to achieve greatness in your prayer life, it's not about things will just happen, no you need to be deliberate about your prayer life. We really need to plan in terms of our spiritual life as we do with anything in our life. Without a disciplined prayer life, it will be difficult for us also to be stable in our Christian walk. A prayerless life leads to a faithless life. They will be days when we will walk out naked and days when we will walk out clothed with his glory. We are crying for consistency. Being consistent will bring you a desired life with no surprises. The word of God said we must never give a room to the devil. Chances of drawing back are few. I know you really want to serve God, so do it right. Have your own prayer time and stick to it. Today I am asking you, how do you value your prayer time? Do you pray every day? Has the world caught up with us that we no longer have time for God? Are you too busy for God? If your prayer life is none-existent just know that your love of God is growing cold. We really need to be in the presence of God, that's where we get our strength, get our joy and peace and we also get our victory. When we become prayerful, we also become fearless, faithfully, reliable, joyful and powerful. A prayer less life will make you to become a danger to yourself and other people, consequently you will draw back. God bless you.


**Prayer**

We pray that Lord Jesus, you help us to have consistency in our prayer life. After waking up every morning we should pray.

Before we eat, we should pray and before we sleep, we should pray. Your word says, "And pray in the Spirit on all occasions with all kinds of prayers and requests. With this in mind, be alert and always keep on praying for all the Lord's people." We shall never give a room to the devil. We shall never rely on yesterday's anointing. We will always be thirsty for you Lord. We shall seek you God, day and night. Your word will never depart from our lips, and we will do according to it. Amen


**Bible verses to study.**

1 Corinthians 15:58; Galatians 6:9; Luke 16:13; Mathew 5:37; Psalms 9:10; Proverbs 8:17; Hebrews 11:6; Mathew 6:33; 1 Chronicles 16:11

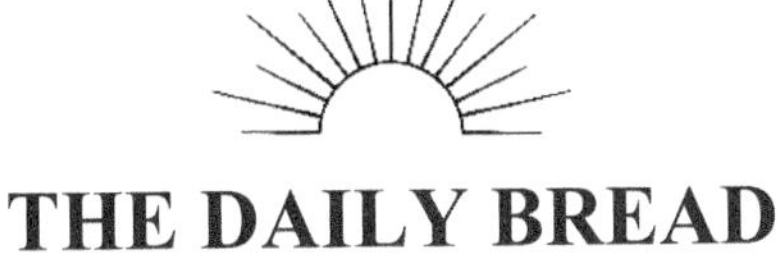

# THE DAILY BREAD

They Know Your Power More Than You Do....Have you seen how much your enemies know about your power. They seem to be obsessed with knowing your capabilities, your weaknesses and your desires. That is why the devil will never tempt you with money if your weakness is sex. The devil knows you and your power probably more than you know it yourself. That is why Joseph was hated by his brothers even though he did not know the interpretation of his own dreams. (Genesis 37:6-8) Your enemies know your dreams and their interpretation. They know where you are going that is why King Herod put Peter under heavy guard. As the Bible says, "When he had arrested him, he put him in prison, and delivered him to four squads of soldiers to keep him, intending to bring him before the people after Passover." (Acts 12:4) Why would you put an unarmed fisherman/ preacher under such heavy guard? Your challenges are directly proportional to your anointing. You are a champion that is why you are under siege. "Be sober, be vigilant; because your adversary the devil walks about like a roaring lion, seeking whom he may devour. (1 Peter 5:8) The devil knew Job's weakness that why he said to God, "Does Job worship God for nothing". Job was blessed by God with wealth and a great family. Job lost everything, his wealth, his family and his health. After losing everything the word of God says "Then Job got up, tore his robe, and shaved his head; then he fell to the ground and worshiped. And he said: "Naked I came from my mother's womb, And naked shall I return there. The LORD gave, and the LORD has taken away; Blessed be the name of the LORD. In all this Job did not sin nor charge God with wrong." (Job 1:19-21) The enemy knows about you more than you. The more anointed you are the bigger the giants you will face. David faced the lion, the bear and Goliath before he became a King. The word of God reminds us that, ".…. : Yet in all these things we are more than conquerors through Him who loved us." (Romans 8:37) God bless you.


**Prayer**

Thank you, Lord, because you have put a hedge around us. Our homes are blessed, our families are blessed, our finances are blessed, our health is blessed, and our business are blessed. We are walking in power; we are walking in miracles, and we live a life of favour because we know who we are in Christ Jesus. There are angels guiding us and protecting us. We are the apple of your eye. Whatever is born of God will overcome the world. Although we walk through the valley of shadow of death, we fear not evil for you are with us. No weapon formed and fashioned against us shall prosper. Thank you, Lord, for your grace is sufficient for us. Amen


**The bible verses to study.**

Genesis 37:6-8; Acts 12:4; 1 Peter 5:8-9; Acts 12:4; Job 1:19-21; Romans 8:37; Hebrews 2:14; John 14:15

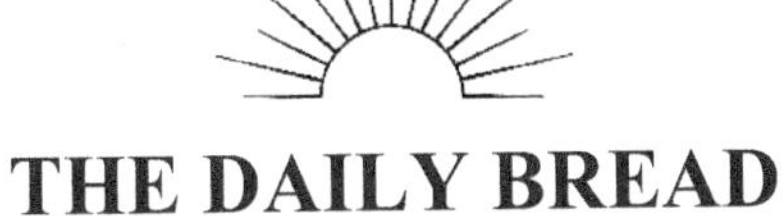

# THE DAILY BREAD

Who is leading you today?" For the flesh desires what is contrary to the Spirit and the Spirit what is contrary to the flesh. They are in conflict with each other, so that you are not to do whatever you want. But if you are led by the Spirit, you are not under the law. The acts of the flesh are obvious: sexual immorality, impurity and debauchery; and witchcraft; hatred, discord, jealousy, fits of rage, idolatry, selfish ambition, dissensions, factions and envy; drunkenness, orgies, and the like. I warn you, as I did before, that those who live like this will not inherit the kingdom of God. But the fruit of the Spirit is love, joy, peace, forbearance, kindness, goodness, faithfulness, gentleness and self-control. Against such things there is no law" (Galatians 5:17-23). If we feed our flesh and neglect our Spirit, the acts of the flesh will manifest in our lives. Our flesh is contrary to the Spirit. You can't live a life feeding your flesh only and do what the Spirit wants. If you relax in your Spiritual life, your old self will creep up. Paul warned us "Be very careful, then, how you live--not as unwise but as wise making the most of every opportunity, because the days are evil. Therefore, do not be foolish, but understand what the Lord's will is. Do not get drunk on wine, which leads to debauchery. Instead, be filled with the Spirit," (Ephesians 5:15-18). Today let us be filled with the Spirit. The fruits of the Spirit will be seen in our lives. The word of God said to be carnal minded is death but to be Spiritual minded is life. The devil is not far away but very close so let's be wary and vigilant because he is roaring like a lion seeking whom he may devour. It's easy to see who is leading you. If its flesh, flesh fruits will show up and if its Spirit, Spirit fruits will show up. "For every tree is known by its own fruit. For men do not gather figs from thorns, nor do they gather grapes from a bramble bush." (Luke 6:44). If you spend more time listening to worldly music and watching worldly programs don't ever think you will be led by the Spirit. It's a choice that you need to make whether it's feeding the flesh or the Spirit. "For those who are led by the Spirit of God are the children of God." (Romans 8:14). God bless you.

**Prayer**

Your word says, "For those who are led by the Spirit of God are the children of God." We pray that we shall be led by the Holy Spirit. Like Paul we shall say, "I have been crucified with Christ; it is no longer I who live, but Christ lives in me; and the life which I now live in the flesh I live by faith in the Son of God, who loved me and gave Himself for me." "For we walk by faith, not by sight". Your word teaches us that, to be carnal minded is death but to be Spiritual minded is life. We shall feed our Spirit and starve my flesh by spending more time in the presence of God. As your word says, "For every tree is known by its own fruit. For men do not gather figs from thorns, nor do they gather grapes from a bramble bush," we shall abide in Jesus Christ the true vine and bear much fruit. Amen

**Bible verses to study.**

Galatians 5:17-23; Ephesians 5:15-18; Luke 6:44; Romans 8:13-14; Romans 5:5; John 14:26; Galatians 5:16; Romans 8:9; 2 Timothy 1:7; Galatians 4:6

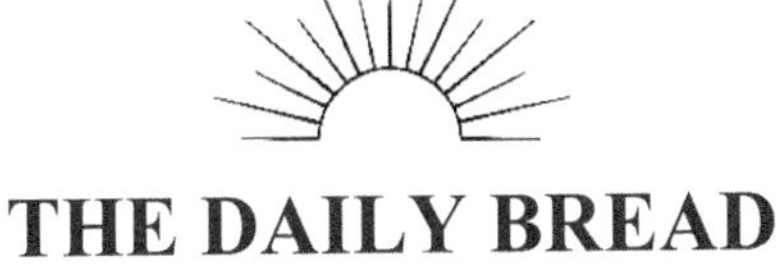

# THE DAILY BREAD

Raise a standard – it's no use for us to complain about what the world is looking like but we forget although we are not of this world, we are also living in it. When they say the world is corrupt, do not be corrupt, when they say the world has lost its morality, are you still living morally upright and when they say the world is wicked, are you living a righteous life. If people walk in whatever you are doing in your private life, will you say amen? It's not okay that you received Jesus Christ as a saviour, but you continue to live a life like you were doing before. When we take someone in the world and compare with you, if there is no difference you are in trouble. Change is needed in our Christian walk of life. But change must start with you. The revival must start with you. Ezekiel was led by God to the waters and the water came to his ankle level and he was brought to the waters again the water came to his knees and again He brought him through the waters: the water came up to his waist and He brought him to a river; that he could not cross for the water was too deep, water which one must swim, a river that could not be crossed. I am asking you where are you in terms of your spiritual growth are, are you at an ankle level. If you remain at an ankle level, you will never experience the knee level. When you are in grade six, for you to learn grade seven material, you need to get to grade seven. There is a certain level of life which God wants us to live but if we remain where we are, it will remain as a pipe dream. I ask you again to carry out a stocktake in your life and start working on those areas where you know they are still grey areas. "Therefore, seeing we also are surrounded with so great a cloud of witnesses, let us lay aside every weight, and the sin which does so easily ensnare us, and let us run with patience the race that is set before us," (Hebrews 12:1) Be blessed.

**Prayer**

We pray that we raise our standards in our walk with Christ. Lord make us a burning bush that can turn people to you. Let us be like Jeremiah and say "Then I said, I will not make mention of him, nor speak any more in his name. But his word was in mine heart as a burning fire shut up in my bones, and I was weary with forbearing, and I could not. We pray that our faith grows to experience a relationship with you at a river level. Let the revival starts with us. As your word says, "the fear of the Lord is the beginning of the wisdom", let us shun evil and honour you, Lord. Let us be like a pregnant woman to understand that what we are carrying is very special. We are moving from glory to glory because of the grace of our Lord Jesus Christ. Amen.


**Bible Verses to study**

Galatians 2:20; Proverbs 9:10; Colossians 1:9-10; 2 Peter 3:18; Galatians 5:22-23; Mathew 5:6; Ephesians 4:15

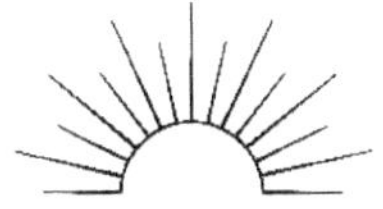

# THE DAILY BREAD

Grasshopper mentality. Today I refuse to have a grasshopper mentality. This when you look at yourself and say I am very small. This is an inferiority complex. When you regard yourself as powerless to change your circumstances. You live a faithless life. You cannot see yourself leaving beyond a mediocre life. People who think like this are selfish and they think we know everything, so they continue to fight against the will of God. Therefore, they will miss God's blessings. Instead of them seeing God's blessings, they will see problems. They magnify the problems than the blessings, so they never attempt possess the blessings. 12 spies were sent out to view the land by Moses, 10 came back with a bad report. "We saw Nephilim there (the descendants of Anak come from the Nephilim). We seemed like grasshoppers in our own eyes, and we looked the same to them" (Numbers 13:33). God is not pleased with the grasshopper mentality because he created you in his own image. "For God has not given us a spirit of fear, but of power and of love and of a sound mind" (2 Timothy:1-7). He gave you the gifts and the talents. He sent his only son to die for you. He has prepared a great future for you. These 10 spies saw that they were grasshoppers in their own eyes. They cursed themselves; undermined God and they gave up. The life you are living today maybe a result how you see yourself. With a grasshopper mentality you will remain small and think small is good. I pray today that you will not limit the plan of God over your life by a grasshopper mentality. Joshua and Caleb came back with a good report. "And Caleb stilled the people before Moses, and said, Let us go up at once, and possess it; for we are well able to overcome it" (Numbers 13:30). I choose to see the milk and honey in the promised land than the giants. "What then shall we say to these things? If God is for us, who can be against us?" (Romans 8:31).

When you look at South Africa, what do you see? Do you see giants or a land full of honey and milk? They are giants of inflation, giants of crime, giants of unemployment and giants racism but I choose to see a land full of honey and milk. South Africa is a country full of honey and milk but to those with grasshopper mentality its terrible country without hope and future. Some people have already given up on their lives just waiting to die. I pray that the word of God can renew your mind. If God said stay in South Africa, be obedient and stay, the blessing is inside of you than outside of you, he will make your ways prosperous. God bless you.


**Prayer**

We refuse to have a grasshopper mentality because your word teaches me that, "For God has not given us a spirit of fear, but of power and of love and of a sound mind". We have faith of the word of God and know that all things working together for good for us. We choose to see the milk and honey in the promised land than the giants. We do not walk by sight but by faith. We pray that God, we do not curse ourselves by speaking against your blessings. As your word says "A man's stomach shall be satisfied from the fruit of his mouth; From the produce of his lips, he shall be filled. Death and life are in the power of the tongue, and those who love it will eat its fruit", from my mouth shall proceed blessings not curses.


**Bible verses to study**

Numbers 13:30-33; Romans 8:31; 2 Timothy:1-7; Joshua 1:9; Psalms 23:4; Romans 8:37; 1 Samuel 17:41-52

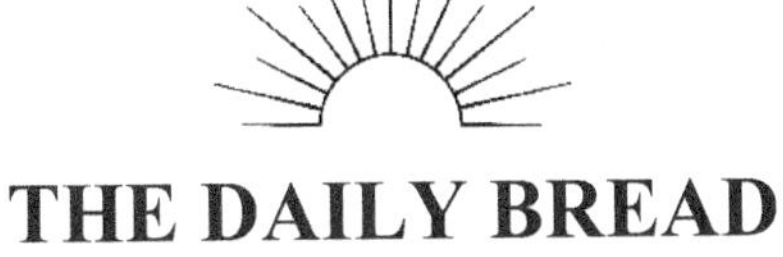

# THE DAILY BREAD

God help can us to live again. People die whilst living. They lose expectation of the next day. How many people now who believe that they do not deserve the best out of life? They live a defeated life. They stay too long in their hurts of the past and devoid them to see a better future. They have believed the devil's definition of their life. People become like a dried fruit, no more juice. People lose their self-esteem. The devil stole their joy. You cannot be a Holy Spirit filled Christian who live in the presence of God and live a depressed life. If you live a sad life, you must seek the presence of God in your life. The far we live away from God's presence, is more we give up on life. Sinful life kills something's in your life. We were created to have a relationship with God. When we don't have a relationship with God, a void is created. That's why people end up filling this void with drugs, alcohol, alcohol, gambling and pornography. It's like we reject ourselves. We believe God made a mistake to create us. When you live a sad life, it's like you are telling God that you are not good enough. God says before I formed you, I knew you. Let me tell you, you are not mistake, you are the apple of God's eye, and you are fearfully and wonderfully made in the image of God. There is no one like you in town. So, you need to remain connected to source of Joy that is God. People committed suicide with millions in their accounts. Only Jesus can satisfy you. Even if you lose something or someone dear to you, do not mourn forever because you may miss God's next best thing. Regardless of your circumstances, choose to live, make every-day counts, surround yourself with people who value you and rejoice in the Lord. The word of God says" Then he said to them, "Go your way, eat the fat, drink the sweet, and send portions to those for whom nothing is prepared; for this day is holy to our Lord. Do not sorrow, for the joy of the LORD is your strength." (Nehemiah 8:10). Sinful live makes you dead whilst living.

That's why the word of God says, "When you were dead in your trespasses and in the uncircumcision of your sinful nature, God made you alive with Christ" (Colossians 2:13). As we know that the wages of SIN is death, lets live a life that honour God. We need to give our lives to God because there is a resurrection power in Christ Jesus. The word of God says, "And if the Spirit of him who raised Jesus from the dead is living in you, he who raised Christ from the dead will also give life to your mortal bodies because of his Spirit who lives in you." (Romans 8:11). God bless you.

**Prayer**

Please God, resurrect everything dead in our lives and by the grace of God they shall live again. As your word says, "The thief does not come except to steal, and to kill, and to destroy. I have come that they may have life, and that they may have it more abundantly", we shall live a life of abundance of Joy through Jesus Christ. We pray that we dwell in the presence of God all the days in my life so that we can have fullness of joy. Your word says "Go your way, eat the fat, drink the sweet, and send portions to those for whom nothing is prepared; for this day is holy to our Lord. Do not sorrow, for the joy of the LORD is your strength." Amen.

**Bible verses to study**

John 10:10; Nehemiah 8:10; 1 Samuel 16:1; Psalms 91:1; Psalms 23:4; Psalms 51:11; 2 Corinthians 3:17

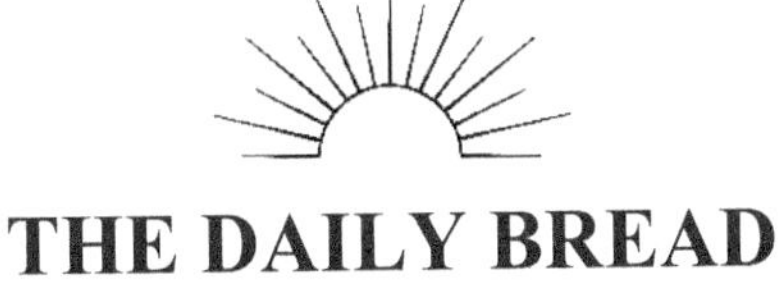

# THE DAILY BREAD

Association. The garden of Eden was a fine place but there was a snake. The earth is a fine place, but we live with the devil. Adam and Eve were fine before they started to associate with a snake. Eve chose a wrong company. The snake came and moved into Eve's life. Eve was not aware of what she is giving away by associating with the snake. This association of Eve and the ungodly made her to start acting like the snake. The snake crawled into her world to the point of her believing the word of the snake than the word of God. It was a continuous moral decay. At last Eve could not stand the temptation because she ate the fruit and fell. Today check your association. Stay away from evil company. Evil company corrupts good character. Be alert and of sober mind. Your enemy the devil prowls around like a roaring lion looking for someone to devour. (1 Peter 5:8). The devil is a thief, "The thief comes only to steal and kill and destroy. I came that they may have life and have it abundantly." (John 10:10). The word of God teaches us that, "Do not be yoked together with unbelievers. For what do righteousness and wickedness have in common? Or what fellowship can light have with darkness?" (2 Corinthians 6:14). Are your friends leading to heaven or to hell. Someone said show me your friends, I will tell you your future. The people who you spend most of your time with will influence you. You cannot be friends with gossipers if you do not gossip. Its high time you to tell the evil company that I am taking a new direction in my life and our association has ended. Loving people does not mean you need to associate with them, you can love them from afar. The sooner you realise that the life God called you for greatness requires you to separate yourself with the darkness is better. I pray that you associate yourself with people that build you than people who gossip with you. God bless you.

**Prayer**

We pray that God you take away bad people in our life and bring good people to our life as your word says, "Do not be deceived: "Bad company corrupts good character". As you separated light from darkness, we shall be separated from the evil company. Your word says, "Blessed is the man Who walks not in the counsel of the ungodly, nor stands in the path of sinners, nor sits in the seat of the scornful;" But his delight is in the law of the LORD, And in His law, he meditates day and night. He shall be like a tree Planted by the rivers of water, that brings forth its fruit in its season, whose leaf also shall not wither; And whatever he does shall prosper. Amen


**Bible verses to study.**

1 Peter 5:8; John 10:10; 2 Corinthians 6:14; 1 Corinthians 15:33; Romans 16:17; Deuteronomy 7:2-4; Psalms 1:1; Psalms 26:4; Proverbs 1:10

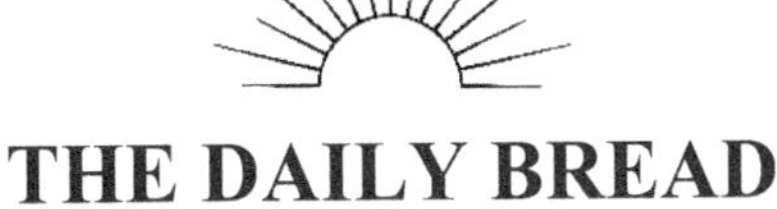

# THE DAILY BREAD

Identity. Moses was raised in the palace as a son of Pharaoh's daughter. His mother was his nurse. His mother must have told him that you do not belong here. The palace must have had everything that Moses wanted or dreamed for in life. Surrounded by all the riches, there was a voice that was speaking to him. There must have been a voice that told him, look at your brothers and sisters how oppressed are they? The most important truth is that Moses knew who he was because his mother told him. "By faith Moses, when he had grown up, refused to be known as the son of Pharaoh's daughter" (Hebrews 11:24). Now we have people living in the devil's palaces. They are caught up in the world. They have lost their identity and now they have accepted that they belong in the world. We have a duty to raise the Moses and tell them who they are? There is a power in the spoken word because even at creation God spoke and things became to existence. Although Moses grew up in the palace, he despised it and as a result his life was not defined by the palace. Moses was in the palace, but it was not his destiny. We have a duty to speak to those who have taken refuge in the world, enlighten their minds about Jesus Christ and tell them who they are? One day the word of God will bring life to their dead state, and they will rise up again to fulfil their purposes in life. There was a farmer who picked up an eaglet and he put it together with the chickens. It grew up thinking it was a chicken. When the eagles used to come and attack chicken, it used to run away like chickens. It ate drops of food in the dust like a chicken. But one day the Farmer told it that you are not a chicken but an eagle, it must fly high into the sky. The eagle one day managed to fly high into the sky. Today just know you are not a chicken but an eagle, so you soar above the clouds like eagles. God bless you.

**Prayer**

We praise You, for we are fearfully and wonderfully made. Marvelous are Your works, and we know this very well. We are created in the image of God and after his likeness. As you spoke through Prophet Jeremiah "Before I formed you in the womb I knew you, And before you were born, I consecrated you; I have appointed you a prophet to the nations," you knew us before the foundations of the world. For we are His workmanship, created in Christ Jesus for good works, which God prepared beforehand that we should walk in them. For in You we live and move and have our being.' As some of your own poets have said, 'We are his offspring.' Amen

**Bible verses to study.**

Genesis 1:27; 2 Corinthians 5:17; Jeremiah 1:5; 1 Peter 2:9; John 1:12; Hebrews 11:24; Ephesians 1:14; Ephesians 1:5; John 15:5

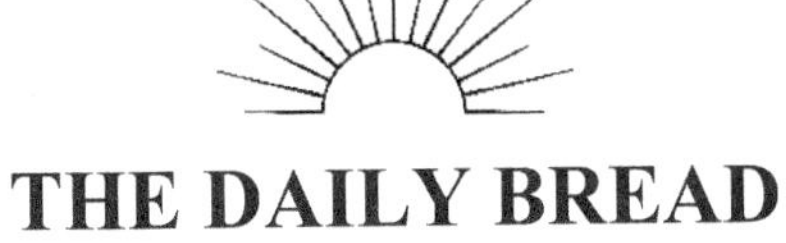

# THE DAILY BREAD

The rod. A shepherd carried the rod always in the country looking after the sheep and in fact, was an extension of the owner's own right arm. It stood as a symbol of his strength, his power, his authority in any serious situation. The rod was what he relied on to safeguard both himself and his flock in danger. And it was, furthermore, the instrument he used to discipline and correct any wayward sheep that insisted on wandering away. Today what do you have? "And the LORD said unto him, what is that in your hand? And he said a rod. The LORD said, "Throw it on the ground." Moses threw it on the ground, and it became a snake, and he ran from it. And the LORD said unto Moses, Put forth thine hand, and take it by the tail. And he put forth his hand, and caught it, and it became a rod in his hand:" (Exodus 4:2-4). God asked Moses to throw the rod on the ground. When he threw it on the ground, there was a transfer from Moses's hand to God. Moses let go the most precious equipment he relied on. Moses did put all his trust on God. When he threw it on the ground, he let it go and it was no longer in his possession. After that, God gave back the rod to Moses in a different state than it was before. God need something to work on, it might be your time, finances, gift and something of value to you. We can never have an impact on this world if we continue to hold back what we have from God. The rod was used by Moses to part the red sea, to hit a rock and then the water came out and when Joshua fought the Amalekites. A lot of Miracles were performed through the rod. When we give what we have to God, it may come back as good marriage, promotion at work, good health and peaceful life. God want to bless us, but He needs us first to put our trust on Him. Sadly, people are not ready to let go because they do not know who God is. Today let it go what you are holding, and your life will transform beyond measure. To the boy it was just his lunch but in the hands of Jesus 2 fishes and five loaves were enough to feed 5000 men. The word of God is saying "But seek first the kingdom of God and His righteousness, and all these things shall be added to you." (Mathew 6:33) God bless you.


**Prayer**

As word says, "Thy rod and Thy staff, they comfort me" let us not despise your correction so that we can learn and grow. Our lives starts with you and ends with you. You are our Alpha and Omega, the author and the finisher of our faith. Help me to let go of me so that I can get you in my life. As your word say, "Trust in the LORD with all your heart and do not lean on your own understanding". Let us surrender all to you Lord Jesus. As your word says, "Whoever finds their life will lose it, and whoever loses their life for my sake will find it", we shall give away our lives so that we can gain it. Lord, you restore our souls. Thank you Lord Jesus for loving us and blessing us. Amen.


**Bible verses to study.**

Exodus 4:2-4; Mathew 6:33; Psalms 23:4; Proverbs 3:5; Psalms 37:7-17; Psalms 28:7; Psalms 46:10; Romans 8:28; Joshua 1:9

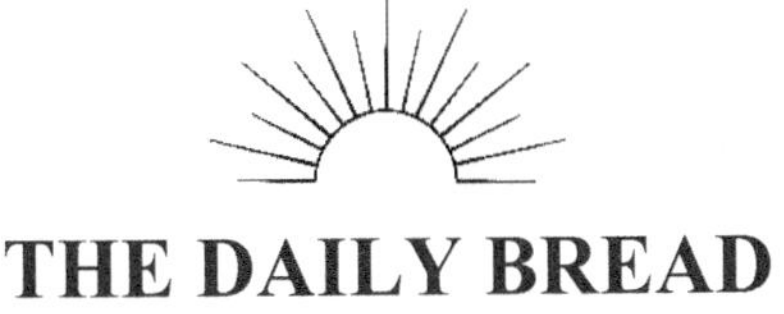

# THE DAILY BREAD

What will you be known you for. Job was known for his righteousness, Abraham was known for his faith, Ananias and Sapphira were known for their deception, Daniel was known for his righteousness, Paul was known for his great encounter will Jesus and his ministry to the gentiles, Pharaoh was known for his hard heart and Cain was known for killing his brother Abel. What will the people know you for? What legacy you are going leave? You can rewrite your life through grace. You will testify that mercy rewrote my life. It's never too late. David committed adultery but he repented and wrote great psalms, Lazarus died but Jesus resurrected him, and Peter denied Jesus 3 times, but he repented led 3000 people to Christ and God used him mightily. Each day you are living, God is giving you a chance. Never settle for less. Let me tell you that you are an eagle not a chicken. A farmer picked an eaglet and raised it with chickens. The Eaglet thought it was a chicken because it grew up in chicken life and surrounded by chickens. Do not adjust your level to suit your environment. One day the farmer told the eaglet when it had grown that you are not a chicken, but you are an eagle. That's why our barometer of life should not be subject to our peers, family and our background. Only a dead fish goes where the water flows. The word of God should speak to our lives who we are. We should not conform to the patterns of the world but renew our minds through the word of God. You shall leave a great legacy. Through you, nations and your family shall be blessed. You are a prophet to your family. Do not be fooled, evil company corrupts a good character. Never give a place to the devil. Job shunned away evil, and he left a great legacy. Have faith in God and live a godly life, you shall leave a good legacy. God bless you.

**Prayer**

Thank you, lord, for fixing us. Thank you, Jesus, for giving us a new character, we are no longer whom we used to be. We have put off the old men which grows corrupt and put on the new man that is after the righteousness. Create a new heart in us O Lord that is after you. Help us live a righteous life like Job and shun away evil. Forgive our sins as we forgive those who trespass against us. We shall leave a great legacy in the name of Jesus. Your word says, "I have been crucified with Christ; it is no longer I who live, but Christ lives in me; and the life which I now live in the flesh I live by faith in the Son of God, who loved me and gave Himself for me." Amen


**Bible Verses to study.**

Proverbs 13:22; Psalms 112:2; Psalms 78:4; Deuteronomy 6:5-7; Psalms 112:2; Proverbs 3:35; Proverbs 22:1; Ezekial 46:17

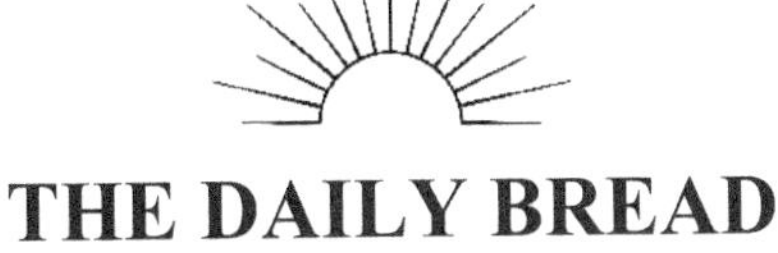

# THE DAILY BREAD

Today I am writing this message pleading with you to understand that they are stages in life. You are going through various challenges because you are not yet there where you want to be in life. God is building your life. Let's compare your life to a process of constructing a big building. The first stage you will be a land with grass which they will dig a big whole. Then you move to foundation level, no one sees anything else, but God knows that there is 15 stories building being built. There is a computer-generated picture for a building. People might see only the hole but there is a computer-generated picture for you and God know how you are going to be like. "Before I formed you in the womb, I knew you; Before you were born, I sanctified you; I ordained you a prophet to the nations." (Jeremiah 1:5) You might be at foundation level, window level and roof level just know, being confident of this, that he who began a good work in you will carry it on to completion until the day of Christ Jesus. (Philippians 1:6). Do not let anything take away your joy. For we walk by faith, not by sight. (2 Corinthians 5:7). Do not compare your lives with other people. Rejoice in the Lord always. I will say it again: Rejoice! "(Philippians 4:4). Life is too short to worry about what if. Make every moment count. Let your days be full of joy regardless of circumstances. "For we are the circumcision, which worship God in the spirit, and rejoice in Christ Jesus, and have no confidence in the flesh". (Philippians 3:3) Be still and know that he is God. You are under construction and God will make something special with you. "Does not the potter have power over the clay, from the same lump to make one vessel for honour and another for dishonour? "(Romans 9:21) No matter where you are, you must be faithful like Joseph who was tried and tested, but he came on top always. God promoted Joseph from prison to a ruler in Egypt. The way you are today is not the way you are going to be tomorrow the resurrection power of Jesus Christ is working upon your life. "For we are his workmanship, created in Christ Jesus unto good works, which God has before ordained that we should walk in them." (Ephesians 2:9). When you get to a restaurant drive through, you will find that they are some people who are ordering, paying and others collecting. If you are in the queue and you still have to order do not worry because you shall collect too if you continue to be in the queue. God bless you.


**Prayer**

O Lord, we thank you for being the Lord in our lives. How excellent is thy name O Lord? Thank you for finding us O Lord Jesus. Without you, we do not know where we will be. As your word says, "He raises the poor from the dust and lifts the beggar from the ash heap, To set them among princes And make them inherit the throne of glory. "For the pillars of the earth are the LORD's, And He has set the world upon them," you have raised us from the ashes to sit with the Kings. We are moving from glory to glory. The way we are today is not the way we are going to be tomorrow, the same spirit that raised Christ from the dead dwells in us. The grace of God is sufficient for us. We walk in power; we walk in miracles, and we live a life of favour. We are blessed, for you are the Father of glory. Amen.


**The bible verses to study.**

Jeremiah 1:5; Philippians 1:6; 2 Corinthians 5:7; Philippians 4:4; Philippians 3:3; Romans 9:21; Ephesians 2:9

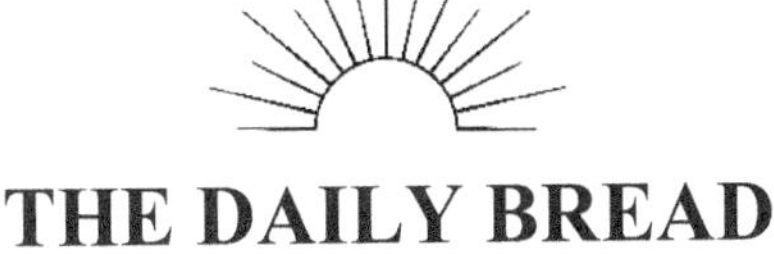

# THE DAILY BREAD

Realisation- Joseph knew who he really was. In house of Potiphar, he did not stoop down to the level of fellow slaves, he served diligently until everything was put under him. He knew that he was not serving Potiphar but the living God. The value of Joseph was not directly related to his conditions. Because of faith and relationship, he had with God, he saw that the grace of God was much more than his conditions. He did not have confident in himself but in God changing his life. Your value should not be determined by the country you are, the job you do, the economy, the money which you make but what God says who you are? "But you are a chosen people, a royal priesthood, a holy nation, God's special possession, that you may declare the praises of him who called you out of darkness into his wonderful light" (1 Peter 2:9). Like money, its value will not change whether it's folded, dirty and on the floor, it has the same purchasing power. Do not let your setbacks become the story of your life, you serve a living God. Do not camp in your past disappointments, one day is one day, you shall testify the goodness of God in the land of the living and that day is near. God is our present helper "I will lift my eyes to the hills – from whence comes my help? My help comes from the Lord, who made heaven and earth "(Psalms 121:1). God bless you.


**Prayer**

As your word says, "If you have faith as a mustard seed, you can say to this mulberry tree, 'Be pulled up by the roots and be planted in the sea,' and it would obey you", help us O Lord to have faith in you. We know that our success is not determined by the country we are, the level of education we have, our jobs, the economy, the money that we make but God who made the heavens and earth. Your word says, "But you are a chosen people, a royal priesthood, a holy nation, God's special possession, that you may declare the praises of him who called you out of darkness into his wonderful light". We are blessed, Abraham blessing are ours. Greater he that is in us than he that is the world. Amen


**Bible verses to study**

1 Peter 2:9; Psalms 121:1; Romans 8:37; Genesis 39:1-12; Mathew 10:31; Psalms 139:13-16; Isaiah 43:4; Isaiah 60:1; Mathew 6:26

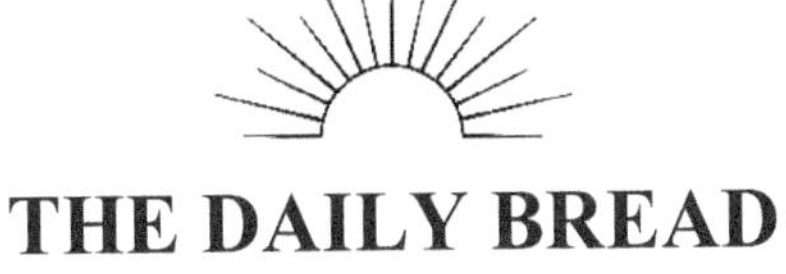

# THE DAILY BREAD

We are running a race. To be an athlete, you need to be much disciplined. There is a strict diet we must follow. This is not a sprint but a marathon. The spiritual diet is when we feed our spirit not our flesh. The word of God says Man shall not live by bread alone but by every word that proceeds from the mouth of God. Faith comes by hearing and by hearing the word of God. Our spiritual diet includes hearing the word of God daily. Our flesh gets tired as we continue to run the race but fasting helps us to kill the voice of the flesh and activate the voice of the spirit. So many people start the race so well but not all will complete the race. Paul said you started the race very well but who hindered you. What I can say it's not easy to run the race of life without Jesus because when storms of life come on your way your boat will be destroyed. Jesus said if you want to come after me, you must first deny yourself and carry your cross daily. When the Holy Spirit comes and dwells in you amen it's like you are pregnant, you cannot eat everything. You need to realize; I cannot live life as I was doing before. The word of God says I beseech you brethren by mercies of the Lord that you present your bodies as a living sacrifice, Holy, acceptable to God, which is a reasonable service. (Romans 12:1) For you to endure the race, living the life of righteousness will take you through. We must just remember that it's by the grace of God not by our strength we have been saved. This morning I am saying, the grace of God is sufficient for you, you will run the race of faith and complete it. When you fall the Lord shall pick you up and your faith shall never fail." Therefore, we also, since we are surrounded by so great a cloud of witnesses, let us lay aside every weight, and sin which so easily ensnares us, let us run with endurance the race that is set before us, looking unto Jesus the author and finisher of our faith, who for the joy that was set before Him endured the cross, despising the shame, and has sat down at the right hand of the throne of God. (Hebrews 12:1-2) As we run the race, we must make sure, we practise what we preach. Paul said, "But I discipline my body and bring *it* into subjection, lest, when I have preached to others, I myself should become disqualified". Just remember winners are not quitters. God bless you.

## Prayer

Thank you, Lord, for all the blessings. We pray that we shall fight a good fight of faith like Paul until we get hold the life you have set before us. We shall run this race of life with you Lord Jesus until we complete it. Let us be able to put you God first in our lives. As your word says, If we say that we have fellowship with you Lord and walk in darkness it's a lie", let us walk in the light and forsake our ways of darkness. Let us keep our eyes on you God. Let us trust in the Lord with all our hearts and souls and not to lean in our own understanding. By the grace of God, we will run this race and complete it. Give us the strength lord Jesus to hold on no matter what comes our way and complete this race. All we need is you Lord in our lives and with you Lord we shall not stumble. Amen

## The bible verses to study.

1 Corinthians 9:24; Hebrews 12:1-3; Galatians 5:7; Mathew 24:13; Isaiah 40:31; Romans 12:1; 2 Timothy 4:17; Habakkuk 2:2

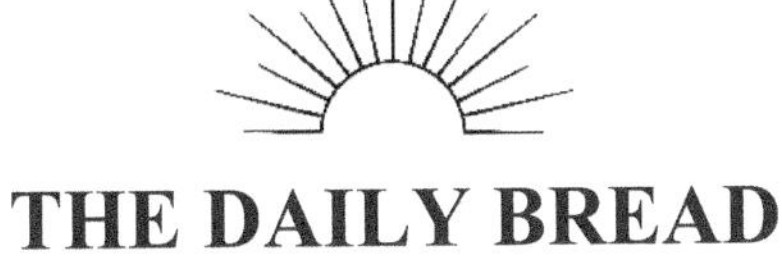

# THE DAILY BREAD

"……..Not by might, nor by power, but by my spirit, said the LORD of hosts." (Zechariah 4:6). You have God as your father, and you need to realise that it's not about you alone. God is with you. If you are a minister do not rely on your own strength, let the Holy Spirit lead you and guide you. My heart is very close to the praise and worship team, if you lead praise and worship, it's not about your gift, it's about you surrendering to the Spirit of God. People must not see you in the worship, but God. Praise and worship is not a place of performers. Whatever ministry you are involved with at church just remember it's the grace of God that is carrying you through. If you operate in the flesh amen you will have a burden to carry and you will burn up. You will be choked. You need to step up. God called us but it does not mean we are more important than his work. The work of God will continue even if you are not around. When Jesus entered Jerusalem ridding on donkey, the people shouted Hosanna and they were praising Him. It would be a mistake for the donkey to think people were praising it because without Jesus, it would not have received such a great entrance. With the things of God, you cannot rely on yourself, you need to be connected. Thus, why it's important to stay in the presence of God. I pray for you that you decrease in yourself and let God increase in your life, do like what Moses said that if your presence does not go with us, do not let us go there. We must be led by the Spirit of God. God bless you.


**Prayer**

As your word says, "it's Not by might, nor by power, but by my spirit, said the LORD of hosts," let us not rely on our own strength but your Spirit. We have all come from you, to be alive it's you, to have a job it's you and to be healthy comes from you.

You are Jehovah Jireh, you are Jehovah Nissi, and you are Jehovah El Shaddai. For we are convinced that neither death nor life, neither angels nor demons, neither the present nor the future, nor any powers neither height nor depth, nor anything else in all creation, will be able to separate us from the love of God that is in Christ Jesus our Lord. Your word says, "seek first the kingdom of God and his righteousness and all the things shall be added unto us." Help us O Lord to seek you first in our lives.


**Bible Verses to study**

Zechariah 4:6; Genesis 41:16; 1 Samuel 14:6; 1 Samuel 17:47; 2 Chronicles 32:8; 1 John 4:4

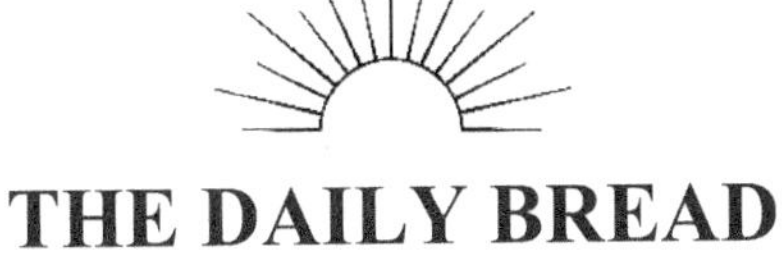

# THE DAILY BREAD

The journey. You can never be prepared for this journey. It's a learning process. Life has a certain way of bringing surprises. Most of the children of Israel who left Egypt did not see the Promised Land. They did not have faith on God. God did not tell them the challenges they were going to experience but promised to be with them. "The LORD replied, "My Presence will go with you, and I will give you rest." (Exodus 33:14). God did not promise us a trouble-free life but that we shall overcome. "You are of God, little children, and have overcome them, because He who is in you is greater than he who is in the world." (1 John 4:4) In our everyday life, we also face challenges. These challenges must bring us closer to God and not to complain against him. "My brethren, count it all joy when you fall into various trials, knowing that the testing of your faith produces patience". (James 1:2-3) Everyone wants the blessings, but they do not want the challenges associated with them. The children of Israel lived a supernatural life, they crossed the red sea by walking on the dry land, drank water from rock and ate manna from heaven but they did not believe. All these things tested their faith. God did not take them through the wilderness to destroy them but to teach them and grow their faith. The intention of God was to lead them all to the Promised Land. Because of the challenges, they gave up on the journey not God. The word of God says "Beloved, think it not strange concerning the fiery trial, which is to try you, as though some strange thing happened unto you: but to the degree that you share the sufferings of Christ, keep on rejoicing, so that at the revelation of His glory you may also rejoice and be overjoyed." (1 Peter 4:12-13) Today, do you still have faith that God will take you to your promised land? Are you able to have faith on God in the storm? When you look back and compare your life with where you are now, do you not see the hand of God upon your life? God is faithful. His plans are to prosper you not to harm you. Keep on trusting on him. Do not walk by sight but rather be led by the Spirit of God. God will deliver you. Be strong and of good courage, God has already given you victory. God bless.

**Prayer**

We thank you Lord Jesus that we are not in this journey of life alone. Your word says, "the LORD replied, "My Presence will go with you, and I will give you rest." You have put a hedge around us like job. They are angels that are guiding us and protecting us. Your word is thy lamp upon thy feet, and they light upon thy path. Your word says, "My brethren, count it all joy when you fall into various trials, knowing that the testing of your faith produces patience". We know that God you will never give up on us so we will never give up on ourselves. Like Paul, I will "Fight the good fight of the faith. Take hold of the eternal life to which I was called when I made my good confession in the presence of many witnesses". Amen

**Bible verses to study.**

Exodus 33:14; 1 John 4:4; James 1:2-3; 1 Peter 4:12-13; Psalms 3:6; Joshua 1:9; Romans 8:11; Romans 8:18; 2 Corinthians 12:9-10; Philippians 4:12-13

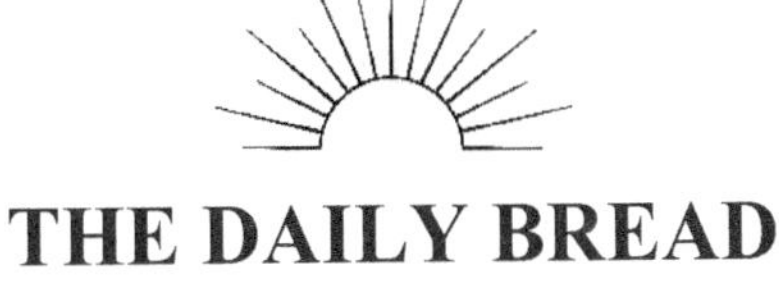

# THE DAILY BREAD

Do not live for yourself only. The word of God says you are the light of the world so literally it means as a light, when you shine, you are not providing light to yourself only but to the other people. Being a born-again Christian it's only good for you, if you only live for yourself but when you touch other people there is the big deal bringing the kingdom of God here on earth. You can find someone who is living in Australia paying school fees other people who are disadvantaged in Africa. What are you doing to touch and change the world? Just imagine as Christians we bring the ministry to the people who are in need. I pray that God shakes you in your sleep, those who are living a selfish and defeated life. Moses thought his dreams were over and looking after sheep and God brought a burning bush to his attention. Jonah needed a drowning experience. Your brothers and sister are living in bondage and what are you doing about it. We are blaming the evil on how the world is looking like but actual we must be blame ourselves. We are lights that have failed to shine. What are you doing to change the world before you can blame the devil? Yes, there is so much evil so what. Do you know when you win a soul there is a party in heaven. If they are so many parties in heavens because of you winning souls, your life will never be same. You will be known in heaven like Paul. Tell yourself that I refuse to conform to the pattern of the world. I will not let my misfortunes, hurts, brokenness, and emptiness in the past makes me to hate my brothers and sisters. Love people, care for people and lead them to Christ. Do not be satisfied by having finances to take care of yourself, pray to God to give you more finances to take care of others. Africa is lagging BEHIND in terms of development and there is so much poverty but let God use us to be the solution of this world. The world is melting financial, and they do not have solutions. We as the children of God we are ahead of the world because we can tap into the spiritual world and bring those things which are not in existence here on earth to become physically available. My prayer for you today is for you to become a Joseph of this generation. "If my people, which are called by my name, shall humble themselves, and pray, and seek my face, and turn from their wicked ways; then will I hear from heaven, and will forgive their sin, and will heal their land". (2 Chronicles 7:14). God bless you.


**Prayer**

We pray that Lord we become the Light of world and bring light to many sitting the darkness. Use us O Lord, to touch the need and use us to heal the sick. May we be a living epistle as we may the only bible which someone will ever read. Your word says, "for as the body without the spirit is dead, so faith without works is dead also." We pray that when we preach about a revival, let the revival starts with us. Let us answer your call. Your word says, "Therefore go and make disciples of all nations, baptizing them in the name of the Father and of the Son and of the Holy Spirit,". Amen


**Bible Verses about to study.**

2 Chronicles 7:14; Galatians 2:20; Galatians 5:24; Galatians 6:14; Romans 14:7-12; John 12:24; Acts 20:24; Mark 12:31

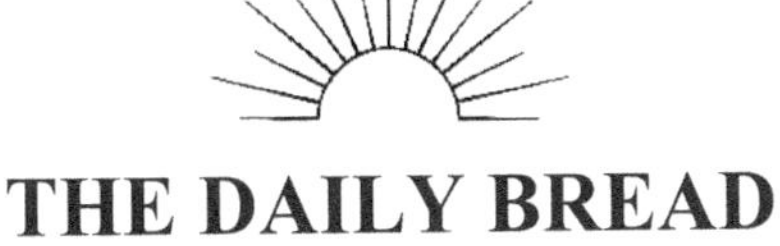

# THE DAILY BREAD

Motivation. Today what is your motivation to come to church? Some people are motivated by needs as soon as that need is met, they leave. People who came looking for jobs to church as soon as they got a job, they left; people who came looking for marriage at church, soon they got married their needs were met so they left and people who came looking for healing soon they got healed, they left. They were people who followed Jesus because of miracles. After the feeding of the 5000 men, some followed Jesus and he noticed that they were following him because of the miracle. We call them rice Christians. Your worship of God should not be attached to your bank balance, your health, jobs, marriage, cars and houses. What will happen if you lose those things? When my bank balance is low, I will praise God the same as when it's high because my joy for the Lord is not directly related to the material things. Paul warned us "Brethren, join in following my example, and note those who walk, as you have for a pattern. For many walk of whom I have told you often, and now tell you even weeping, that they are the enemies of the cross of Christ, whose end is destruction, whose god is their belly and whose glory is in their shame - who set their minds on earthly things" (Philippians 3:17-19). We cannot worship the blessings instead of God. You should not be identified with your circumstances. Let your motivation be for the things of God not on the material things but on the love of God. By this you will be able to rejoice in every season which you are. "............ for the joy of the Lord is your strength" (Nehemiah 8:10). But seek first the kingdom of God and His righteousness, and all these things will be added unto you." Mathew 6:33). Delight yourself also in the LORD, And He shall give you the desires of your heart. (Psalms 37:4). David had this testimony "I was young and now I am old, yet I have never seen the righteous forsaken or their children begging bread". (Psalms

37:25). Your motivation should be to live a righteous life as the word of God says "Blessed is the man Who walks not in the counsel of the ungodly, nor stands in the path of sinners, nor sits in the seat of the scornful; But his delight is in the law of the LORD, And in His law, he meditates day and night. He shall be like a tree Planted by the rivers of water, that brings forth its fruit in its season, whose leaf also shall not wither; And whatever he does shall prosper. (Psalms Chapter 1:1-3). God bless you.


**Prayer**

We shall never be motivated by materials things (Money and fame) but living a life right with you God. When we lose materials things, we pray that we should say like job. "and said: "Naked I came from my mother's womb, and naked I will depart. The LORD gave and the LORD has taken away; may the name of the LORD be praised." Lord Jesus Christ give us a new heart and put a new spirit in us; You will remove from us our heart of stone and give me us a heart of flesh. Your word says, "Unless the LORD builds the house, its builders labour in vain; unless the LORD protects the city, its watchmen stand guard in vain." You are the Alpha and the Omega, the Author and finisher of our faith, we shall delight ourselves in you so that you can give us the desires of our hearts. Amen.


**Bible verses to study**

Philippians 3:17-19; Nehemiah 8:10; Mathew 6:33; Psalms 37:4; Psalms Chapter 1:1-3; Romans 8:1-2; 2 Timothy 1:7; Philippians 4:13

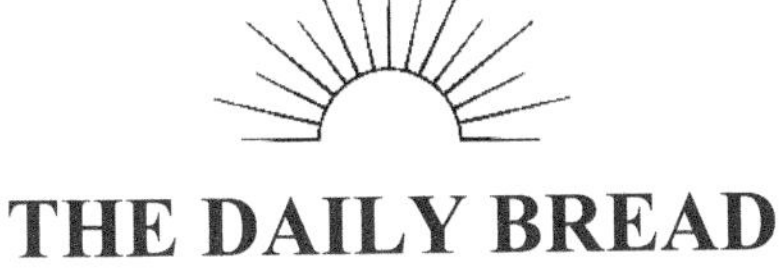

# THE DAILY BREAD

Live your dreams as a child of God. Are you still pursing your dreams, or you have given up. What is hindering you to live your dreams? When someone has dream is like he/she is pregnant. When someone is pregnant, she is expecting. When you have a dream, you are also expecting. But a lot happens throughout carrying of the child for nine months. Unfortunately, not all carry their pregnancy to term. Some decide to terminate the pregnancy because they cannot bear the pain of carrying the child for nine months and others, they fear the financial burden that will be incurred when the child is born. Are you prepared to suffer for your dreams, sacrifice some comfort, not to care what will the people say, taking a journey into the unknown and go out of your comfort zone. God allows us to go through uncomfortable zones so that when we make it, we will not glorify ourselves, but we will give glory to Him. Do not give up. You will make it. The only impediment that is stopping you to achieve your dreams it's you. Start to focus your life towards your dreams. Do not allow yourself to be carried away with other things. You can never have complete fulfilment, peace and joy in life unless you pursue your dreams. That is living life in your purpose. A Journey of one thousand miles begins with one step. Do not forsake the humble beginnings. Whatever you have started, you are sowing a seed, another will water it and God will give an increase. "And Jesus said unto them, Because of your unbelief: for verily I say unto you, if you have faith as a grain of mustard seed, you shall say unto this mountain, remove from here to yonder place; and it shall remove; and nothing shall be impossible unto you" (Matthew 17:20). "Jesus said unto him, If you can believe, all things are possible to him that believes" (Mark 9:23). Dreams become a fantasy if you fail to pursue them. To live your dreams involves you taking action towards fulfilling them. That's why the graveyard is the richest place because of dreams which were never pursued. What you will regret for in life when you are old is not the dreams you pursued and failed but those dreams you never pursued. God bless you.

**Prayer**

Your word says, "For I know the plans I have for you," declares the LORD, "plans to prosper you and not to harm you, plans to give you hope and a future. Help us O Lord by showing us the plans you have for us because your plans are already blessed. Help us O Lord to grow our faith since your word says, ".. for verily I say unto you, if you have faith as a grain of mustard seed, you shall say unto this mountain, remove from here to yonder place; and it shall remove; and nothing shall be impossible unto you" Our faith shall never fail. God you are faithful. You are the same God who made the way for the children of Israel in the wilderness, you shall make a way for us. Our God you are a way maker, miracle worker, a promise keeper and our dreams shall come to fruition. Amen

**Bible Verses to study**

Daniel 1:17; Philippians 4:13; Joel 2:28; 2 Chronicles 15:7; Ephesians 2:10; Ephesians 3:20; Mathew 6;33; Psalms 23:1-6; Joshua 1:8; Philippians 1:6

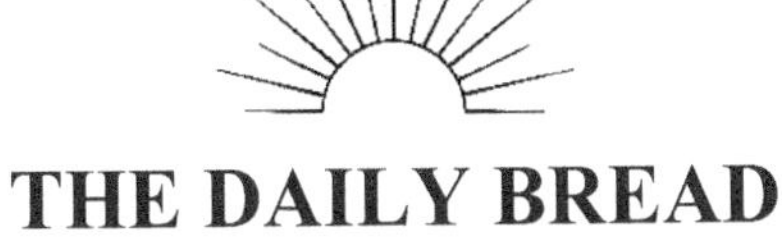

# THE DAILY BREAD

Earning Pounds. The soccer players develop in stages. They may start playing for a none league football clubs. The players may be bought by a lower league club and end up playing in premiership in South Africa. Then the players are bought again by an English premier league club and start earning pounds in England. When we look where the soccer players started it was long way off. The players have a target to play soccer at the highest level. They are so many players who want to grow in their football careers. Few of them make it and ask you why? It is due to lack of commitment, lack of focus, lack of vision, lack of aspiration and lack of ambition, being too comfortable in their position and pleasures of the world. To be successful in life you need to write down your vision and your goals. "Then the LORD answered me and said, "Write down the vision and inscribe it clearly on tablets, so that one who reads it may run." (Habakkuk 2:2) When we look at our Christian walk, when we received Jesus, we had a great zeal and fire burning. Where did that fire go to? Who killed the fire of God in your life? But some of the people have remained stagnant in their Christian walk. They are neither cold nor hot but lukewarm. People have remained in lower league club because of lack of ambition. They cannot move from there. They allowed the spirit of mediocre life to control them and settled for less. They have deprived themselves some of the finer things in life. The children of Israel had to get to the Promised Land to receive the promise but most of them never reached it because they perished in the wilderness due to unbelief. They are lot of promises in the word of God but until we move to where God wants us to be, we will not be entitled to them. You cannot do Grade seven stuff in grade four. You need to move up grades until you reach grade seven. God is hoping you will move to the next stage. You need to grow and by growing you become more responsible and being entrusted with more responsibility. Tell yourself this morning that I will not remain a baby in Christ, but I will grow to get to the life God has purposed for me. God bless you.


**Prayer**

We thank you Lord Jesus Christ for dying for us. Now the life we are living is through the hope of Him that died for us. The way we are today is not the way we are going to be tomorrow. The grace of God is sufficient for us. Your word says we overcame them by the word of the testimony and the blood of the lamb. We testify that our future is bright, we will keep fighting the good fight of faith. As your word says, "Write down the vision and inscribe it clearly on tablets, so that one who reads it may run," we shall write the vision and run with it. Your word says, "For I know the thoughts that I think toward you, says the LORD, thoughts of peace and not of evil, to give you a future and a hope." Amen.


**The bible verses to study**

Habakkuk 2:2; Jeremiah 29:11; 2 Corinthians 1:2; Joshua 14:10-15; Genesis 13:15

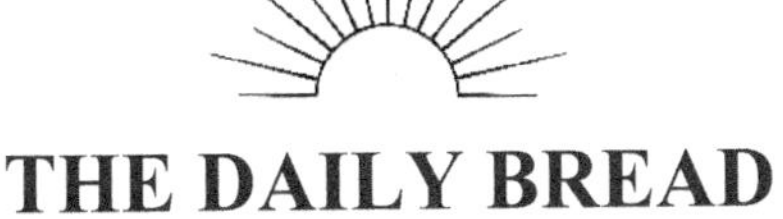

# THE DAILY BREAD

Act. Now it's the time to act on your faith. God gave you the land. Yes, you have prayed for the land. You praised God for the land but you still empty handed. Fear has gripped you. You are doubting and you are saying, "Did God really give me this land". Everyone else can dream but a few can follow their dreams. There is no perfect time. Another Pastor once said if you wait to clear the junk in the trunk, you may spend 20 years clearing it before you set on your journey. Everyone have junk in their trunks. There were 4 lepers sitting at the gate. They said if we stay here, we will die, if we go into the city we will die because of famine, let's go to the camp of the Syrians if they kill or save us it's okay. You can't stay and do nothing. It depends on how desperately do you want it. The lepers had nothing to lose. They found the camp of the Syrians empty. "For the Lord had made the host of the Syrians to hear a noise of chariots, and a noise of horses, even the noise of a great host: and they said one to another, Lo, the king of Israel has hired against us the kings of the Hittites, and the kings of the Egyptians, to come upon us" (2 Kings 7:6) The lepers ate and drank food they found in the tent. They even took gold and silver and hide it. Faith is the currency of heaven. God will go before you. Wait a minute don't look at yourself, look at God. We spoke too much about the promised land, let's go and take it. We have stayed too long on this mountain. We are taking the land as your words says, "And from the days of John the Baptist until now the kingdom of heaven suffers violence, and the violent take it by force." (Mathew 11:12) Like what God told Joshua that every land you step on it shall be yours, we shall go and take the territory for God. Devil I am coming for what is due for me, I have lived a defeated life too long, now I am a changed man, it's no retreat no surrender. "For as the body without the spirit is dead, so faith without works is dead also" (James 2:26). God bless you.

**Prayer**

We pray that we should not procrastinate to follow our calling. We pray that we should not wait for rain to start sowing as your word says, "Whoever watches the wind will not plant; whoever looks at the clouds will not reap." Like what Caled said, "We should go up and take possession of the land, for we can certainly do it." Your word says, "And from the days of John the Baptist until now the kingdom of heaven suffers violence, and the violent take it by force." Your word says, "For as the body without the spirit is dead, so faith without works is dead also". Amen


**Bible verses to study.**

2 Kings 7:6; James 2:26; Mathew 11:12; James 2:19; Hebrew 11:1; Luke 1:37; Hebrew 11:6; Mark 11:24; Mark 9:23

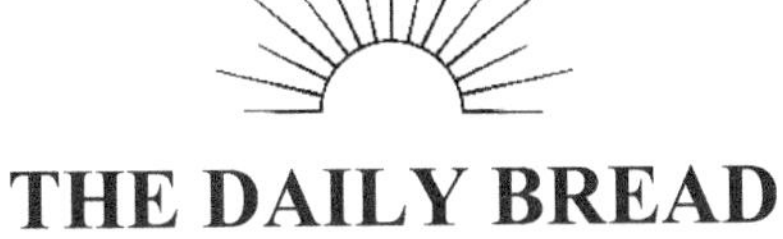

# THE DAILY BREAD

Saturate yourself with the word. "So, then faith comes by hearing, and hearing by the word of God" (Romans 10:17). " In the beginning was the Word, and the Word was with God, and the Word was God"(John 1:1). "And the Word was made flesh, and dwelt among us, and we beheld his glory, the glory as of the only begotten of the Father, full of grace and truth. (John 1:14). The word became flesh and dwell among us amen. Joshua was told by God to meditate on the word day and night neither deviate from it right and left and I will make your ways prosperous. This word can become flesh in your life amen. You can now start to have the nature of God, live a life of faith and having the promises of God manifest in your life. Jesus said that man shall not live by bread alone but by the word that proceeds from the mouth of God. Its high time to grow. Some of you lack the word in your body. Spiritual you have kwashiorkor. There is blessing in meditating on the word. The word exposes you to a different atmosphere and dynamics. You can't live without the word, just like a flower without water you will die spiritual. Let's get back to basics, let's eat this word. There is power in the word like salt to preserve your soul. David said, "I have hidden your word in my heart that I might not sin against you." (Psalms 119:11). The word of God gives your direction your life. "Your word is a lamp to my feet and a light to my path". (Psalms 119:105). God want to lead you and guide you. The steps of a good man are ordered by the LORD, And He delights in his way." (Psalms 37:23) The word of God brings healing in your life. "He sent His word and healed them and delivered them from their destructions." (Psalms 107:20). God is faithful to fulfil his promises in his word, "For all the promises of God in Him are Yes, and in Him Amen, to the glory of God through us." (2 Corinthians 1:20). The word of God spoken over your life shall not go back to God empty handed. "So is my word that

153

goes out from my mouth: It will not return to me empty but will accomplish what I desire and achieve the purpose for which I sent it." (Isaiah 55:11). When Jesus was tempted by Satan, he quoted the word of God, you need the word of God to fight the temptations. God bless you.


**Prayer**

As your word says, "So, then faith comes by hearing, and hearing by the word of God", we shall saturate ourselves with the word. We shall meditate on your word day and night neither deviate from it right and left and you will make our ways prosperous. Like David, "I have hidden your word in my heart that I might not sin against you." Your word is a lamp to our feet and a light to our path". Your word has healed us and saved us from destruction. We pray for you to let your word be a lamp to my feet and a light to our path. Amen.


**Bible verses to study**

Romans 10:17; John 1:1; John 1:14; Psalms 119:11; Psalms 119:105; Psalms 37:23; 2 Corinthians 1:20; Isaiah 55:11

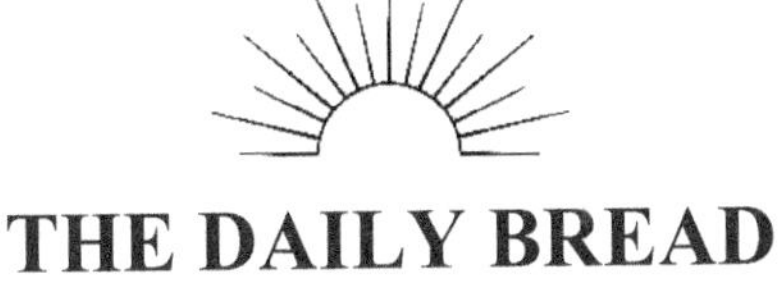

# THE DAILY BREAD

Prison cannot contain you. Paul was put in prison several times by the enemy. A prison is a place where literally you are cut off from the society, broken, doomed and your dreams have died. The devil is threatened by your existence. He wants to see you in prison so that he can kill your dreams. People are in prisons without knowing. Lot of Christians are in debt and even blacklisted. They are owned by banks, credit shops and loan sharks. Do you know someone in financial prison? "So, Peter was kept in prison, but the church was earnestly praying to God for him." (Acts 12:5). God sent an angel to open the gates of the prison for Peter and took him out of prison. It may be alcohol addiction, gambling addiction, phonograph addiction and sex addiction. The prisons are there. I want to tell you that you don't belong in prison. Jesus has set you free by his blood on the cross. "So, if the son sets you free, you will be free indeed." (John 8:36) That prison holding you does not have power over you. Whatever has imprisoned you, I pray that it set you free in the name of Jesus. The word of God says, they overcame them by the blood of the lamb and the word of their testimony. You shall be free. "Then you will know the truth, and the truth will set you free." (John 8:36) If God is for you, who can be against you, debt cannot hold you down, any addictions and sicknesses. We are more than conquerors through Christ Jesus who gives us strength. Being in prison its temporary, God has sent his angels to release you. God is with you, have courage. The enemy does not have hold over you. It's a setback. Praise God. He is a faithful God. I say rejoice always rejoice. The peace God gave us is different from the world. You are an overcomer. "For a righteous man may fall seven times and rise again, But the wicked shall fall by calamity". (Proverbs 24:16). The same Spirt that raised Jesus Christ from the dead dwells in you. "Rejoice not against me, O mine enemy: when I fall, I shall arise; when I sit in darkness, the LORD shall be a light unto me." (Micah 7:8). Just remember that they are some prisons that you can come out only through prayer and fasting. "So, He said to them, "This kind can come out by nothing but prayer and fasting." (Mark 9:29) God bless you.


**Prayer**

No prison can get hold over our lives. "Yet in all these things we are more than conquerors through Him who loved us." We shall never be imprisoned by any addition, financial institution and sickness as your word says, "So, if the son sets you free, you will be free indeed". As your word says, "If God is for you, who can be against you", debt cannot get hold us down, even any addictions and any sicknesses . Your word says, "For a righteous man may fall seven times and rise again, But the wicked shall fall by calamity". Your word says, "Rejoice not against me, O mine enemy: when I fall, I shall arise; when I sit in darkness, the LORD shall be a light unto me." Amen.


**Bible verses to study**

Acts 12:5; John 8:36; Proverbs 24:16; Micah 7:8; Mark 9:29; Mathew 25:36; Isaiah 61:1; 2 Corinthians 3:17

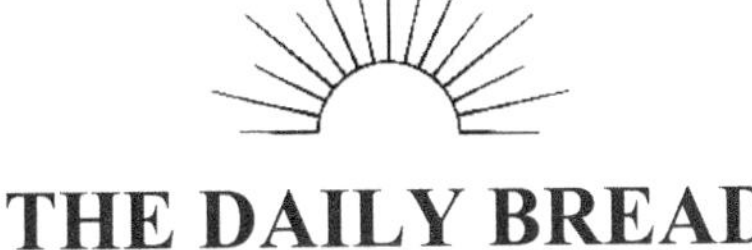

# THE DAILY BREAD

Mediocre life. Do not forget what God says you are and take up the world's definition. "But you are a chosen generation, a royal priesthood, a holy nation, a peculiar people; that you should show forth the praises of him who has called you out of darkness into his marvellous light;" (1 Peter 2:9). I know today, you are surrounded by chickens, but you are not a chicken but an eagle. Don't let the chickens drag you down to their level. Remember you are in this world but not of this world. See yourself up there in the sky. Soaring up in the air like an eagle. Know your worth, you shall not settle for less. Where you are today cannot define your life. It's just temporary. You need to believe. Walk out of your comfort zone. "Come," he said. Then Peter got down out of the boat, walked on the water and came toward Jesus. (Mathew 14:29) Out of 12 disciples in the boat only Peter walked on top of the water. Not everyone has the zeal to get out of the boat (comfort position.) If you want greatness get out of your boat and walk on water. Greatness is not for those who live like everyone and want to be identified with the crowd. Jesus is with you, you will not drown. Keep trying no matter how many times you fall. Walk through the narrower path and do not to take short cuts. Do not keep living in your past and move to God's next best thing. To achieve that excellent life God set for you, it will cost you something. Jesus went through the cross. Do not lose hope, do not forsake the humble beginnings. God is faithful so don't live a mediocre life. Today choose the higher life that God has set up for you. Never subscribe to mediocre life. God said, "I know your works, that you are neither cold nor hot. I could wish you were cold or hot. So then, because you are lukewarm, and neither cold nor hot, I will vomit you out of My mouth." (Revelations 3:15-16). God does not reward mediocrity but excellence. "But without faith it is impossible to please Him, for he who comes to God must believe that He is,

and that He is a rewarder of those who diligently seek Him."
(Hebrews11:6). God bless you.


**Prayer**

We pray that we shall not subscribe to life of mediocrity and
forsake the higher life you have called us to. You called us from
darkness into your marvellous light for your great works. We are
a chosen generation, a royal priesthood, a holy nation and a
peculiar people. Even we know today that we are surrounded by
chickens, we are not a chickens but an eagles. We shall soar up
in the air like eagles. We shall never keep living in our past and
move to God's next best thing. We shall never live a life of
mediocrity as your word says, "I know your works, that you are
neither cold nor hot. I could wish you were cold or hot. So then,
because you are lukewarm, and neither cold nor hot, I will vomit
you out of My mouth." Amen


**Bible verses to study.**

1 Peter 2:9; Mathew 14:29; Revelations 3:15-16; Hebrews
11:6; Colossians 3:23-24; Romans 12:2; Proverbs 10:4; Romans
8:18

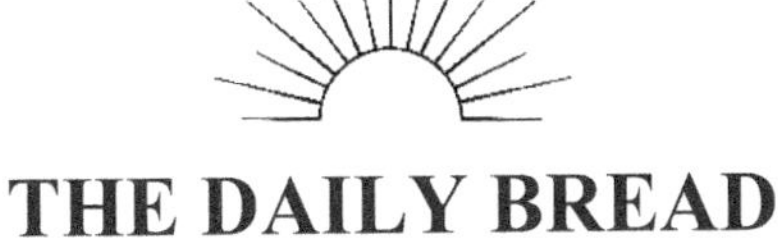

# THE DAILY BREAD

Suspect demon you have been caught. The nature of the demon can clearly be defined in John 10:10 to steal, kill and destroy. They are different demonic activity that operates on people. They are people who fall in the category of demonic influenced. Because of the nature of their life amen, they are easily influenced by the demons. Largely because of their lifestyle. Demons love to operate in the groups. When the demon was casted out, and came back and found the house empty, well swept and put in order, it brought more wicked demons, and the state of the person became worse than before. People can be demonic influenced and fail to know it. Take a closer look at the people in your life do they fall under intentions to kill, destroy and steal. Demonic influenced people they will hold you back, steal from you, hurt you, destroy you and kill you. Check what they are introducing you to in life, is it gambling, womanizing, alcohol, crime and drugs. A person who is a drug addict, someone introduced him or her to drugs. Demonic influenced people sow wrong seeds in people lives sometimes unaware. Do not be enticed by the pleasures of this world. What looks like a devil, dress like dress like a devil, talk like a devil , sound like a devil and walk like a devil, it's a devil. Demonic influenced people are full of deception and devoid of the truth. The demonic activity strives because of lack of knowledge and living a life to please one's fleshy desires no matter what the word of God says. People think they feel so good but in fact the devil is robbing them. How to protect yourself from demonic influenced people. Show me your friends, I will tell you your character. Do not befriend people who you know they are living life out of the will of God. Are your friends pulling you to God or away from God ? "Do not be misled: Bad Company corrupts good character." (1 Corinthians 15:33) "For the love of money is a root of all kinds of evil. Some people, eager for money, have wandered from the faith and pierced themselves with many griefs." (1 Timothy 6:10). Stay away from people who live uncontrolled life, busy bodies who are frivolous, selfish, without love and do not have compassion over you. The word of God says neither give a place to the devil. They are people who are living a broken lives in prisons, lost everything they have, go to work and have nothing show off and ruined marriages. They were not operating in the Spirit, too much flesh not able to hear the voice of the Holy Spirit, lack of discipline and all this allowed people who are demonic influenced in their life and the result in that they were robbed, destroyed and killed. God bless you.


**Prayer**

Thank you, Lord, for the gift of life. Help us O Lord to live the life that is pleasing to you. Give us wisdom to live a blessed life as your word says, "Walk circumspectly not as fools but as wise, redeeming the time, because the days are evil. Therefore, do not be unwise, but understand what the will of the Lord *is*. And do not be drunk with wine, in which is dissipation; but be filled with the Spirit," Your word says, "blessed is the man who walks not in counsel of ungodly, nor stand in path of sinners nor sit in the seat of the scornful but his delight is the law of the Lord. And in his law his meditate day and night. He shall be like a tree planted by the rivers of the water that brings forth its fruits in its season who leaves shall not wither". Let us delight ourselves in you O Lord and resist the devil he will flee. Today, Lord, I choose you, I choose life. Amen


**Bible Verses to study**

James 2:19; Mathew 12:43-45; 2 Corinthians 4:4; 1 Peter 4:1; Luke 8:10; 1 Corinthians 10:21; Luke 8:27; Mathew 17:19; Psalms 106:37

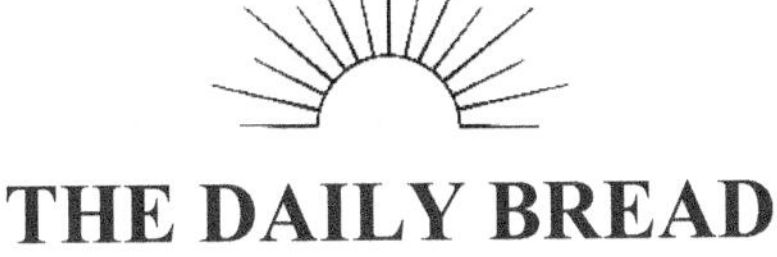

# THE DAILY BREAD

The familiarity spirit. This is a really very dangerous spirit because people become used to the things of God and as a result, they become complacent. Let me warn you, no one have arrived yet. People often make a mistake by saying I am now a great man/woman of God, I do not need to pray and read the word of God. People say I read the whole bible in previous years, but we do not rely on the past that's why the word of God says "Do not conform to the pattern of this world but be transformed by the renewing of your mind. Then you will be able to test and approve what God's will is--his good, pleasing and perfect will" (Romans 12:2). Renewing of your mind is daily not once off. Do you still pray as you used to be? Do you still attend church and cell groups as you used to be? Do you still read the word of God as you used to be? Do you still fast as you used to be? The familiarity spirit limits the power of God to be manifested in our lives that's why people are asking why the miracles are not happening in their lives. People are used to giving in church in a way that when they give its no longer out of their hearts but just like a duty. "In the spring, at the time when kings go off to war, David sent Joab out with the king's men and the whole Israelite army. They destroyed the Ammonites and besieged Rabbah. But David remained in Jerusalem" (2 Samuel 11:1) David did not go to war like any other king during his idleness he walked on top of the roof and saw Bathsheba bathing and committed adultery with her. An idle mind is a devil's playground. David got used to the things of God and forgot his duties as a King. People have a wrong perception of saying why things are not going well in their lives. They always say it's not my season but one day my season will come. If you are not careful that season may never come. The word of God says "we are like trees planted by the rivers of the water that brings forth its fruits in its season and whose leaves shall not wither. Do not blame God if things are

161

not going well in your life, you need to return to the place of worship and seek God Day and night mediating of his word. "Even now," declares the LORD, "return to me with all your heart, with fasting and weeping and mourning. And tear your hearts, and not your garments, and turn unto the LORD your God: for he is gracious and merciful, slow to anger, and of great kindness, and relents from sending calamity" (Joel 2:12-13). God bless you.

**Prayer**

We pray against familiar spirit, so that we do not get used to the things of God. As your word says "Therefore, my beloved, as you have always obeyed, not as in my presence only, but now much more in my absence, work out your own salvation with fear and trembling;", we will work on our faith with fear and trembling. We shall never be complacent with the word of God and renew my mind daily as your word says "Do not conform to the pattern of this world but be transformed by the renewing of your mind. Then you will be able to test and approve what God's will is--his good, pleasing and perfect will" Your word says, "Even now," declares the LORD, "return to me with all your heart, with fasting and weeping and mourning. And tear your hearts, and not your garments, and turn unto the LORD your God: for he is gracious and merciful, slow to anger, and of great kindness, and relents from sending calamity". Amen

**Bible verses to study**

Romans 12:2; 2 Samuel 11:1; Joel 2:12-13; Leviticus 19:31; 1 Timothy 5:17; Hebrews 11:6; Jeremiah 29:13;

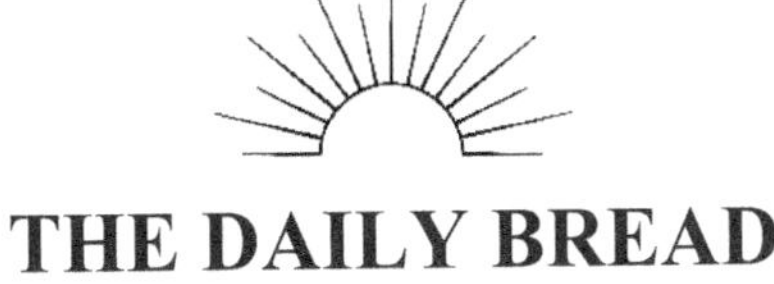

# THE DAILY BREAD

Your dream shall never die. Do you know that they are dream killers? They are people who are very negative. People who will try by all means to kill your dreams. The dream killers are not far because they come in the form of family and friends. People who you really trust. How many people who failed even before they tried? How many people who gave up on their dreams? The reason being they got into wrong hands and were advised that they are not good enough. Today ask yourself if you are helping others to fulfil their dreams or not? My prayer is for God to bring that fire back. May God awaken that hunger in you again? The fire that died down to burn again. Like Moses, may God to send a burning bush in your life. You are not perfect, but God will make you perfect, you are weak, but God will make your stronger and you just have a little, but God will multiply it. The word of God is saying this morning "For I the LORD your God will hold your right hand, saying to you, Fear not; I will help you" (Isaiah 41:13). Today I urge you to live a life of purpose and pursue your dreams. When you pursue your purpose that's when you will live life in abundance. My prayer is, let me not be the one who will kill other people's dreams. Let us build one another and glorify God with the talents he gave us. May God grant you wisdom and be able to pursue your purpose. God bless you.

**Prayer**

We pray that we shall never give up on our dreams and also, we shall never kill other people's dreams. When the dreams killers come in our lives, help us to identify them and uproot them. We pray that God you bring destiny connecters in our lives. Our dreams shall never die, if we lose the passion, help us to bring the fire back. We shall be hungry again to fulfil our purposes. We are not perfect, but God will prefect us, we are weak, but God you are strong, and we just have a little, but God you will multiply it . Your word says, "For I the LORD your God will hold your right hand, saying to you, Fear not; I will help you". We pray for us to build one another and glorify God with our talents. Amen.


**Bible verses**

Isaiah 41:13; Philippians 1:6; John 3:16-17; Acts 2:17; Joel 2:28; Ecclesiastes 5:7; Mathew 6:33; Psalms 138:8; Romans 8:37; Philippians 4:12-13

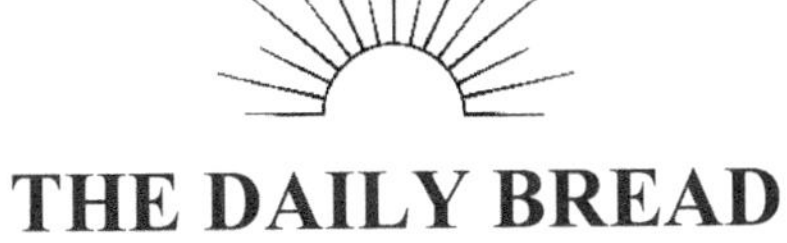

# THE DAILY BREAD

Quantity vs quality. In the ministry if we are not carefully, we will be motivated by quantity and fail to give much focus on the quality. Producing quantity is easier than producing quality. It's easier for the ministry to grow in numbers than to grow the people spiritual. People naturally follow miracles and prosperity gospel. That's why we now find some ministries now concentrate on miracles and prosperity gospel to get the quantity. Those who preach on repentance, righteousness, bible scriptures and the receiving of the Holy Spirit are the ones busy growing the people spiritual that's the quality. Developing quality, it's not easy; to see a Christian grow from a baby to a man it takes much effort and sacrifice. They are people who really need to be encouraged to grow. During the time of the early church people really saw that their lives they were living was not right after the word was preached and desired change "When the people heard this, they were cut to the heart and said to Peter and the other apostles, "Brothers, what shall we do?" Peter replied, "Repent and be baptized, every one of you, in the name of Jesus Christ for the forgiveness of your sins. And you will receive the gift of the Holy Spirit" (Acts 2:37-38). As the body of Christ, it's high time now we should seek the face of God. We must be on fire for God. Let's raise a level so that we can also pull others to that level. We do not want to produce only Sunday Christians but to develop them to the level they understand that Christianity is a way of life. People need to have a personal relationship with God. People really need to live a Christian way of life. They must reach a certain level where they practise what is preached. It is important for people to know the living God because if not they may end up worshiping Mammon the God of this world. Finally, quality should not be sacrificed for quantity. God bless you.

**Prayer**

We pray that we can grow Spiritual as your word says "I gave you milk to drink, not solid food, for not yet were you able. In fact, now you are still not able, for you are still fleshly. For where jealousy and strife *are* among you, are you not fleshly, and are walking according to man? As your through Apostle Paul says, "When I was a child, I spoke as a child, I understood as a child, I thought as a child; but when I became a man, I put away childish things", help us O Lord to put away childish things. You taught us, that you put off, concerning your former conduct, the old man which grows corrupt according to the deceitful lusts, and be renewed in the spirit of your mind. We shall be led by the Spirit of God not by flesh. Amen


**Bible verses to study.**

Acts 2:37-38; 1 Corinthians 3:1-8; 1 Corinthians 13:11; 1 Samuel 3:7; 2 Peter 3:18; Colossians 1:9-10; Galatians 5:22-23; Mathew 5:6; 2 Timothy 3:16-17

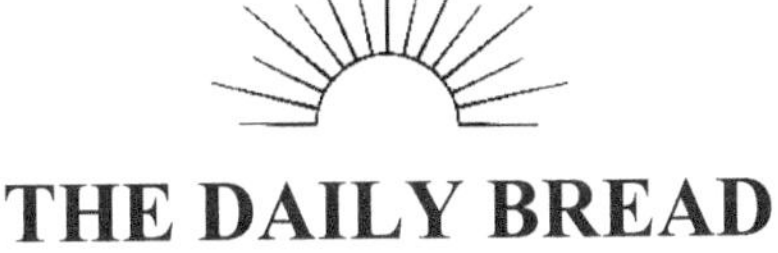

# THE DAILY BREAD

God can fix you. When the manufacturers make a bucket, they make it in a way that water does not leak. Imagine having a leaking bucket. It's a defect bucket. It's not usable. No matter how much water you put in it, it will be empty very soon. God wants to bless us more abundantly more than we can ask for, but our buckets are there not leaking. The prodigal son got so much wealth from his inheritance, but it was in and out. In a short period of time the bucket was empty. God is faithful. David said my cup runs over. (David's bucket had no holes) Your situation and circumstances are due to a leaking bucket. There is no need to fill the bucket if its leaking. Paul spoke about sins that easily ensnares us. Sinful life pokes our buckets. The devil is a thief, all he wants us to do is to miss the best from God. Have you ever seen someone who had a great family, a great job, great company and a great future but all just vanished? God poured and filled the bucket with blessings. It's about the condition of your heart. The word of God says, "Guard your heart with all diligence, for from it flow springs of life." (Proverbs 4:23) Lot was blessed by God but because of his heart, he lived in Sodom and Gomorrah. But at the end Lot lost everything and even his wife. Pray for God to fix you first before you pray for those blessings. The word of God spoke about renewing our minds so that we do not conform to the pattern of the world. If you move away from Jerusalem (God)to Jericho (World), you will fall among thieves. The story and Samson and Delilah show us how evil company can corrupt us and dispossess our blessings. If you live a sinful life, you live in past tense, I used to be rich, a manager, married, have a house and I used to have a car. God want us to be rich without sorrow (without holes). Let's do operation reset, let God fix our bucket when the wholes are closed then we can pray for God to bless us. The first step to an abundant life is to repent,

God closes the holes and then the blessings from God will flourish in our lives. Amen.


**Prayer**

We Know that God you can rebuke the devourer in our lives if we return to you. We are living a cursed life if we do not honour you with our tithes and offering. Help us understand that silver and gold belongs to you. Jesus, you came so we can have life abundantly. Your word says, "Come to Me, all who are weary and burdened, and I will give you rest," We shall be restored according to the prophet Joel, "So I will restore to you the years that the swarming locust has eaten, The crawling locust, The consuming locust, And the chewing locust, My great army which I sent among you." "And my God shall supply all your need according to His riches in glory by Christ Jesus." Amen.


**Bible verses to study.**

1 John1:9; John 10:10; Hebrews 13:8; Psalms 34:18; Revelations 3:19; James 5:16; Proverbs 3:5; Galatians 6:1; Philippians 4:13; Joel 2:25-32

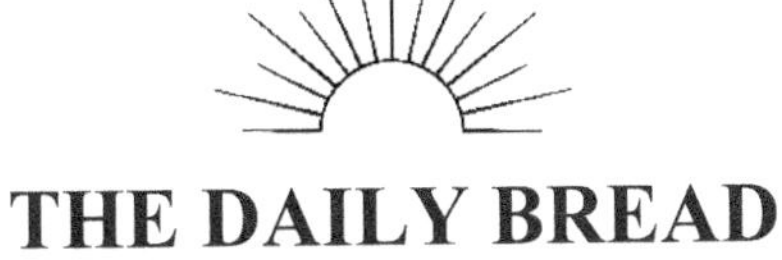

# THE DAILY BREAD

Failing. It's disingenuous for a person to fail once and quit. Failing it's not a final destination but it's a setback which can be turned into success. If you fail do not stop to keep on trying. When children are learning how to walk, they may fall several times until one day they will manage to walk properly. But if the father holds the child and does not allow the child to fall, he/she may never walk. God allows us to fail as a learning process that will lead us to success. They might be a reason why people fail in life. Failing might be a lesson to you so that you will be able to handle your success. Too much success too early might stifle your growth. Failing may humble yourself so that when you become successful you do not glorify yourself but God. When we look into the word of God, you will find that many people failed but God gave them another chance. God knew that you were going to fail like Moses; he will raise a Joshua in your life. Do not judge your life by a single event. The word of God says, "Rejoice not against me, O my enemy: when I fall, I shall arise; when I sit in darkness, the LORD shall be a light unto me" (Micah 7:8). God is saying this morning "For I know the plans I have for you," declares the LORD, "plans to prosper you and not to harm you, plans to give you hope and a future" (Jeremiah 29:11). Today when you fall do not remain on the ground, rise up, dust yourself and walk again. The devil will want to hold you in your past failures and make you believe that you are not good enough, but God want you to have faith that I can do all things through Christ Jesus who strengthens me. God bless you.


**Prayer**

Help us O Lord to understand that failing in not our final destination, we shall never stop trying and we shall never give up. God, you knew that we were going to fail, and you have made a way for us. Your word says, "Rejoice not against me, O my enemy: when I fall, I shall arise; when I sit in darkness, the LORD shall be a light unto me". Your word says, "For I know the plans I have for you," declares the LORD, "plans to prosper you and not to harm you, plans to give you hope and a future". We are fearfully and wonderfully made in the image of God and failure is not our portion. Our faith shall never fail. Amen.


**Bible verses to study.**

Micah 7:8; Jeremiah 29:11; Proverbs 24:16; Psalms 37:24; Psalms 55:22; Deuteronomy 31:8; Philippians 4:12-13; Romans 12:12; Joshua 1:9; Isaiah 41:10

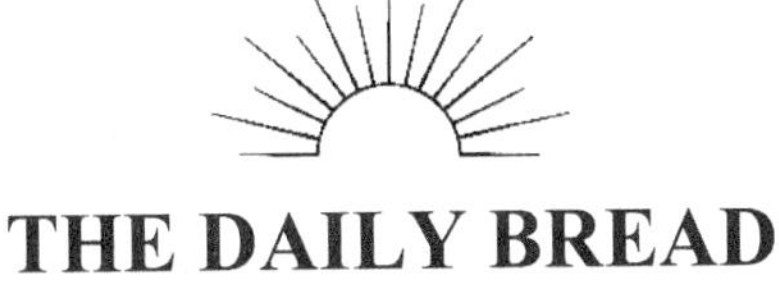

# THE DAILY BREAD

Soul winner. The fruit of the righteous is a tree of life, and the one who is wise saves lives. (Proverbs 11:30") "And they that are wise shall shine as the brightness of the firmament; and they that turn many to righteousness as the stars forever and ever" (Daniel 12:3). Are we hot to turn others hot who are cold? Do we have a great conviction in our life that Jesus is the only way, the truth, and the life? God gave his breath to everyone, and no one is supposed to go to hell. "Do I take any pleasure in the death of the wicked? Declares the Sovereign LORD. Rather, am I not pleased when they turn from their ways and live?" (Ezekiel 18:23). They are many wolfs wearing sheep's clothing instead of leading the sheep to Christ they are busy devouring them. The time is now to win more souls. Do you know if you are going to be alive in the next 24 hours, only God knows? "I must work the works of him that sent me, while it is day: the night comes, when no man can work" (John 9:4). People are suffering, possessed with demons, sick, addicted to drugs and alcohol, and bent on committing evil. "When he saw the crowds, he had compassion on them, because they were harassed and helpless, like sheep without a shepherd" (Matthew 9:36). Take every opportunity to minister the word of God every time when you meet a new person. You must ask them if they are saved. For a man you might miss the opportunity to minister to a lady because you are in flesh you lust after her and miss a soul. When we meet people, what do we see, for a thief it's a chance to pick pocket and for beggar it's a chance to ask for money, for an Evangelist it's an opportunity to win a soul. Make every opportunity counts. You are the salt of the earth, and the light of the world lets win more souls. God bless you.

**Prayer**

As you said in your word "The fruit of the righteous is a tree of life, and the one who is wise saves lives" And they that are wise shall shine as the brightness of the firmament; and they that turn many to righteousness as the stars forever and ever," let us have passion for soul winning O my Lord. Your word says" Do I take any pleasure in the death of the wicked? Declares the Sovereign LORD. Rather, am I not pleased when they turn from their ways and live?". Help us O Lord to populate heaven and depopulate hell. Amen.


**Bible Verses to study.**

Proverbs 11:30; Daniel 12:3; Ezekiel 18:23; Matthew 9:36; Mathew 28:19; Daniel 12:3; Mark 16:15; Romans 6:23; Romans 5:8; John 3:16; Romans 3:10; Acts 20:20-21

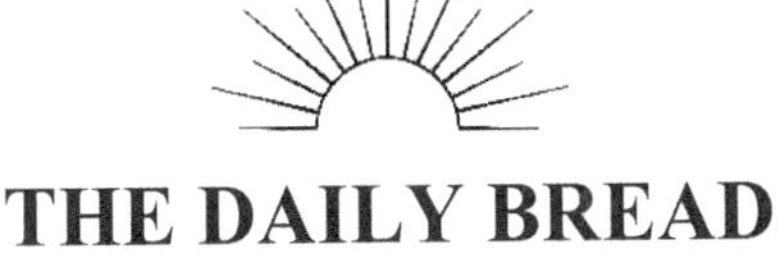

# THE DAILY BREAD

"Whoever watches the wind will not plant; whoever looks at the clouds will not reap. As you do not know the path of the wind, or how the body is formed in a mother's womb, so you cannot understand the work of God, the Maker of all things. Sow your seed in the morning, and at evening let your hands not be idle, for you do not know which will succeed, whether this or that, or whether both will do equally well" (Ecclesiastes 11:4-6). I learnt a lot at business excellence meeting this Saturday. Some Christians when they hear that there is a giant outside, they will lock themselves in the house and do not go out. Today God want you to face the giants. The world is taking the opportunities whilst the Christians are scared. When we go out there and defeat the giants, it shows faith. David defeated the lion, the bear and Goliath because of the anointing. David defeated a giant before he became a King. We need to have faith to sow the seeds before the rain. When the anointing of God is upon your life, it does not matter what qualifications you have? And where you are from? God will raise you up. Joseph was in the prison when God made him a ruler of Egypt. The anointing took him from the prison into the King's palace. Even his brothers ended up bowing to him. Everyone bows down to the anointing. Daniel changed the whole country because of the anointing. What matters most is what is inside of you than what is outside. The anointing will cause you to sow in a draught and reap a hundred-fold. Anointing will cause you to eat manna from heaven. Today we need to be prayerful, live a righteous life and shun away evil. God will make all things work together good for us. The difference between a good idea and God's idea is that a good idea you will supply for it but a God's idea, he will supply for it. We are not dependent on the on worldly economy but on the heavenly economy. What is sinking the world is rising us up.

Having the anointing is a secret to success in doing business. God bless you.


**Prayer**

As your word says, "Whoever watches the wind will not plant; whoever looks at the clouds will not reap. As you do not know the path of the wind, or how the body is formed in a mother's womb, so you cannot understand the work of God, the Maker of all things. Sow your seed in the morning, and at evening let your hands not be idle, for you do not know which will succeed, whether this or that, or whether both will do equally well", we shall never procrastinate and we shall now our seeds in the morning. Help us to understand that difference between a good idea and God's idea is that a good idea we will supply for it but a God's idea, you will supply for it. Your word says, "For I know the plans I have for you," declares the LORD, "plans to prosper you and not to harm you, plans to give you hope and a future." Amen.


**Bible verses to study**

Ecclesiastes 11:4-6; Jeremiah 29:11; Haggai 2:9; Zechariah 4:10; Genesis 8:22; Proverbs 3:5-6; Proverbs 12:24; Proverbs 13:4; Ecclesiastes 9:10

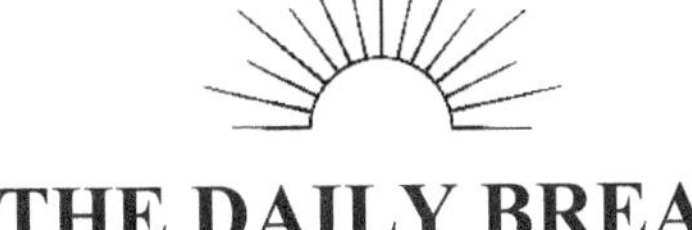

# THE DAILY BREAD

Lazarus come forth. Jesus called Lazarus from dead. Lazarus came out bound and Jesus said loosen him. People die whilst living because of sin. People stop living their daily life as they used to. They become bound by the devil. Legion is a perfect example of someone who died whilst living. Legion was cut off. Legion lived by the graves and was busy cutting himself. When you die, you become isolated, useless and bound. People they die whilst they are living. The devil put a hold over their lives. Drugs, gambling, pornography, alcohol, sex and other addictions can bring death to someone. There is that sin that brings destruction to a person. The sin that destroys you and your family. That's a stronghold. It's sad that some people they end up dying because of the wages of sin. They think they are okay. You can live again; there is power in the blood of Jesus. You cannot remain dead and bound anymore. Lazarus come forth. You shall be loosed in the name of Jesus. Jesus can restore you. The spirit of death has no power over you. You are a child of God, greater is he that is in you than he in the world. The grace of God has empowered you to say no to a sinful life. I urge you to live life of prayer. Today learn how to discipline your body like Paul so that after you have preached, you don't become disqualified also. What binds you is what you give authority over your life. It's not the water outside the boat that sinks the boat but the water you allow inside the boat. You know what kind of life you are living. God is saying today, "This day I call the heavens and the earth as witnesses against you that I have set before you life and death, blessings and curses. Now choose life, so that you and your children may live" (Deuteronomy 30:19). Being dead whilst you are living affects your family, your finances, you career, your calling and your health. The devil is robing you. "The thief does not come except to steal, and to kill, and to destroy. I have come that they may have life, and that they may have it more abundantly". (John 10:10). When we are bound because of sin, we live a life of lack and life of no purpose. Only Jesus can set you free, he is the way, the truth and the life. The word of God is saying, "Therefore if the Son makes you free, you shall be free indeed." (John 8:36). May the grace of our Lord Jesus Christ keep you and the fellowship of the Holy Spirit for now and forever more amen. God bless you.


**Prayer**

As your word says, "Therefore if the Son makes you free, you shall be free indeed," sin cannot keep us in bondage, we are set free by grace through the blood of Jesus. As your word says, "There is therefore now no condemnation to those who are in Christ Jesus, who do not walk according to the flesh, but according to the Spirit," we shall walk in the Spirit. We shall never give a place to the devil in our lives. As your word says, "This day I call the heavens and the earth as witnesses against you that I have set before your life and death, blessings and curses. Now choose life, so that you and your children may live," we choose life. Greater is He that is in us that he that is in the world. Amen.


**Bible verses to study.**

Romans 6:23; Isaiah 59:2; Romans 3:23; 1 John 3:8; Colossians 3:5; Romans 8:1; Ephesians 2:1; Colossians 3:5-6; Galatians 6:1

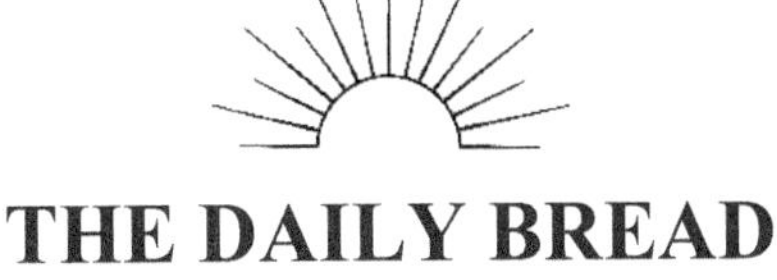

# THE DAILY BREAD

God will use your failure to catapult your future. Failing is not a problem by staying down is a problem. Most of the people who we see very successful, they have failed once upon a time. The recipe to success is not giving up. The word of God says, "Ask, and it will be given to you; seek, and you will find; knock, and it will be opened to you. For everyone who asks receives; he who seeks finds; and to him who knocks, the door will be opened." (Mathew7:7-8) . Failing should be a lesson to be better prepared next time, to work harder next time , equip you properly how to deal with disappointments and teach you how to deal with pain. We learn more in the valley than on top of the mountains. God is saying, "Do not rejoice over me, my enemy; When I fall, I will arise; When I sit in darkness, The LORD will be a light to me" (Micah 7:8) God want you to face your fears and put your trust in him. You might have failed in business, broken marriage, project and education. Do not stop trying. God will make you stand again and great again. Moses failed and ran away from Egypt, but God sent him back to Egypt again where he failed. Moses faced his fears. It was a mountain to climb for Moses, it was not easy. Moses knew what had happened in Egypt and going back was a dreadfully idea. Moses faced his fears. God made Moses to be successfully. But he had to go and face Pharaoh and talk to his people. We need to play our part and God will do his own part. Moses was now living his life of his own and everything seemed okay. God knew the potential in Moses and called him. You might have been side tracked, defeated and out of destiny but it's not over until God says it's over. Do not just live life for your own. God has made you to be the light of the world and the salt of the earth. Tell yourself that you are not a failure amen I might not be where I am supposed to be but because of the grace of God I will make it. "For I know the thoughts that I think toward you, says the LORD, thoughts of peace and not of evil, to give you a future and a hope." (Jeremiah 29:11) God bless you.


## Prayer

Thank you, Lord, for never giving up on us and for giving us a second chance. We were lost and now we are found . Your word says, "Do not rejoice over me, my enemy; When I fall, I will arise; When I sit in darkness, The LORD will be a light to me". In our weakness, you are strong. We are not failures, but success is in our veins through the blood of Jesus. He who has begun a good work in us shall continue until Lord Jesus Christ comes. We are head not a tail, we are always above not beneath. We are more than a conquerors through him who gives us strength. You word says, "For a righteous man may fall seven times And rise again, But the wicked shall fall by calamity." Amen


## Bible Verses to study

Proverbs 24:16; Job 5:19; Psalms 34:19; Micah 7:8; Proverbs 24:16; Psalms 37:24; Psalms 121:1-2; Psalms 145:14

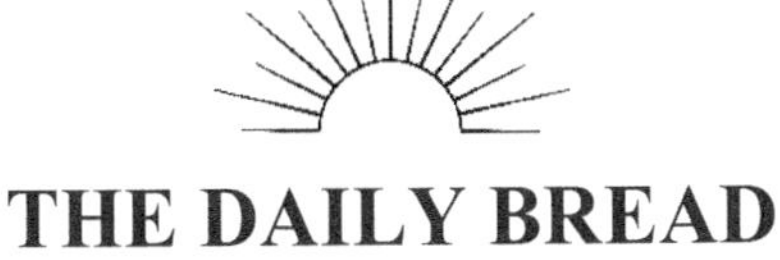

# THE DAILY BREAD

Thankful – Be thankful this morning. Take a time to thank God. In midst on all the evil and chaos around this world, God is protecting you, God is providing you and God is also blessing you. Most of the times we look at what we do not have and complain to God. This morning I am content, and I have joy because of the grace of God in my life. Although there is so much sickness, I am health; although there are so many wars, I live in a peaceful country. Paul said, "I am not saying this because I am in need, for I have learned to be content whatever the circumstances. I know what it is to be in need, and I know what it is to have plenty. I have learned the secret of being content in any and every situation, whether well fed or hungry, whether living in plenty or in want. I can do all this through him who gives me strength." (Philippians 4:11-13). God has put good people in my life. I am counting my blessings this morning. God is really good to me, and I hope you will see that too in your life. 'Praise the Lord! Oh, give thanks to the Lord, for he is good, for his steadfast love endures forever! Who can utter the mighty deeds of the Lord, or declare all his praise" (Psalms 106:1-2)? God is faithful. The greatest gift God gives us is life. When you are still breathing, tell yourself that God has plans with my life. It's a blessing that you have a roof above your head, you have food to eat, you are married, you are healthy and have a job. God is faithful. You must thank God for the precious gift of life. Jesus said, "Peace I leave with you, My peace I give to you; not as the world gives do I give to you. Let not your heart be troubled, neither let it be afraid." (John 14:27). In everything give thanks: for this is the will of God in Christ Jesus concerning you. (1 Thessalonians 5:18). O give thanks unto the God of heaven: for his mercy endures for ever." (Psalms 136:26). Your word teaches us that, "Enter His gates with thanksgiving, And His courtyards with praise. Give thanks to Him, bless His name." (Psalms 100:4) God bless you.

**Prayer**

We thank you God for the gift of life, we are healthy, we have a job, we have a place to stay, and we have businesses. Jesus, you came so that we can live life more abundantly. Blessed is our name. Greater is He that is us than he that is the world. God, you love us. We are blessed. Goodness and mercy is following us for the rest of our lives. We thank God because we are lying in the greener pastures. All we need is you, Lord and nothing else matters. There is no darkness in our finances, at my workplaces and in our families and our children. Your word says, "Enter His gates with thanksgiving, And His courtyards with praise. Give thanks to Him, bless His name." Amen

**The bible verses to study**

Philippians 4:11-13; Psalms 106:1-2; John 14:27; 1 Thessalonians 5:18; Psalms 136:26

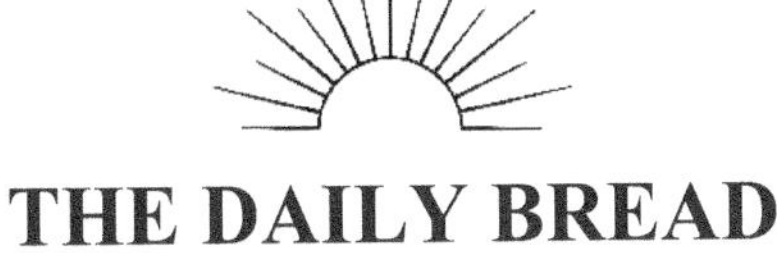

# THE DAILY BREAD

Denying yourself and carrying your cross daily. Then Jesus said to his disciples, "Whoever wants to be my disciple must deny themselves and take up their cross and follow me. (Mathew 16:24) . Why deny yourself, our flesh has a sinful nature. The denying is acting against the flesh. People who diet amen they deny themselves certain delicacy for a certain period. After that they will restore that food in their diet. When we deny ourselves, it's not supposed to be temporary it must be permanent. For us to deny ourselves we need to carry our cross daily. When you carry your cross daily amen you will be a prisoner of Jesus Christ. Only prisoners carried the cross. That means you will have surrendered your previous life and now living a new life. As a prisoner, you do not live in the way you want but according to prison rules. It's not easy to carry your cross daily because it involves a lot of suffering. Some of the Christian do not like the part denying themselves. But according to the word of God, you cannot serve 2 masters. Also, the cross symbolizes dying to yourself. You have to die to yourself daily." So, then they that are in the flesh cannot please God". (Romans 8:8). Christianity it's a way life. You need to say no to your former life. "That you put off, concerning your former conduct, the old man which grows corrupt according to the deceitful lusts, and be renewed in the spirit of your mind, and that you put on the new man which was created according to God, in true righteousness and holiness. Ephesians (4:22-24) As a child of God before you aspire other things in the ministry, the first step is to deny yourself. But why it's difficult to deny ourselves. Confusion, people not yet decided to follow Christ or leave their former life. Friends, people who have much influence on your life but not yet saved. Unrenewed mind, not studying the word of God therefore your way of thinking is very carnal . Airtime , how you spend your time if you spend your time watching only worldly programmes on TV and listening to worldly music you will also become worldly and stunt your growth. Some people they say you are what you eat . As a result, there is no time to spend with God. Lies, the devils always have a way to make you miss your former life and make you think about it , the more you think about it , those cravings come, and you will fall back . Do not be fooled the wages of sin is death. God bless you.


**Prayer**

Dear God, help us to be strong in our faith so that we do not waiver. Give us strength to continue holding on even our past is calling us. Give us the wisdom like Paul to continue to fight a good fight of faith. We pray that we become more of you Lord and less of ourselves. We pray that you direct our footsteps, and as the footsteps of a righteous man are ordered by God. Your word says, "That you put off, concerning your former conduct, the old man which grows corrupt according to the deceitful lusts, and be renewed in the spirit of your mind, and that you put on the new man which was created according to God, in true righteousness and holiness." Amen


**Bible Verses**

Mathew 16:24; Mathew 10:38; Luke 14:27; 1 Peter 2:21; Romans 8:8; Galatians 5:16; Romans 8:6; Luke 9:23-24; Titus 2:11-12

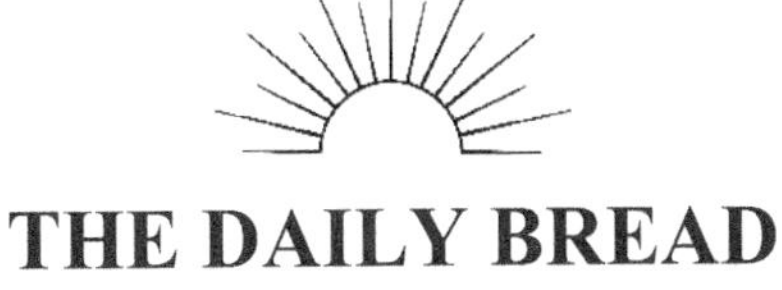

# THE DAILY BREAD

Excellence. Serena Williams won 23 Grand Slam titles in her legendary career. How many girls who played tennis and yet she proved to be the best. People they paid a lot of money to watch her play. The people paid for her talent that has been perfected through excellence. Money follows her. For her to remain the best for a longer period, she must have be doing something that is of excellence. Joseph is an example of someone who lived a life of excellence. Living with his family, he was a dreamer, in the Potiphar's house everything was put under him; in the prison he was made a leader and later a ruler in Egypt. You do not have an excuse of not living a life of excellence. In the Ministry some have only focused on anointing and forgot about excellence. That's why some Ministries are failing to attract people in the world. Although the Gospel music is growing but excellence is still lacking sometimes. People have a choice. Places in the world that sells alcohol, they provide an excellent service because they are selling a product. The churches need to move towards excellence. We are a head not a tail, the world must look for excellence from us. What you do in your time alone will lead you to excellence. Life is like a comrades marathon. You need you need to run it before the day of the race. You must see yourself winning. If you can see yourself winning in your practise time nothing can stop you. You cannot do whatever everyone is doing then you will be successful. Spend more time, take care of every detail, do not fear to take risks, hard work pays, look at what others are doing, challenge yourself, do not be afraid of criticism and learn from your mistakes. Paul said to Timothy, "Neglect not the gift that is in you, which was given you through prophecy, with the laying on of the hands of the presbytery".( 1 Timothy 4:15)God bless you.

**Prayer**

We pray for the Spirit of excellence, the one you gave to Joseph, Daniel, and Solomon. Open my eyes see the path you have set up for us. Let us work on our faith with fear and trembling. Let us understand that all things are working together for good for us. If God is for us who can be against us and Christ in us, is the hope of glory. Greater is He that is in us than he that is in the world. All things are possible to those who believe. We are head not a tail and always above not beneath . The same Spirit that raised Christ from the dead dwells in us. Amen

**Bible Verses to study**

Philippians 4:8; Colossians 3:23; 2 Corinthians 8:7; Psalms 16:3; 2 Peter 1:5; Daniel 6:3; Colossians 3:23; 1 Peter 2:9

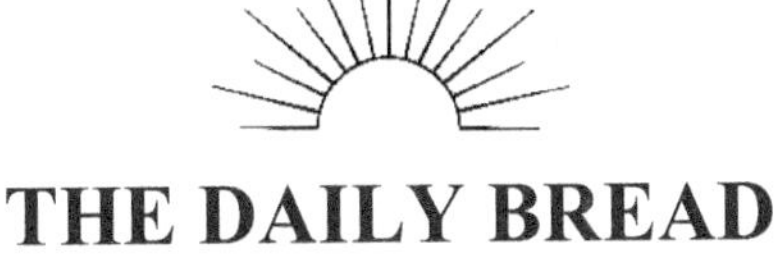

# THE DAILY BREAD

Fallen off. How many of you who have fallen? How many of you who have grown cold now sitting on the side lines. You started sitting in the front row of the church, now you are sitting at the back of the church, now you are in the parking lot and now you are out of the church. I know you are disappointed with God; you are angry at God, and you have given up on God. Why can't you come back to the house? Why are you still staying in exodus? Why are you running away from the good that once nourished you before? Why did you let the devil to blind your heart. "A Song of Ascents. Of David. I was glad when they said to me, "Let us go into the house of the LORD." (Psalms 122:1) There is no life apart from God. Remember those days you used to be the mighty man/woman of valour for the Lord, the days when the fire of the Lord burned in your life, when you walked in the glory of God and when you used to be that city built on top of the hill. You can come back; God has never forgotten about you. How long shall you let this bitterness tear you apart. God is faithful. God wants to restore you. Don't be like a child who hate his father and mother who love him/her dearly. Return to your first love. Return to God. He is just and faithful. It will be shortsighted for us to be like dogs and go back to our vomit, that is our past life. Off ramping from the life God called us may have a far-reaching consequences to us and our generations to come. God is saying today, "Return, O backsliding children," says the LORD; "for I am married to you. I will take you, one from a city and two from a family, and I will bring you to Zion." (Jeremiah 3:14). May you come back to the house of worship and God is faithful to his word, "I will give you a new heart and put a new spirit within you; I will take the heart of stone out of your flesh and give you a heart of flesh." (Ezekiel 36:26). Like a Parodical son you shall come back, the father will cloth you with the best robe and put a ring on your finger and sandals on your feet. Bring the fattened calf and kill it and prepare a feast and celebrate., for his son he thought was dead, is alive again; he was lost and is found. God bless you.


**Prayer**

Lord, we shall never fall off, we shall never grow cold and sit in sidelines in our walk of faith. As your word says, "I was glad when they said to me, "Let us go into the house of the LORD". We shall dwell in the House of the Lord Forever. We are the light of the world, the salt of the earth, a city that is built of the Hill that can never he hidden. Your word is saying, "Return, O backsliding children," says the LORD; "for I am married to you. I will take you, one from a city and two from a family, and I will bring you to Zion." Your word says, "I will give you a new heart and put a new spirit within you; I will take the heart of stone out of your flesh and give you a heart of flesh." Thank you, Lord, for saving our souls. Amen


**Bible verses to study.**

Psalms 122:1; Jeremiah 3:14; Ezekiel 36:26; Hebrews 10:24-25; Mathew 18:20; Acts 2:42; Hebrews 3:13

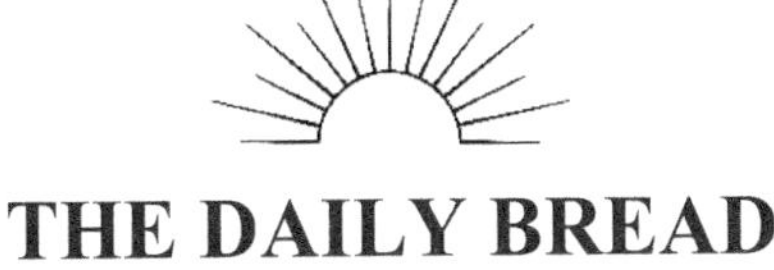

# THE DAILY BREAD

Character. The world has a created a criminal record and credit record to check the Character of a person. If people they do not know who you are, they can mistake you. They want to know if they can trust you. We have people who say today you will know who am I. Which means they have been hiding for all their life their character? Samson was a powerful man of God and much anointed, but he lacked Character. "Your gift, talents and abilities can take you to great heights but only character can sustain you there " Dr AR Bernard. The devil wants to attack your character like Job. The devil knew Job was wealthy, loved his children so much and he was a righteous man. The devil destroyed his wealth, children and his health to test his character. The devil asked a question does Job worship God for nothing. If the devil can ask that question in your life what will happen. Where is your faith? Is your faith in what you have than in God? It takes very long time to build a character but to destroy it takes a moment. "I am the vine; you are the branches. If you remain in me and I in you, you will bear much fruit; apart from me you can do nothing. (John 15:5). We need to remain in Christ and David said let your word be thy lamp upon thy feet and let be thy light upon thy path. Our character needs to reflect what we stand for that is Christ like life. Without that we are not different from anyone else. The word says, if you say that you have fellowship with him and still walks in darkness it's a lie. Our character should be shaped by the word of God. You cannot serve two masters. You cannot serve God and mammon. It's not the water that is outside the boat that sinks it but it's the water that is allowed inside the boat. Be careful of corruption because God hates corruption. Choose to live life that glorify God. What happens if a temptation comes in your way, will you be able to overcome it? Where is your faith? Your character will be able to sustain you in the time of a storm. When God looks like He is not hearing your prayers, will you compromise. Paul warned us about evil workers, dogs and mutilators in Church, there is also corruption in Church. The word of God says, "…… bad company corrupts good character." (1 Corinthians 15:33). God bless you.


**Prayer**

We thank you LORD Jesus Christ for the gift of life. You said come unto me those who are weary and heavy burdened, and I will give you rest. Please grow our faith so that we can learn to trust on you. Let us be able to live a life that glorifies you. We pray that the word of God to be thy lamp upon thy feet and thy light upon thy path. Strengthen our inner man and open our eyes to understand the hope of our calling. You said we are the light of the world and the salt of the earth. You called us from darkness to glorious light for a reason. Your grace is sufficient for us. Thank you for saving us and giving us a new life. Amen


**The bible verses to study**

John 15:5;1 Corinthians 15:33; Judges 16:1-31;Romans 5:3-4; 1Timothy3:2;Galatians 5:22-23

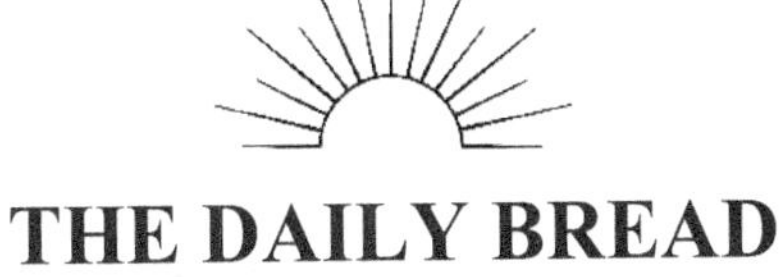

# THE DAILY BREAD

Salt. When you put salt on the food, it changes the taste of the food not the food changing the taste of salt. Salt is used to preserve food. The word of God say we are the salt of the earth (Mathew 5:13). So, when we look closely, we realize as Christians we have a great responsibility, as the salt of the earth, to preserve the world. The issue of morality now takes place in that we need teach the word of God and live the word of God. Paul said, " But I discipline my body and bring it into subjection, lest, when I have preached to others, I myself should become disqualified."(1 Corinthians 9:27) With our saltiness, we are empowered by God over the enemy. We have to affect our environment not to be affected by the environment. We must not reflect the worldly life but the kingdom principles. Your word says, "You are the salt of the earth. But if the salt loses its saltiness, how can it be made salty again? It is no longer good for anything, except to be thrown out and trampled underfoot" ( Mathew 5:13). We are in world but not of this world. Have the people shortchanged you, robbed you, did not keep their promise and did not show compassion to you. Now don't take it as an excuse to be bitter and copy their behaviour. You are the salt of earth nothing should change you. If they hate you, love them more, look at people how God look at them and give them a second chance. Some people cannot show love anymore because they were hurt, some people cannot borrow anymore because people were stingy to them, and some people cannot give because when they were poor growing up. Hey, it's not about how the world has treated you; it's about who you are. I am in Christ therefore I am grounded and rooted in love. Nothing will change me. Greater is He that is in me than he that is in the world. Do not return evil for evil but with good. You are the light of the world and in you there is not darkness. You are a city that is built on the hill that cannot be hidden. God bless you.

**Prayer**

Thank you, God, for shining your light in our lives. We were sitting in darkness, and now we are sitting in light. We are now the salt of earth and light of the world. God you are love, teach us how to love. Let us look at people the way you look at them and not to give up on anyone. We shall cast all burdens and cares unto you Lord Jesus. Our hope and trust are in you. We glorify your name. Who can be like you Lord? You are high and lifted up. Your mercies endures forever. We cannot seize to thank you. Amen


**The bible verses to study**

Mathew 5:13; 1 Corinthians 9:27; Job 6:6; Mark 9:50; Luke 14:34-35: Colossians 4:6; Hebrew 6;4-6

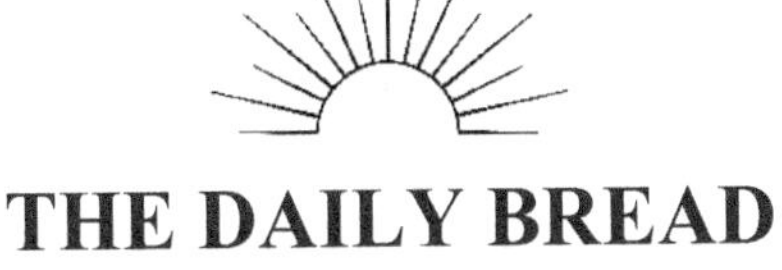

# THE DAILY BREAD

Do not hold on to manna, move into the Promised Land. For the children of Israel manna was nice, great, and awesome but it was not what God had promised them. God had promised them the land full of honey and milk in Canaan that's why when they entered into the promised land and ate the first produce, it seized. We call manna the transition period, a shadow of what was going to come. All of us, we are moving towards what God had promised us in his word. In this aspect, there is a problem of not being able to see God's vision. We know it but do we believe it, that God has the best plan for lives. So, soldier on and get to where God has promised you. You are not there yet so do not stop. If you keep holding onto the manna, you are delaying yourself to enter into the promises of God. Get out of that comfort zone. Grow some tooth so that you can chew meat. The milk you are drinking does not have all the nutrients you need to develop in the next level. God wants you to have life and live more abundantly. The manna was nice but now I have faith to move to the next level. The manna it's just a shadow about what is going to come. I cannot keep holding on yesterday's anointing, I used to fast, pray for the sick and pay tithes, I will backslide. I need to move to the next level. Do not stay at place where the presence of God has left. Move with God. Do like Moses who said to God if your presence does not go with us, do not send us up from here. Be hungry and thirsty to move to the next stage. God did not promise us manna but the land of milk and honey in the promised land. Although manna is great its temporary, it should not destruct us and settle on manna. The word of God says the just shall live by faith. God bless you.

**Prayer**

We thank you God for the manna from heaven you gave us, but we are yearning for the milk and honey of the promised land. Your word says , "For all the promises of God in Him are Yes, and in Him Amen, to the glory of God through us." Help us O Lord not to settle for less as your word says, "For I know the plans I have for you," declares the LORD, "plans to prosper you and not to harm you, plans to give you hope and a future." We will never rely on yesterday's anointing and stay at a place where the presence of God has left. Create in us a hunger for you Lord. "As the deer pants for the water brooks, So pants my soul for You, O God." Amen

**The bible verses to study**

Exodus 16:1-36; John 6:38; Psalms 78:23-25; Joshua 5:12; Numbers 11:6-9; Nehemiah 9:15; Mathew 4:4; Revelation 2:17

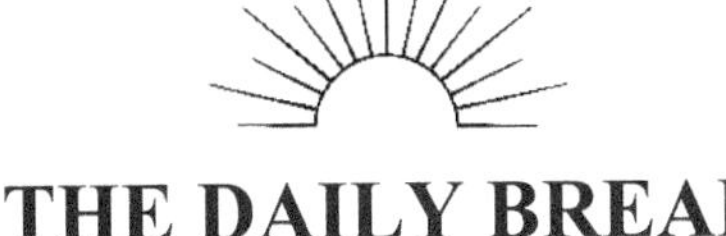

# THE DAILY BREAD

Pray for other saints. Paul did not cease to pray for other saints. When was the last time you prayed for your local pastors, leaders and fellow Christians? We are in a spiritual welfare. "Be sober, be vigilant; because your adversary the devil, as a roaring lion, walks about, seeking whom he may devour" (1 Peter 5:8). We do not know what other fellow Christians are going through. At school there are dropouts, people that fail to complete education. There are some people who came to church and disappeared. The word of God says, "neither give place to the devil."(Ephesians 4:27) Sinful life drives people out of Church. If your fellow brother and sister, no longer come to Church or cell do not cease to pray for them. We need to pray for those whose love of God has gone cold. As we are soldiers of Christ we need to be there for fellow wounded soldiers. Part of Paul's prayer to Philippians "I thank my God upon every remembrance of you, Always in every prayer of mine for you all making request with joy". I once had a dream of fellow Christians praying for me and I know they were saints praying for me because I once off ramped , left Church and went back into the world. But because of the prayers of other saints, I was freed from my bondage and Satan let me go. "Therefore, confess your sins to each other and pray for each other so that you may be healed. The prayer of a righteous person is powerful and effective. "(James 5:16) They are Christians who are still babies in Christ. They are Christians who have backslidden. They are also Christians who are in different seasons. We must be intercessors, who can stand between the gaps. We must pray for their spiritual growth, revelation of the word and God to give them strength. Please pray for the body for Christ, in the same aspect God will also intervene in your situations. "Many are the afflictions of the righteous, But the LORD delivers him out of them all". (Psalms 34:19) Job prayed for his friends when he was still in a predicament. God restored Job after he prayed for his friends. Your breakthrough may come after you have prayed for your boss, wife, family, friends or enemies. Peter was in a prison and bound with the chains. But because the Church prayed, God sent an angel to take him out of the prison. The chains fall off and the prison doors opened. God bless you.


**Prayer**

We pray for the body of Christ. We pray for the Pastors, the Evangelists, Teachers of the word, Apostles, Prophets, ushers, praise and worship, hospitality, cleaners, chefs, givers, tithers, protocol, security, car guards, children's church, partners and the congregation. Please Lord cover our families and friends from the evil one. Deliver us for evil. May their souls prosper and their health too in the name of Jesus. We pray against the spirit of poverty, sickness and death. We pray for those who does not know God to give their lives to Jesus. We pray for Christians facing prosecution as your word says, "Many are the afflictions of the righteous, But the LORD delivers him out of them all". Bring back the fire to those who have backslidden and grow cold. Amen.


**The bible verses to study**

1 Peter 5:8; Ephesians 4:27; James 5:16; Psalms 34:19; Job 1:7; Mark 4:15; 2 Corinthians 2:11 2 Timothy 4:17; James 4:7; 1 Peter 1:13; Mathew 4:1-11; Job 2:2

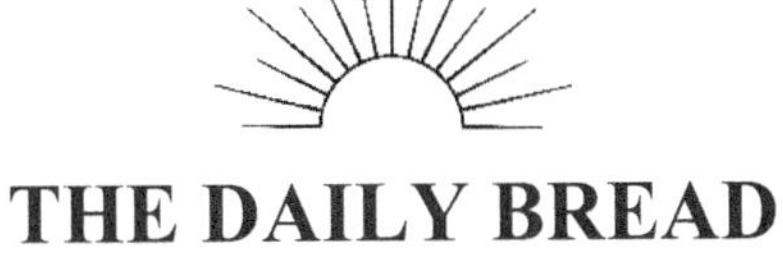

# THE DAILY BREAD

Go further. You cannot be at the same stage with people you are leading. Moses is an epitome of good leadership. Moses would go to the mountain and spend time with God. He managed to balance his time with people and with God. Moses spent more time in the presence of God. You could not identify him with the crowd. When they were murmuring and crying in the camp, it did not come from Moses. Moses was spiritual ahead of his followers. He was leading by example. Because of His closeness to God, He was used by God to do mighty miracles. Because of Moses's obedience, God used him to fulfil his will on earth. When God wanted to destroy the sinful people, who created and worshiped a golden calf, Moses interceded for them, and He did not want them to be destroyed. I encourage you as leaders to be filled by the Spirit of God. Spend more time in the word and prayer. Do not let this destructive world to take your time for things of God. You must be a channel which God can use you to change the lives of his people. You need to go ahead, go further, dig deeper and search for God. (Psalms 1:1-3) says "Blessed is the man that walks not in the counsel of the ungodly, nor stands in the way of sinners, nor sits in the seat of the scornful. But his delight is in the law of the LORD; and in his law he meditates day and night. And he shall be like a tree planted by the rivers of water, that brings forth his fruit in his season; his leaf also shall not wither; and whatsoever he doeth shall prosper." This morning I challenge you to be a full tank. Remember you are the salt of the earth. Salvation is freely given but to apply the principles in the kingdom of God, you need to work on your faith. To harvest, you need to be a Sower. You cannot want to live a supernatural life whilst your prayer life is just like everybody. You need to go further and be hungry for the things of God. God bless you.

**Prayer**

God, we pray that we can go further. We are not satisfied with the level we are today. We will continue to grow from glory to glory. May you create a hunger in us for you. May we delight ourselves in the law of the Lord. May the book of the Lord not depart from our mouths. Your word says, "Create in me a clean heart, O God, And renew a steadfast spirit within me". We pray that we die to ourselves so that you can live through us. We pray that we decrease so that you can increase in us. We pray that we forsake our evils ways and follow you. Amen


**The bible verses to study**

Psalms 1:1-3; Ezekial 47:5; Hebrews 11:6; Exodus 34:28; Mathew 4:2; 2 Timothy 2:15

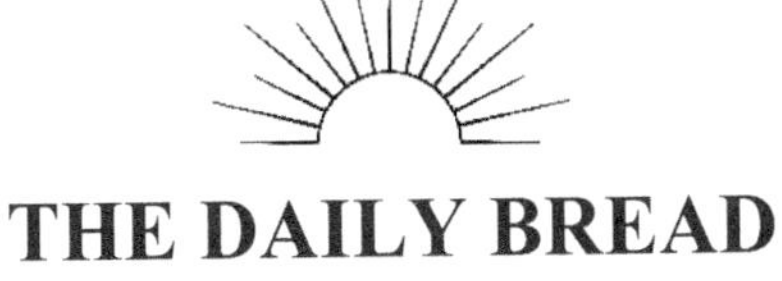

# THE DAILY BREAD

Please God make me to be the instrument of peace. "Blessed are the peacemakers, for they shall be called sons of God." (Mathew 5:9). Where there is strife, let me move away for the sake of peace. Let me be like Abraham when there was strife between him and Lot, he chose to let Lot go to maintain peace. Let me be the first one to say I am sorry. You taught us to pray, " forgive our trespasses and we forgive as we forgive those who trespass against us". Let the sun not go down when I am angry with anything. I shall love my enemies and not to return evil with evil but with good. Let me not close a door on anyone and give people a second chance. Let me not Judge people by what I hear and what I see but let the Holy Spirit guide me. Help me to keep my mouth shut and not to spread rumours and say words I will regret tomorrow. Let me not touch your anointed and not say negative things of other people. "Love suffers long, *and* is kind; love envies not; love vaunts not itself, is not puffed up, Does not behave itself rudely, seeks not her own, is not easily provoked, thinks no evil; Rejoices not in iniquity, but rejoices in the truth; Bears all things, believes all things, hopes all things, endures all things. Love never fails....." 1 Corinthians (13:4-8). The word of God says neither give a place to the devil. God is love; may I be like you Lord. Let me be able to love my enemies. Teach me Lord, how to love the unlovable. Teach me Lord Jesus your ways. Let me not throw stones at anyone. Let me be fair with all men and not be a false witness. Where there is peace God commands a blessing. "I pray that out of his glorious riches he may strengthen you with power through his Spirit in your inner being, so that Christ may dwell in your hearts through faith. And I pray that you, being rooted and established in love, may have power, together with all the Lord's holy people, to grasp how wide and long and high and deep is the love of Christ, and to know this love that surpasses knowledge—that you may be filled to the measure of all the fullness of God." (Ephesians 3:16-19). God bless you.


**Prayer**

As your word says, "Be angry and do not sin; do not let the sun go down on your anger, we pray that the sun shall not down whilst we are angry. We thank you God because you have given us the peace that passes all our understanding. Let us be used by you to be peacemakers. Forgive us as we forgive those who trespass against us. Let us not hold on to the grudges. Let us also give people second chances. May we not look for the specks of dust in their eyes and forget that we have logs in our eyes. We pray for healing for those who have been wounded so that they do not wound others. Amen


**The bible verses to study**

Mathew 5:9; Mathew 6:14; Ephesians 4:26-27; 1 Peter 3:7; Mark 12:31; Mathew 7:12

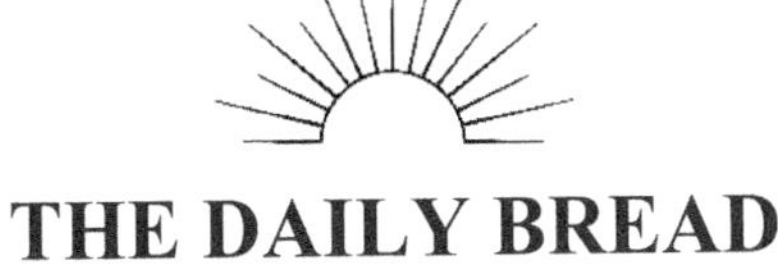

# THE DAILY BREAD

At face value. After Jesus fasted for 40 days and nights, He was tempted by the devil. Jesus was fasting and concentrating on the heavenly things whilst the devil on the earthly things. The word of God says, "Set your mind on things above, not on things on the earth. For you have died, and your life has been hidden with Christ in God. When Christ *who is* our life appears, then you also will appear with Him in glory". (Colossians 3:2-4) Jesus was focused on the heaven and could not be tempted by earthly things. Fasting and prayer help us on concentrating on heavenly things. He saw the devil at his face value. What were the devil's motives? The devil's mission was to make Jesus lose the heaven by focusing on earthly things. This morning, I am asking you where your focus is. "Store your treasures in heaven, where moths and rust cannot destroy, and thieves do not break in and steal". (Mathew 6:20) "For where your treasure is, there will your heart be also." (Luke 12:34). Your heart and treasure they go hand in hand. If your focus is on earthly things so heart will be stored on earth. Your heart is your treasure. It must be protected and well looked after. The word of God says guard your heart because out of it flows issues of life. Only in heaven it can be free of corruption of rust, moths and thieves. By focusing on heavenly things, you are storing up your heart in heaven. They are lot of things which can make you lose your focus on heaven. But it's about what are you doing with your life here on earth. Is your focus here on earth or on heaven? If you know you are not from here but from heaven start living a life which reflects where you are from. God bless you.


**Prayer**

We pray that we do not gain this world and lose our souls. We pray that we do not conform to the pattern of this world, but we renew our minds to prove that is acceptable and good purpose of God upon our lives, we do not walk in darkness but in light, we do not walk by sight but in Spirit. We pray that we look unto Jesus the author and finisher of our faith. We pray that we do not comprise, lose our birthrights like Esau for a bowl of soup. We pray that for the rest of our lives we will dwell in the house of the Lord forever. As your word says, "Set your mind on things above, not on things on the earth," we shall never set our minds on earthly things but on things above. Amen.


**The bible verses to study**

Mathew 4:1-11; Colossians 3:2-4; Luke 12:34; Mark 8:36; Romans 12:2; Proverbs 4:23

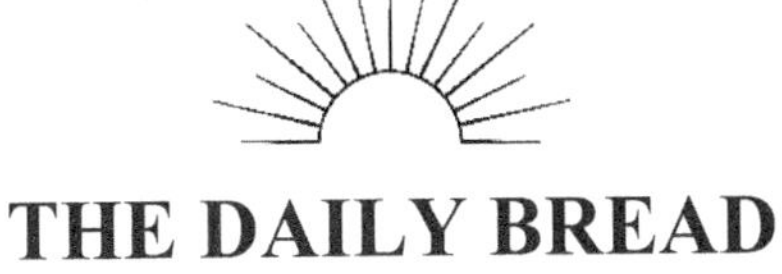

# THE DAILY BREAD

Each of us has hopes and dreams for our lives. God actually designed us to be goal- and vision-oriented Proverbs 29:18 says that without a vision we actually perish. So, it's not a bad thing to have plans, goals and desires for our lives. But what happens when those plans are diverted? (Proverbs 13:12) says that hope differed makes the heart sick. My heart had become sick with disappointments, and I hadn't even realized it. Disappointment is a part of life that every person deals with. Your kids disappoint you; your spouse disappoints you; your friends disappoint you; we even disappoint ourselves. Left unchecked, these disappointments build up and begin to dam up the River of Life that God desires to flow through us. We must regularly ask the Holy Spirit to shine the light of Truth into our hearts and dislodge the hurts, disappointments, and offenses that threaten to cut off the fruit of God's Spirit in our lives. Bearing good fruit is God's greatest desire for our lives (John 15) and so it is no wonder that Satan works overtime to dump garbage there! What we do with it greatly affects our life and the lives of those around us. All those little foxes destroy the vine of our lives! I had to admit that I've had several disappointments over the last several months. Then I had to repent and ask God to forgive me for carrying them. Rather than giving them over to God (Mathew 11:28) and allowing His Spirit to strengthen me, I had 'stuffed' them, causing a dam to be built in me. The word of God says, "Cast your burden on the LORD, and he will sustain you; he will never permit the righteous to be moved." (Psalms 55:22). God bless you.


**Prayer**

God, we pray that you teach us on how to deal with our disappointments. May you give us strength to go past our failures and rejection. Let us know that it's not by might nor by power says the Lord of Hosts but by my Spirit. Your word says a thief comes not unless is to steal, destroy and kill but I come so that you can have life more abundantly. We know the plans you have for us are not to harm us but to give us hope and future. No matter what we are going through we know that weeping may endure overnight but joys comes in the morning. You said that you shall never leave us nor forsaken us. Nothing can separate us from your love O God. Amen


**The bible verses to study**

Proverbs 29:18; Proverbs 13:12; John 15:1-8; John 1:11; Jeremiah 29:11; Philippians 4:6-7; Psalms 34:18; Isaiah 40:28-31

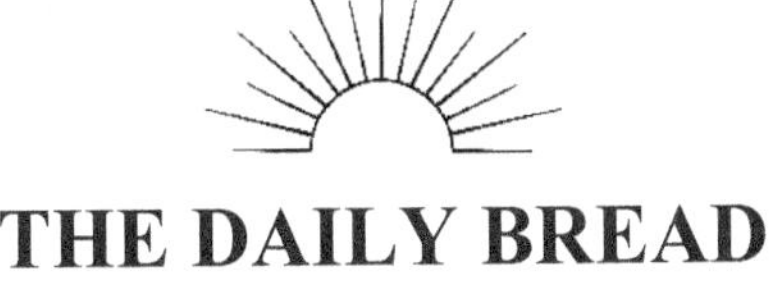

# THE DAILY BREAD

Expiry date. When you buy food in the shop, they have an expiry date. After the expiry date, the shop is not allowed to sale the food. What I am trying to stress is the time period. If the food remains long on the shelf without being sold it will reach its expiry date. All of us have an expiry date. "As for man, his days are like grass; As a flower of the field, so he flourishes. For the wind passes over it, and it is gone, And its place remembers it no more." Psalms 103:15-16). "All go to one place: all are from the dust, and all return to dust." (Ecclesiastes 3:20) One day we will leave this world and we are here temporary. Our body is our earthly suit to function in this world. This issue of time is of paramount importance. The clock is ticking. I know one day I will expire and be taken off the shelf. God has given me one life to live. When you work, they give you a specific time to start work and to finish. And in that time, you are expected to function in a specific way. I choose to live the rest of my days full of joy, not being grumpy, not complaining and not being bitter. What I have learnt is that what you give is what you get, if you sow love, you will reap love. Our time is very limited; do not procrastinate, live for now. Show those who you love that you love them and appreciate their effort too. One day they will leave this world and you will too. Always thank God our Father for giving you the gift of life. Paul said, "For to me to live is Christ, and to die is gain." (Philippians 1:21). We should work whilst it is daytime when the nighttime comes no one can work. Your problems too have expiry date. I am not sure which season you are but hold on to your faith in the Lord Jesus Christ. Paul spoke about running a race and completing it. For you to complete it, you need to discipline your body. Fight a good fight of faith. When I die, I want God to say, "Well done, good and faithful servant; you have been faithful over a few things, I will make you ruler over many things. Enter into the joy of your lord." Mathew 25:23) God bless you.


**Prayer**

We thank you Lord for the gift of life. May we live the lives that glorify you God. Let us be a living epistle that someone can read. May you satisfy us with long life and show us your salvation. Let us be able to fight a good fight of faith. Use us to bring light to those still sitting in the darkness. We will serve you God for the rest of our lives. We are the salt of the earth, the light of the world and a city that is built on the hill that cannot be hidden. The grace of God is sufficient for us. The just shall live by faith.        We pray that when we die Lord you will say, "Well done, good and faithful servant; you have been faithful over a few things, I will make you ruler over many things. Enter into the joy of your lord." Amen


**The bible verses to study**

103:15-16;  Ecclesiastes  3:20;  Philippians  1:21;  Mathew 25:23; Psalms 30:5; 2 Corinthians 4:17; John 9:4

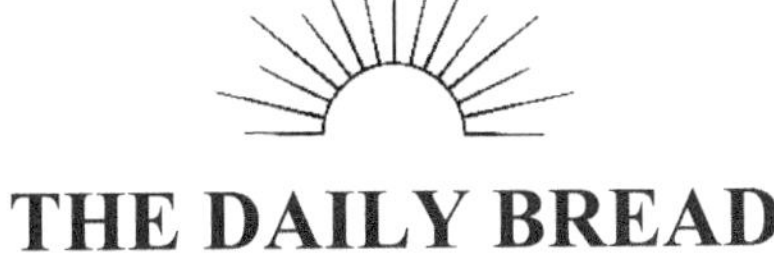

# THE DAILY BREAD

God is the one, who can raise you from the ashes. Job found himself living in the ashes and dust. "He raises the poor from the dust And lifts the beggar from the ash heap, To set them among princes And make them inherit the throne of glory. "For the pillars of the earth are the LORD's, And He has set the world upon them". (1 Samuel 2:8) Job was a righteous man. Being righteous does not exclude you from suffering but will guarantee you that God will be with you in the trouble. "Many are the afflictions of the righteous, But the LORD delivers him out of them all". (Psalms 34:19) His wife told Job curse God and die. Job was never hopeless, Job hoped on God. "For I know *that* my Redeemer lives, And He shall stand at last on the earth;"(Job 19:25) Being hopeless makes you vulnerable and developing negative thoughts and thereby creating a doubt that God will take out of your situation. Job knew God. He was never moved because of his circumstances. His faith was not hinged on materials things. He did not have confidence in the flesh. It shows how humble Job was in this ordeal when he said naked, I come from my mother's womb and naked should I go. He knew that God has power to make him prosper. Are you in a dire situation, are you in a storm, are you saying why me, you are saying does God hear me? Jesus said I am closer to you that a brother. God said if you call unto me, I will answer you and show you great and mighty things. It's just your faith being tested. Let your problem bring you closer God. Praise God in every season. Neither give a place to the devil. I pray this morning that your faith shall never fail. God said I will never leave you nor forsake you. God is faithful. Weeping may endure overnight but joy comes in the morning. You should not commit suicide; it will not always be like this. Your situation is not permanent but temporary. Have faith in God. The just live but faith. God bless you.

**Prayer**

We pray that we put our faith on you God not on physical things which are temporary. Let us count our blessings not our curses. Help us to understand the things we cannot change. Let us have a thankful heart. Thank you, God, even for the small things we cannot notice. You are a faithful God. As your word says, "Many are the afflictions of the righteous, But the LORD delivers him out of them all", we shall keep having my trust on you Lord. Thank you, God, for blessing us financial and good health. Amen


**The bible verses to study**

1 Samuel 2:8; Psalms 34:19; Job 19:25; Jeremiah 33:3; Job 1:21; Job 36:7; Job 42:10-12

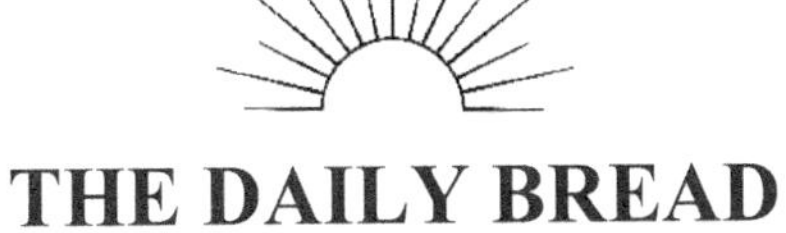

# THE DAILY BREAD

Bearing much fruit. Today I thought I should remind you that your minimum expectation is to bear much fruit. "But the manifestation of the Spirit is given to everyman for a profit withal ". (1 Corinthians 12:7). We are blessed to be a blessing. The word of God stated it that, "Neither do people light a lamp and put it under a bowl. Instead, they put it on its stand, and it gives light to everyone in the house"(Mathew 5:15). They are no invisible Christians ( James Bond 007). The parable of talents is a perfect example of what we must do while waiting for Jesus Christ to come back. It likened the kingdom of God as a man traveling to a far country and gave his goods to his servants. The one gave 5 talents, the other 2 and to other 1 according to their ability. He who received 5 talents went and traded and made 5 and also the one who received 2 made 2 but the one who received 1 went and dug in the ground and hid his Lord's money. When the Master came back the ones who traded and made more were rewarded and added more but the one who hid the talent was called lazy and the talent was taken away from him. The other reason why servant hid the talent was fear. Fear will paralyze you and make you fruitless. We are God's hands and legs here on earth. We are the body of Christ. We cannot stand and complain and say there is so much evil in the world. What I am asking is; what are you doing about it. It was not by accident you are saved. You were called from darkness into the marvellous light for a purpose. God has a purpose for you to bear much fruit. Shine your light at work, home, streets and in every area of influence. You may be the only bible the other people may read for the rest of their lives. Just as our fathers here on earth have expectations of our lives, God's expectation in us is very high. Jesus cursed a fig tree which had no fruit on it. Being fruitless is not the nature of God but the works of the enemy. When God looks at your life, he must say, "His master replied,

'Well done, good and faithful servant! You have been faithful with a few things; I will put you in charge of many things. Come and share your master's happiness!" (Mathew 25:23). God bless you.

**Prayer**

Thank you, Lord, for making us abide in you. As long as we abide in you, we shall bear much fruit. We are blessed at our workplaces, in our homes, in our businesses, in our families and in our health. We pray that we serve you God faithful. Help us to become fruitful in all aspects of our lives . We pray that, we shall fight a good fight of faith and lay hold the eternal life you have set before us . Let us be thirstier for you. Your grace is sufficient for us. We serve a faithful God. Your word says, "Arise, shine; For your light has come! And the glory of the LORD is risen upon you." Thank you, Lord. Amen

**The bible verses to study**

1 Corinthians 12:7; Mathew 5:15; Mathew 25:14-30 Genesis 1:28; John 15:1-8; Mark 11:12-14

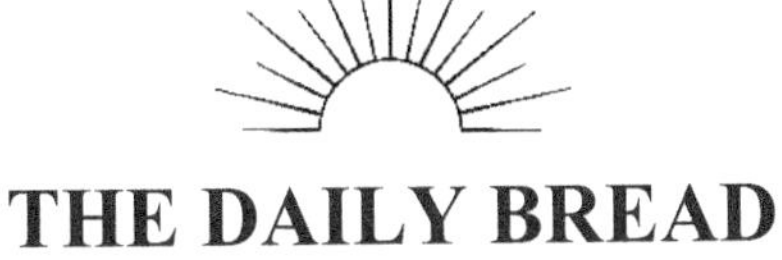

# THE DAILY BREAD

God will take care of you. The world can be a frightening place to live. Fear is all around us. Sometimes the fear is personal: Am I wealthy enough, attractive enough, successful enough, clever enough, and good enough? Do others admire me, approve of me, speak well of me? Will my project succeed? Will my marriage last? Will my finances hold out? Will my children flourish? Will my health continue? The world can be a frightening place to live. There are plenty of reasons to be afraid. Think for a moment: What is it that most frightens you? But here is good news: Faith can overcome fear. The psalmist knew the secret to overcoming fear. "When I am afraid," he writes, "I put my trust in [God]" (Psalms 56:3). Know this: faith can overcome fear. Whatever fears you face, whatever troubles loom, "God's going to take care of you." Say with the psalmist, "The Lord is my light and my salvation; whom then shall, I fear? The Lord is the strength of my life; of whom then shall I be afraid…Though an army should encamp against me, yet my heart shall not be afraid; and though war should rise up against me, yet will I put my trust in you." (Psalms 27:1-3). Do not let anything take away your joy "But my God shall supply all your need according to his riches in glory by Christ Jesus". Philippians 4:19". For God has not given us a spirit of fear, but of power and of love and of a sound mind. (2 Timothy 1:7). Fear is opposite to faith. When we fear it's like we are trusting on what the enemy is going to do than God. God bless you.

**Prayer**

We pray that we learn to put all our faith on you God. Let us have the same faith as David had when he said though I walk through the valley of shadow of death, I fear no evil for you are with me. And be able to understand that God you lay table before us in the presence of our enemies. If God is for us, who can be against us. No weapon formed and fashioned against us shall prosper. God you are faithful. God you are in control of our lives; we fear no evil. Thank you, Lord, for protecting us from the evil of the world. Your word says, "For God has not given us a spirit of fear, but of power and of love and of a sound mind." Amen


**The bible verses to study.**

Psalms 56:3; Psalms 27:1-3; Philippians 4:19; 2 Timothy 1:7; John 14:27; Acts 20:24; Zechariah 4:6; Galatians 5:22

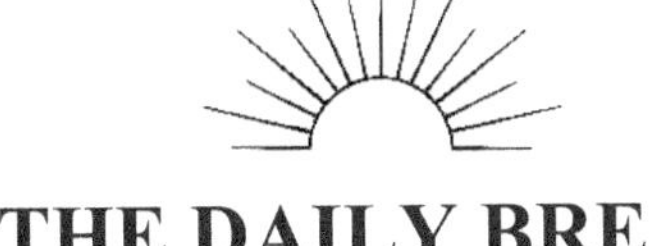

# THE DAILY BREAD

Identity. It's a crushing reality that some Christians live without an identity. They have forgotten who there are. They are lost people. They are there in church, but their hearts are far away from God. They have failed to know who they are. So, they are like dead fish which goes where the water flows. As a Christian you are blessed, and no one can curse you unless you curse yourself. It's like your father left millions in the bank for you and unless you know it, you will leave life of a beggar. Look at the children of Israel in their journey to the Promised Land, they forgot who they are. They complained to God, very ungratefully, lovers of themselves not God and they cried too much instead of praising God, be thankfully and have joy. They were too grumpy. They forgot who there are. They were bitter towards God. They wanted to change God; no God does not change, it's you who need to change. Who said it was going to be easy. God has an identity for you. 'But you are a chosen people, a royal priesthood, a holy nation, God's special possession, that you may declare the praises of him who called you out of darkness into his wonderful light." (1 Peter 2:9). The devil questioned Jesus as a Son of God, "The devil said to him, "If you are the Son of God, tell this stone to become bread." (Luke 4:3). The devil is questioning your identity every day, are you really a child of God, does God care for you, does God answer your prayers. The devil wants to create doubt in your mind. God loves you, that's not questionable. As a Christian, you will face disappointments, hurt, accusations and loss. But all this should not take away your faith from God. I know we are living in the last days, there is so much evil in the world but do not let this darken your hearts. "For we are his workmanship, created in Christ Jesus unto good works, which God hath before ordained that we should walk in them". (Ephesians 2:10). Do not let anything take away your love for God; it might be a man

/woman, car, work and money. If you have problems bring them to God, "Come to me, all you who are weary and burdened, and I will give you rest". (Mathew 11:28) God bless you.

**Prayer**

We know that we are the children of God. Jesus died for us so that we can be called the children of God. The Spirit of God in us me cries Abba Father. We are sitting together with Jesus Christ in heavenly places. Whatever is born of God overcomes the world. We are blessed through our Lord Jesus Christ. God is with us. Your word says, "For we are his workmanship, created in Christ Jesus unto good works, which God hath before ordained that we should walk in them". Your word says, "But you are a chosen people, a royal priesthood, a holy nation, God's special possession, that you may declare the praises of him who called you out of darkness into his wonderful light." Amen

**The bible verses to study**

1 Peter 2:9; Luke 4:3; Ephesians 2:10; John 12:1; 2 Corinthians 5:17; Jeremiah 1:5; Mathew 12:50

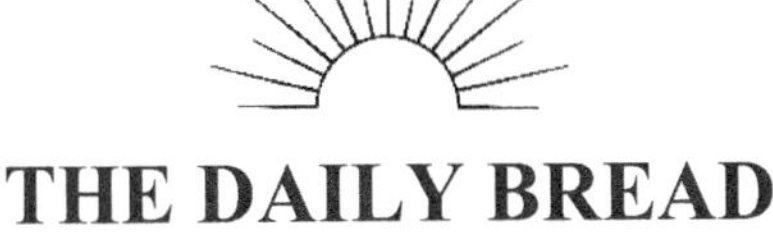

# THE DAILY BREAD

I pray that you let your will be done upon my life. "Thy kingdom come. Thy will be done in earth, as it is in heaven". (Mathew 6:10) Let your Spirit open my eyes. Let your word be thy lamp upon thy feet and thy light upon thy path. I pray that God, you empty me and fill me with yourself. I pray for my first love, that love I had when I got born again. I pray to you God to give me another touch once again. Shine your light upon my life. Deliver me from myself. Create a hunger in me for your righteousness. Jesus you are my rock, my Salvation, my refugee and my strong tower. Every day when I wake up let me be longing for your presence. Let me not hold back but overflow. You are the potter, and I am the clay. Mould me. Touch my mouth and fill me with your word. I cry for my life and my fellow brothers and sisters. Your love is amazing and nothing can separate me from your love. I want to let it go and rest in you. Today is a new day, full of hope, love and joy. My eyes have been opened and I can see clearly now. Direct my footsteps O God as your word says, "The steps of a good man are ordered by the LORD, And He delights in his way."(Psalms 37:23). Create in me a hunger for you as your word says, "As the deer pants for streams of water, so my soul pants for you, my God." (Psalms 42:1). Let me never stop mentioning your name to the world as your word says, "But if I say, "I will not mention his word or speak anymore in his name," his word is in my heart like a fire, a fire shut up in my bones. I am weary of holding it in; indeed, I cannot." (Jeremiah 20:9) . Hide me from the evil one like Job and put a hedge around me. Deliver me from the evil O Lord. All my enemies have been made a footstool to my feet. Our weapons are not canal but mighty to pull down the strongholds. You have exchanged my ashes for beauty. Weeping may endure over night, but joy comes in the moving. This in my morning time, this is my celebration time because God has showed up in my life. God bless you.


**Prayer**

Thank you, Lord for our Jobs, our families, the gift of life, our cars, we are free, we are healthy, and we are loved. We have found the grace in your eyes. You did not consider our sinful life. You love us as we are. You always give us a second chance. You have never left us nor forsake us. You keep on doing great things. We are blessed. As your word says, "The glory of this latter temple shall be greater than the former,' says the LORD of hosts. 'And in this place, I will give peace,' says the LORD of hosts", we have a great future. Your word teaches us that, "I consider that our present sufferings are not worth comparing with the glory that will be revealed in us." Amen


**The bible verses to study.**

Mathew 6:10; Psalms 37:23; Jeremiah 20:9; Psalms 115:109; Psalms 42:1; James 5:16; Ephesians 3:14-21

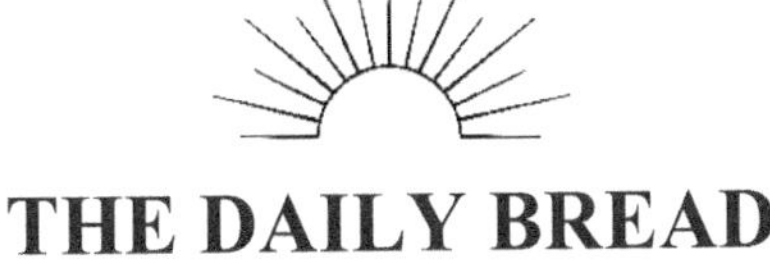

# THE DAILY BREAD

Magnet. A Magnet has its own characteristics. It attracts the metal objects in its magnetic fields. It does not attract everything. When a metal is on the magnet, it can have power to attract other metals that is magnetic powers. I am likening Christ as the magnet and souls as metals. For us to have powers to attract souls (metals) we need to be in Christ. Jesus said, "I am the true vine, and My Father is the vinedresser. Every branch in Me that does not bear fruit He takes away; and every branch that bears fruit He prunes, that it may bear more fruit. You are already clean because of the word which I have spoken to you. Abide in Me, and I in you. As the branch cannot bear fruit of itself, unless it abides in the vine, neither can you, unless you abide in Me. "I am the vine; you are the branches. He who abides in Me, and I in him, bears much fruit; for without Me you can do nothing. (John 15:1-5). We need to abide in Jesus Christ so that we can be fruitful. When we spend more time in the presence of God, we become ignited and light other people. Paul said, "For I am not ashamed of the gospel of Christ, for it is the power of God to salvation for everyone who believes…" (Romans 1:16). When we are connected (in Christ), we become the light of the world and the salt of the earth. Jesus uses us to win souls. We need to make Jesus the centre of our lives. Paul said, "I have been crucified with Christ; it is no longer I who live, but Christ lives in me; and the life which I now live in the flesh I live by faith in the Son of God, who loved me and gave Himself for me." (Galatians 2:20). The more we become closer to God we become more like him. The word of God says, "Therefore, if anyone is in Christ, he is a new creation; old things have passed away; behold, all things have become new." (2 Corinthians 5:17) . When we come to Christ, we get reborn spiritual. Our nature changes in the spirit. We sit together spiritual in the heavenly places in Jesus Christ. When you see us in the spirt you see the blood of Jesus Christ upon our lives. We need to share our story with the world and win souls. Its high time to tell the world what God did for us. The goodness of God brings the people to Jesus Christ. Share your testimony to the world and win souls. God bless you.

**Prayer**

As your word says, " Abide in Me, and I in you. As the branch cannot bear fruit of itself, unless it abides in the vine, neither can you, unless you abide in Me. "I am the vine; you are the branches. He who abides in Me, and I in him, bears much fruit; for without Me you can do nothing", we shall abide in you and bear much fruit. Like Paul, "For I am not ashamed of the gospel of Christ, for it is the power of God to salvation for everyone who believes". As your word says, "The fruit of the righteous is a tree of life, And one who is wise gains souls," we shall tell our stories to the world and win more souls for you. Amen.

**The bible verses to study**

John 15:1-5; Proverbs 11:30; Mark 16:15; Mathew 28:19; Mathew 18:11; 1 Corinthians 9:22

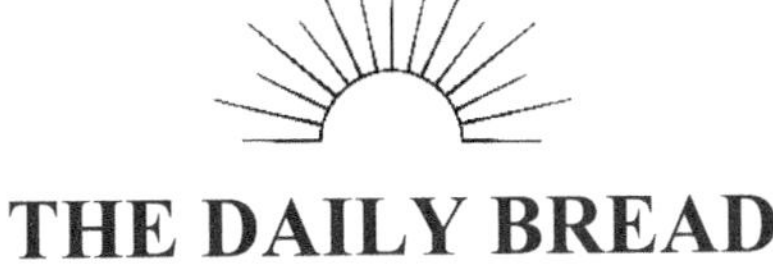

# THE DAILY BREAD

No excuse, what is the excuse do you have today. Our natural default is to give an excuse and give up on the life God has purposed us. Everyone can give an excuse because it's an easy way out. If you are now over 40 years and still blame your parents on how your life turned out to be, you have a problem. There is no excuse for you to live a defeated life. No more procrastinating, going into your shell like a tortoise, allowing people and circumstances to dictate your life . The devil wants you to think you have been defeated, you are not good enough, it was not meant to be and quit. Although Jospeh was sold to slavery, he did not choose to feel sorry for himself and give up. Joseph continued to be faithful even as a slave in the house Potiphar until everything was put under him. Who are you blaming for how your life turned out to be, is it the government. This morning I am encouraging you to waken up a giant in you. No more excuses. When Lazarus died, the people lost hope and buried him that's normal. Jesus told Martha that your brother will rise again that's supernatural. Jesus asked, "where did you laid him?". Where did your dreams die? God want to take you to a place where your dreams have died. God wants you to face your fears. Nothing is impossible with God. Please do not stop trying. You are a head not a tail. You are always above not beneath. "And if the Spirit of him who raised Jesus from the dead is living in you, he who raised Christ from the dead will also give life to your mortal bodies because of his Spirit who lives in you." (Romans 8:11). Look where you came from, whatever you have accomplished in past. Then you can see the hand of God in your life. To stop now it's a no thing. If you quit it's you to blame, Jesus came so that we can have life in abundance. Never give up, Jesus didn't die on the cross for you to quit but to empower you to be a victor. You can make it and God is with you. It's only the battle of the mind. If you can be a winner in your mind, you can overcome anything. Some of you are silent quitters. You are at work or at Church, but you have given up. You need to change the way of your thinking and then you will change the destiny of your life. Never fold your hands and be a victim of circumstances, you need to rise up and face the world head-on . God bless you.


**Prayer**

We pray that we live a life of faith. Your word says my enemies do not rejoice against me, when I fall, I shall arise, when I sit in the darkness, the Lord shall be light upon me. Perfect love cast away fear. We choose to have faith on what God is about to do in our lives than to have fear on what the devil is about to do in our lives. The way we are today is not the way we are going to be tomorrow. The grace of God is sufficient for us. If God is for us, who can be against us. Your word says all things are working together for good for us. We shall never give up on our dreams because we know that you will never give up on us. Your word says, "Against all hope, Abraham in hope believed and so became the father of many nations, just as it had been said to him, "So shall your offspring be". Amen.


**The bible verses to study**

Jeremiah 29:11; Genesis 39:5; Romas 4:20; Luke 1:37; Galatians 6:9; Judges 6:12; Joshua 1:5-9

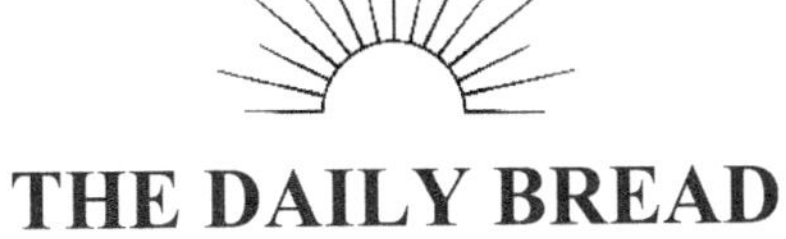

# THE DAILY BREAD

Time alone. We really need to spend time alone seeking the face of God. Jesus before He began His ministry here on earth, He spent 40 days and 40 nights fasting in the wilderness. Jesus would leave his disciples and masses to go and pray. That is away from the people praying. In this way your attention is undivided, and they will be no distractions. Moses would go alone and spend time with God. It's about you and your journey. It's not about saying my church is very good, my pastor is much anointed but what would you say about yourself, your relationship with Jesus Christ. You must have your own personal relationship with Jesus Christ. All those great men of God we read about in the bible, spent considerable time alone praying and seeking God. I know we are very busy but take your time and seek the Lord. Prayerless life leads to faithless life. It's a sacrifice you have to make because you value your relationship with God. Its personal, everyone have their own journey. Set up your time to seek God and go into your closet. When we go on our knees and pray, we activate so much power. We send the angels of God at work. The external things we see in other people's lives is a result of their private prayer times. When you do not walk by sight but by the spirit you will understand why it's important to pray. The word of God says, " Humble yourselves in the sight of the Lord, and He will lift you up." (James 4:10) . "Elijah was a man with a nature like ours, and he prayed earnestly that it would not rain; and it did not rain on the land for three years and six months".(James 5:17). "Confess your trespasses to one another, and pray for one another, that you may be healed. The effective, fervent prayer of a righteous man avails much". (James 5:16). God bless you.

**Prayer**

We pray that we put you Lord first in our lives. May we be thirsty for you Lord. Your word says trust in the Lord with all your heart and do not lean on your own understanding. Jesus you are our everything. Our hope is in you Lord. We are moving from glory to glory. We need your touch Lord once again. Nothing will ever come between us and our prayer time. We shall exalt your name Lord Jesus in the morning, in the afternoon and in the evening. Your word says, "Humble yourselves in the sight of the Lord, and He will lift you up." Teach us how to pray. Thank you, O Lord, for answering our prayers. Amen

**The bible verses to study**

James 4:10; James 5:16-17; Mathew 4:1; Romans 12:12; 1 Thessalonians 5:16-18; Philippians 4:6; Mark 11:24

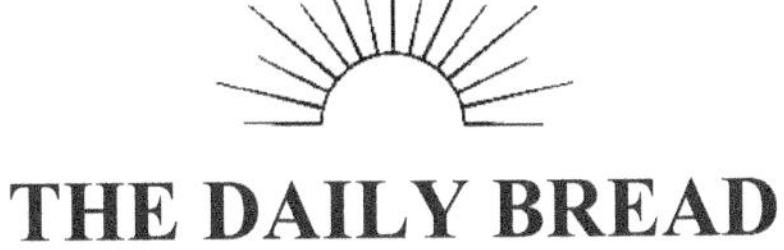

# THE DAILY BREAD

If you say your life is unbearable read this story. "And a certain woman, which had an issue of blood twelve years, And had suffered many things of many physicians, and had spent all that she had, and was nothing bettered, but rather grew worse, When she had heard of Jesus, came in the press behind, and touched his garment. For she said, If I may touch but his clothes, I shall be whole. And straightway the fountain of her blood was dried up; and she felt in her body that she was healed of that plague. (Mark 5:25-29)The story of the woman with the issue of blood reflects a picture of someone who did not have a control of her life and fallen dreams .Even if she will put make up, do her hair, do her nails and wear dolce and gabbana, it was of no help because the blood was still flowing. She was considered unclean. People would ridicule her. Because of this issue, the word of God says she spent all she had but her condition grew worse, it reflects that doctors and various healers became her friends. It was due to her going to their offices every time. The dream of marriage was non-existent. She was a nobody and an outcast. Regardless of her circumstances, she sought for Jesus and touched his garment. She desperately needed healing. Jesus changed her story. If there was no Jesus in her story it was going to be sad story. If Jesus changed her condition, He would change your story. How desperately do you need your healing, change of your finances and to fix your marriage? Jesus is the answer. The word of God through prophet Hosea says, "My people are destroyed for lack of knowledge". Lot of people are suffering and in bondages because they willingly reject God and serve the god of this world. Sickness which flourish in our lives is because of us not having Jesus Christ as our saviour. David knew it when he said, He restores my soul. I pray for divine healing upon your lives, God took the children of Israel from Egypt to the promised land, they were neither sick nor feeble because of the presence of

God was with them. Jesus says, " Peace I leave with you, My peace I give to you; not as the world gives do I give to you. Let not your heart be troubled, neither let it be afraid." God bless you.

**Prayer**

We thank you Lord Jesus for saving our souls. We were lost and now we are found. Whilst we were sinners Jesus Christ you died for us. There is no more darkness in our lives. Your word says they overcame them by the blood of the lamb and word of their testimony. We testify that we are healthy, we have a best marriages, we are the greatest at our workplaces, we are rich, and we are growing Spiritual. Your word says, "But He was wounded for our transgressions, He was bruised for our iniquities; The chastisement for our peace was upon Him, And by His stripes we are healed." As your word says, " He restores our souls', thank you Lord for restoring our souls. Amen

**The bible verses to study**

Mark 5:25-29: Psalms 23:3; Luke 8:50; Psalms 147:3; Isaiah 41:10; Psalms 107.20; 2 Kings 5:14

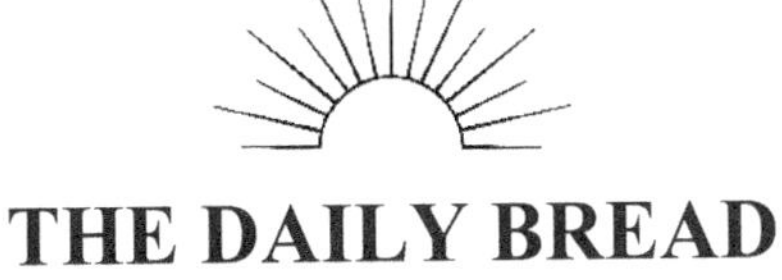

# THE DAILY BREAD

Faith. "So, then faith comes by hearing, and hearing by the word of God". (Romans 10:17) The word faith, it represents the will of God followed. For you to follow the will of God you need to know it. Yes, you need to hear the word of God. They are two principles which are very powerful that is first of all shun away evil and second to meditate of the word of God day and night. The word of God and faith go hand in hand. You need to be immersed in the word of God to be filled with faith. You are a product of what you eat. We consume more worldly programs than the word of God based programs. How do you live your life? Do you create opportunity for yourself to hear the word or you live a wordless life therefore a faithless life? This morning I encourage you to throw away the fruitless magazines, stop watching programmes for leisure always and watch fruitful programs. We need more word to build our faith therefore we need to create an atmosphere to hear the word of God. David said let the word of God be thy lamp upon thy feet and thy light upon thy path. We need the word. I have realized if I continue to listen to a song, I end singing it subconsciously, it get attached to my soul. I found myself singing a song because I have been hearing it and hearing it. Just imagine if you continue playing the word of God and listening to gospel music, at home while driving and at work. You become part of that word and you become inseparable. It will build your faith. Man cannot live by bread alone but by every word that proceeds from the mouth of God. God bless you.

**Prayer**

We pray that, Lord we become separated for you. May we live for you like Paul as he said, " I have been crucified with Christ; it is no longer I who live, but Christ lives in me; and the life which I now live in the flesh I live by faith in the Son of God, who loved me and gave Himself for me." We are forsaking the world for you. We are ready to give ourselves to you. Spirit Lead us to where our trust is without borders. My soul yes to the Lord. You are our everything O Lord. You word says, "If you have faith as a mustard seed, you can say to this mulberry tree, 'Be pulled up by the roots and be planted in the sea,' and it would obey you." Your word says, "But without faith it is impossible to please Him, for he who comes to God must believe that He is, and that He is a rewarder of those who diligently seek Him." Amen


**The bible verses to study**

Hebrews 11:6; Luke 17:6; Mathew 21:22; 2 Corinthians 5:7; Romans 10:17; Hebrew 11:1; James 1:6

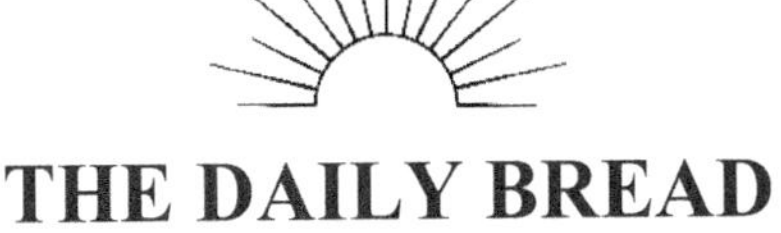

# THE DAILY BREAD

Have you failed some people and yourself? It is an issue of obedience. When we look into the word of God, we have seen the severe consequences of disobedience. First let's start with Jonah. He was used by God mightily and a prophet who decided to be selfish and gave up. God sent him to Nineveh, but he took a boat to Tarshish. They were many souls to be won but fear gripped the man of God. Nineveh was really dangerous, they killed people, skin them and hang them for the public to see. I assume Jonah asked himself why me and I have done so much for God and now I need to rest. As we learn from the story, they were dire consequences. Whilst in the boat, a great storm arose endangering himself and the other people in the boat. They almost perished. Jonah was sleeping. Do we have sleeping, Christians who have gone AWOL? Disobedience to God's plans can endanger other people and your life. Jonah failed himself, people in the boat and the Nineveh people. Jonah repented in the belly of the fish. He prayed but God did not change the plans he had for him. Credit to him, he went to Nineveh and the people repented. Are you a Jonah today running away from God and failing the people? The second person is Samson. He was one of the judges who God has raised. He lacked character, lived against the will of God and lived a reckless life and had weakness for women. Samson failed the children of Israel; he was really anointed but his association with the darkness was his downfall. Delilah was the last straw that broke the camel's back. Samson also failed himself and he was life was cut short. I encourage you this morning stay in the course, do not waiver either left or right because lot of souls need to be won. There is still time. Don't look down on yourself, if God used people who once failed like Moses, Elijah, and Jonah, he will use you. The word of God says, " For a righteous man may fall seven times

And rise again, But the wicked shall fall by calamity".( Proverbs 24:16) God bless you.

**Prayer**

We pray that we do not lose our focus on you Lord. Let us start with you and end with you in everything we do as your word says, "Unless the LORD builds the house, They labour in vain who build it; Unless the LORD guards the city, The watchman stays awake in vain" . Use us to change the world. Let us not grow weary is doing good because in due season we will reap if we do not faint. When we fall, we shall not stay down. The grace of God is sufficient for us. Do not rejoice over me, my enemy; When I fall, I will arise; When I sit in darkness, The LORD will be a light to me. Your word says, " For a righteous man may fall seven times And rise again, But the wicked shall fall by calamity". Amen

**The bible verses to study.**

Proverbs 24:16; Micah 7:8; Jonah 1:2:3:4; Psalms 20:8; Psalms 37:24; Deuteronomy 31:6

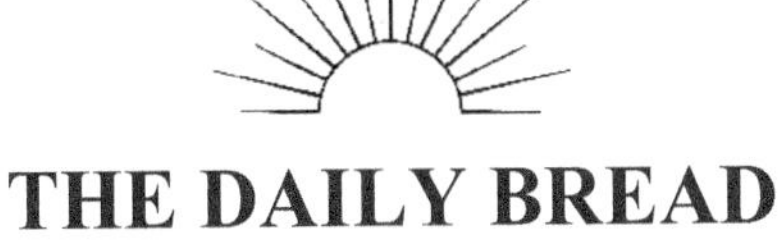

# THE DAILY BREAD

Has your love gone cold? "Because of the increase of wickedness, the love of most will grow cold," (Mathew 24:12). This is one of the signs of the end days Jesus spoke about to his disciples. We are now living in the last days. If your love was measurable with a thermometer, was it not going to be found cold? Now I have to ask myself what is making the love cold which is wickedness. The days we are living are full of evil. Love itself have been perverted. I ask myself why HIV is rampant in Africa, why there is so much teenage pregnancies, why there is so much poverty in Africa, why there is so many divorces, why there are so many single mothers, robberies, suicides and stress related conditions. The decay of the moral society. Let's get back to the basics and live life according to the word of God. Jesus said in (John 15:12) this is my commandment, that you love one another, as I have loved you. God is love so the Devil is hate. As you are moving closer to God, you become more loving but when drifting away; your love will be quenched. Most of the people have turned away from God. Their hearts have been darkened. If we say we love our neighbour as we love ourselves, we won't rape them, steal from them, lie to them and not have compassion over them. "So, ought men to love their wives as their own bodies. He that love his wife loves himself" (Ephesians 5:28) . Do you have love? The story of the good Samaritan shows how some people get involved only with their lives and fail to help others. Another sign of the last days, "People will be lovers of themselves, lovers of money, boastful, proud, abusive, disobedient to their parents, ungrateful, unholy," (2Timothy 3:2). Lack of care of other people, desire for money and bad behaviour shows how the love of people has gone cold. You put monetary value of everything in life and fail to have compassion. The early church shows us true love. Let's return to basics and live life according to the word of God. The word of God should be like a map in our lives. We should use the directions on the map, and we will never get lost. Just like a navigation app, when we about to take a wrong direction, the word of God will tell us make a U-turn. David said let your word be thy lamp upon they feet and thy light in thy upon path. God is love and if we read His word our love will never grow cold. God bless you.


**Prayer**

We thank you Lord for teaching us on how to love. We pray against the spirit of hate. Let us dwell with other brethren in peace. Let us not hold the grudges against anyone. We shall not condemn anyone. We will forgive others as God forgives us. We will do unto others the way we want them to do unto us. We will not return evil for evil. May we love the unlovable. "We pray that out of his glorious riches he may strengthen us with power through his Spirit in your inner being, so that Christ may dwell in our hearts through faith. And we pray that we, being rooted and established in love, may have power, together with all the Lord's holy people, to grasp how wide and long and high and deep is the love of Christ,". We shall love our neighbours as we love ourselves. Amen.


**The bible verses.**

Mathew 24:12; John 15:12; Ephesians 5:28; Mathew 24:11; Revelation 2:4

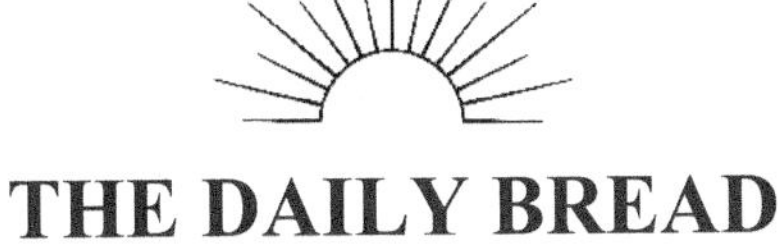

# THE DAILY BREAD

Relationship." I am the true vine, and my Father is the husbandman". (John 15:1) Jesus is the true vine and we are not true vines. God is self-existent but us we rely on God. And we are branches and need to abide in the true vine and thereby bearing much fruit. "Abide in me, and I in you. As the branches we cannot bear fruit of ourselves, except we abide in the vine; no more can ye, except ye abide in me". (John 15:4) Look here the word says abide in me and I will abide you. It's a 2 way, we need to do our own part and God will do His own part. The 2 way can be easy illustrated by a person making a phone call. It's a 2 way, for you to communicate with me, you need to pick a phone and dial a number. It must not be any number amen. It must be my number. You need to speak on the phone, and I need to answer, and the 2-way communication will be complete. So, in the abiding in Christ is to have a relationship with Christ. Can you say I have a relationship with Christ? Having a relationship will make your needs met. My friend is free to come to me in need and I lend him some money because we have a relationship. Our relationship with God is deeper He is our father." ..... That's whatsoever you shall ask of the Father in my name, he may give it you." (John15:16). If you have a relationship with God, ask Him because He said, "ask it shall be given to you and knock it shall be opened to you and seek you shall find". If our earthly wicked fathers know how to give good gifts to us what more will be our father in heaven. God wants us to bear much fruits, therefore if you abide in Jesus Christ your marriage will be fruitful, your finances will be fruitful, your relationship will be fruitful, your businesses will be fruitful and at workplace you will be fruitful. Your word says, "A man who has friends must himself be friendly, But there is a friend who sticks closer than a brother." (Proverbs 18:24) God bless you.

**Prayer**

We thank you Lord Jesus because you are the true vine, we shall abide in you and you in us then we shall bear much fruit. You are our Father. We thank you Lord Jesus for loving us, we boldly come to your thrown, to give you our praises. We are connected to you Lord. We need your presence in our lives. Without you, we are nothing. We need your touch once again. "As the deer pants for streams of water, so my soul pants for you, my God." Your word says, "The steps of a good man are ordered by the LORD, And He delights in his way." You are the Lord our Shepherd; we shall not want." Amen


**The bible verses to study.**

John 15:1-5: Proverbs 18:24; John15:16; John 3:16; John 14:6; John 1:10-13; Proverbs 3:5-6

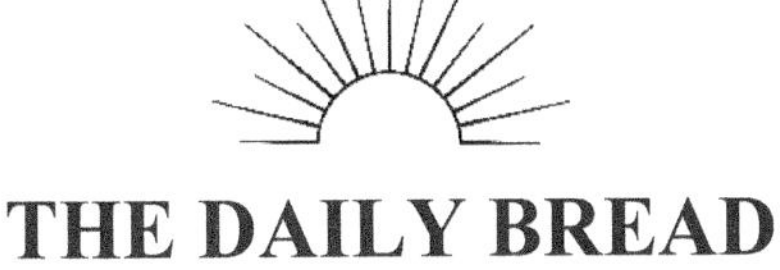

# THE DAILY BREAD

Focus on God not the negatives. Most of the times we dwell so much on the negatives. Those things can easily depress us. I encourage you this morning not dwell not on your negatives. Being negative does not only depress you but it can bring also conditions like high blood pressure and ulcers. I was listening to the preaching about a King Asa whose heart was really after God. He was attacked by troops from Ethiopia under the leadership of General Zerah. Asa cried out to the Lord for help, and the Lord defeated the Ethiopians, and Asa and the army of Judah triumphed as the Ethiopians fled. The Ethiopians were many as compared to the army of Judah. Asa cried to God because his focus was on God. "Give your burdens to the LORD, and he will take care of you. He will not permit the godly to slip and fall." (Psalms 55:22) "Casting all your care upon him; for he cares for you". (1 Peter 5:7). When you are prayerful and waiting upon the Lord, you will mount up your wings like eagles. You will fly above every problem. The challenges may come on your way but there will neither get any of your airtime nor bring them to your heart, but you bring them to God. Elijah was suicidal when Jezebel threated him with death, he ran away and sit under a tree waiting to die. Elijah had Just killed 450 prophets of Baal but chose to believe on what Jezebel had said than having faith on God. The fear of Jezebel's words made him to give up. If we focus on the negative things, we end up in depression. Fear is believing on what the devil is going to do than having faith in God. No matter how dark is it outside the sunshine shall come through tomorrow. Weeping may endure overnight but joy comes in the morning. God is good all the times, we must praise him on top of the mountains and in the valley. David said through I walk through the valley of the shadow of death, I fear no evil for you are with me. Negative reports are part of life . The word of God says, "Many are the afflictions of the righteous,

But the LORD delivers him out of them all."( Psalms 34:19). God bless you.

**Prayer**

We pray that we must focus on you God than to focus on our problems . Your word says weeping may endure overnight but joy comes in the morning. We pray that no matter how its rains in our lives, we should have faith the sunshine will come out tomorrow. We shall never live a life in disappointments, but being grateful always for what the Lord has done in our lives. We are not a failure, the way we are today is not the way we are going to be tomorrow. The power of God is working in us. Your word says, "Many are the afflictions of the righteous, But the LORD delivers him out of them all." Like David, though we walk through the valley of shadow of death, we fear no evil for you are with us. Amen

**The bible verses to study**

Psalms 55:22; 1 Peter 5:7; Psalms 34:19; 1 Kings 19:1-4; Psalms 23:4; 1 Peter 5:7; Mathew 11:28

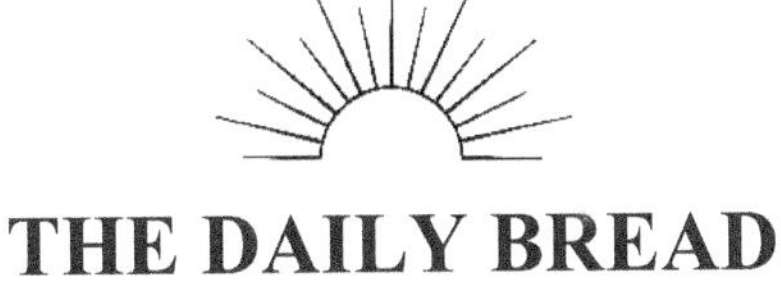

# THE DAILY BREAD

God did not create you to be a cheap copycat. You are very special and the only one in town. Your fingerprints are unique, and no one have them in town. So do not copy another person's life. There was one Moses in the bible and one Joseph. Your life is different and cannot be compared to anyone else. Allow the Holy Spirit to teach you so that you can discover who you are. Take your time to learn yourself and see the advantages you have over others. Pursue the passion God gave you. Follow that which speaks louder to your life. It might not have been seen yet but if you can see it which means God gave you that's your vision. Because everyone is operation a tuck-shop you also want to have one no you are not everyone. This I say to you, do not burry your head in the sand like a tortoise but go out there and act upon your faith. Isaac sowed in the famine and reaped a hundredfold. God deposited in your life something special if you cannot see it no-one will see it. Invest in your future God will give the increase no matter how small it is. Take a step of faith and leave the rest to God. In the parable of talents, the word of God says, "And to one he gave five talents, to another two, and to another one, to each according to his own ability; and immediately he went on a journey. (Mathew 25:15). No one is without a talent, so do not envy other people's talents but work on yours God will add more. God is saying today, "For I know the plans I have for you," declares the LORD, "plans to prosper you and not to harm you, plans to give you hope and a future." (Jeremiah 29:11) God bless you.

**Prayer**

We thank you God for showing confidence in us. When you went on the cross you never doubted us. Whilst we were sinners Jesus Christ died for us. We are fearful and wonderful made in your image. The life we are living now is in confidence that who has begun a good work in us shall continue until Jesus Christ comes. Your word says, "For I know the plans I have for you," declares the LORD, "plans to prosper you and not to harm you, plans to give you hope and a future." Amen.


**The bible verses to study.**

Mathew 25:14-30; Jeremiah 29:11; Psalms 139:14; 1 peter 2:9; Habakkuk 2:2; Isaiah 60:1

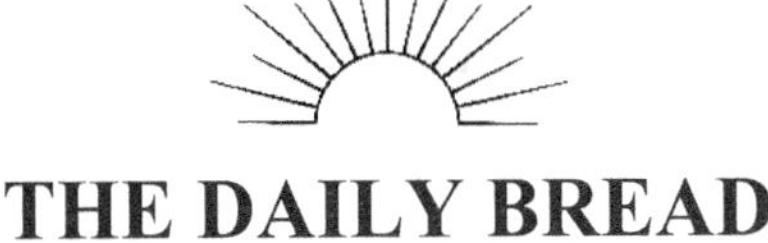

# THE DAILY BREAD

This morning what is your will? What do you want? Jesus asked the 2 blinds what you want me to do for you. People they can pray for you but if your will is not to be healed it's a waste of time. It is also aligned when people get saved, you confess Jesus Christ as their Lord and saviour with you own mouth. What is your will this morning, to choose to live a prosperous and God-fearing life or choose to live according to your strength? Let go of you. We can have all night praying, fasting and but if your will is not aligned with the word of God your situation will not change. You need believe that God will change your situation and you want God to change your situation in his own way. Some people they have already made their decision of how they are going to prosper so they want God to get along their plans. If Jesus asked you today what you want me to do for you what will you say. Are you ready for change? Some people have become accustomed to their situations and conditions and believe now this is the perfect will of God upon their life. Largely is because they are eagles, but they hang around chickens and end up living a chicken life. I encourage you this morning to know the perfect will of God upon your life and live it. "'if you can'?" said Jesus. "Everything is possible for one who believes."(Mark 9:23) There was a crippled man who was carried daily to the beautiful gate but there is nothing beautiful about his life. You can be in a country full of honey and milk but go to bed hungry because of your wrong focus. The word of God says, " But seek first the kingdom of God and His righteousness, and all these things shall be added to you.'' (Mathew 6:33) . The man at the beautiful gate had a career in begging. He was subject to money. But he never got enough of the money. When Peter and John passed through the beautiful gate on their hour for prayer, he looked at them expecting money. They told him silver and gold we don't have but in the name of Jesus rise up and walk. After receiving the healing, he went into the synagogue praising God and it was his last day of him begging. Jesus has the living water, and if you drink this water, you will never be thirsty again. The word of God says, "Set your mind on things above, not on things on the earth."(Colossians 3:2). God bless you.

**Prayer**

Thank you, Lord, for the perfect will you gave us. You gave us the choice to choose between death and life. I choose Jesus today; I choose life today so that me and my family can live. We pray that we do not conform to the culture of the world, but we renew our minds to prove what is good, perfect will of God upon our lives. Let our will be aligned to your plans. Your word says, "But seek first the kingdom of God and His righteousness, and all these things shall be added to you." Your word says, "If you are willing and obedient,You shall eat the good of the land;" Amen.

**The bible verses to study.**

Mark 9:23; Mathew 6:33; Colossians 3:2; Deuteronomy 30:15; Isaiah 55:7; Romans 12:2; Psalms 34:8

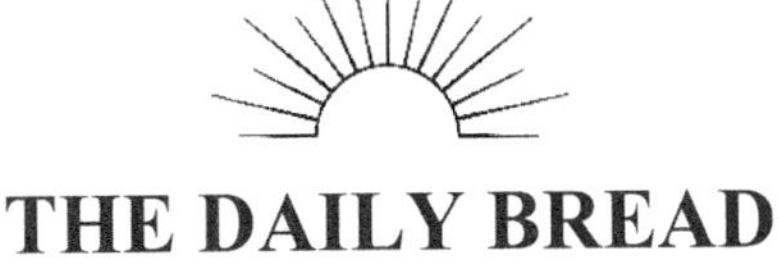

# THE DAILY BREAD

When we reflect to the life we are living, does it point to the fact that God paid the highest price for me and you. There is no doubt God loves me and you. Jesus died for us, and the curse was broken. God loved us first. God wants the best for us. Parents often open savings account for their children because they want a brighter future for them and deposit money there. When the children of Israel left Egypt for the promised land, they did not leave empty handed. "And I will give this people favour in the sight of the Egyptians; and it shall be, when you go, that you shall not go empty-handed. But every woman shall ask of her neighbour, namely, of her who dwells near her house, articles of silver, articles of gold, and clothing; and you shall put them on your sons and on your daughters. So, you shall plunder the Egyptians." (Exodus 3:21-22) God deposited in our lives before even we were born. Do you know Abraham blessing are ours? God did not send his son to die for you to just live by and have a bleak future. "The thief does not come except to steal, and to kill, and to destroy. I have come that they may have life, and that they may have it more abundantly."( John 10: 10) We are created in the image of God. Success is written all over us. Tell yourself I am success; I am the glory of God; greater is He that is me than he that is in the world. "For the earnest expectation of the creation eagerly waits for the revealing of the sons of God". (Romans 8:19) If you can audit your life, you can see how God has blessed you and begin to look at your future with so much excitement. You made it against all the odds, the favour of God is upon your life nothing can hold you back because Christ in you, is the hope of glory. What I can say, all is well despite of all the negatives news in the world, God is still on the throne. God made a distinction between Goshen and the place where Egyptians were staying. The best is yet to come in your life. "However, as it is written: "What no eye has seen, what no ear has heard, and what no human mind has conceived" -- the things God has prepared for those who love him--" (1 Corinthian 2:9). 'The glory of this latter temple shall be greater than the former,' says the LORD of hosts. 'And in this place, I will give peace,' says the LORD of hosts." Haggai 2:9. "For I consider that the sufferings of this present time are not worthy to be compared with the glory which shall be revealed in us". (Romans 8:18) God bless you.


**Prayer**

We thank you God for the blessed lives you have given us. Our homes are blessed, our finances are blessed, our health is blessed, our business are blessed, and our workplaces are blessed. We cannot live without your presence . The Lord is our Shephard we shall not want; he makes us to lie down on greener pastures. Your word says, "Then you will lay your gold in the dust, And the gold of Ophir among the stones of the brooks." For the earnest expectation of the creation eagerly waits for the revealing of the sons of God" . "For I consider that the sufferings of this present time are not worthy to be compared with the glory which shall be revealed in us". 'The glory of this latter temple shall be greater than the former. Amen


**The bible verses to study**

Exodus 3:21-22; John 10: 10; Romans 8:19; 1 Corinthian 2:9; Haggai 2:9; Job 22:24

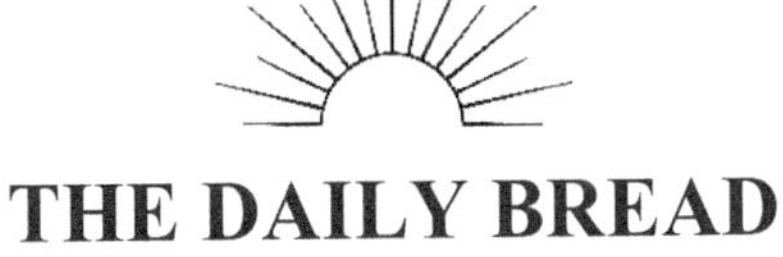

# THE DAILY BREAD

Be sensitive. It is the truth that God loves us, He cares for us, the Holy Spirit dwells in us and we have a relationship with him. In the garden of Eden Adam and Eve God had a very close relationship with God. Today our relationship with God is also very close because of the in dwelling of the Holy Spirit. Take a moment during the day; see how everything is coming together. Appreciate those small things. You have driven to work safely, you have a cup of coffee, you are laughing and everything is cruising throughout the day. When you have that joy in your spirit, take a moment to praise God. Appreciate the presence of God in your life. Do not just go through your day blindly. Be sensitive to the Holy Spirit. There is favour upon your life and the power of God is working in your life. You are special to God therefore you receive many blessings during the day. Now you know when everything is coming together it is what God promised in His word." Peace I leave with you, my peace I give unto you: not as the world gives, give I unto you. Let not your heart be troubled, neither let it be afraid." (John 14:27). The word of God teaches us that, "And do not grieve the Holy Spirit of God, by whom you were sealed for the day of redemption."(Ephesians 4:30) As a Holy Spirit filled person, you can't curse throughout the day, drink alcohol to excess and share your temple with harlots. When we do not spend time in the presence of God and always giving attention to worldly things, we grieve the Holy Spirit. They are things that kill the fire is us like going clubbing, having bad friends, listening to the worldly music always and watch demonic programs on Tv. Do like what a pregnant woman does, she understand that what she is carrying is very special. She can't drink alcohol, smoke and eat other foods. It's a conscious decision we make that we want things in our lives that edify my spirit man. The word of God says, "See then that you walk circumspectly, not as fools but as wise, redeeming the time, because the days are evil. Therefore, do not be unwise, but understand what the will of the Lord *is*. And do not be drunk with wine, in which is dissipation; but be filled with the Spirit, speaking to one another in psalms and hymns and spiritual songs, singing and making melody in your heart to the Lord," (Ephesians 5:15-19). God bless you.

## Prayer

Thank you, Lord, for this beautiful day. All is well is our souls, it does not matter what the doctors say, our bank account says, our bosses say, it is well in our souls. We are who God says we are, our jobs do not define us, our past does not define us, our failures do not define us. God loves us. The grace of God is sufficient for us. Your word says," Peace I leave with you, my peace I give unto you: not as the world gives, give I unto you. Let not your heart be troubled, neither let it be afraid." I pray that I do not grieve the Holy Spirit by living a worldly life. We shall be filled with the spirit by "speaking to one another in psalms and hymns and spiritual songs, singing and making melody in your heart to the Lord," Amen

## The bible verses to study.

John 14:27; Ephesians 5:15-19; Romans 8:11; Ephesians 4:30; Isaiah 63:10; Ephesians 1:13

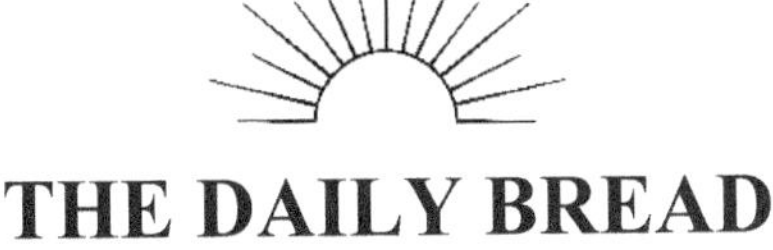

# THE DAILY BREAD

God has given us enough tools to solve our problems. Most of cars have four wheels. During a journey one or two wheels may puncture. A car may have a flat tyre. When you have a flat tyre, you need to stop the car temporarily and change it and move on. When you are driving nicely, you will never perceive that you will have a flat tyre. None of us wants to have a flat tyre. In this country you will have a flat tyre. In a moment the car will stop temporarily. God did not promise us a trouble-free life. As long as we continue to be in the will of God, we will change the flat tyres and continue with our journeys. The word of God says, "Do not rejoice over me, my enemy; When I fall, I will arise; When I sit in darkness, The LORD will be a light to me." We shall fall but we will rise, we shall sit in the darkness, but the Lord will be our light. They are several times in our lives where we will be on mountain tops and other times where we will be in the valley. The problems we experience right now cannot change until we change the way of thinking. We need to go out there, work harder and reach out. The field is ripe but where are the harvesters. The body of Christ needs to take charge, reach out, touch the people and win more souls. The church is empowered, given the tools to change the flat tyres. Us as the body of Christ what are we doing to change the way the people think in this country. God empowered us, through the outpouring of the Holy Spirit; we were given the power and authority. Who is speaking to the people, does the church have the voice? Change is coming, when the enemy comes in like a flood, The Spirit of the LORD will lift up a standard against him . Out of your belly shall flow rivers of living water. We must not look at this country as a lost course. One flat tyre will not stop us completing our journey. God has given us enough tools as the body of Christ, we will change the flat tyres and we will drive again. Do not despair, evil have always been there, but we are stronger than it. Let change start with you. "Behold I have given you the authority trample on serpents and scorpions, and over all the power of the enemy, and nothing by any means hurt you" (Luke 10:19). God bless you.


## Prayer

We are highly blessed, highly favoured and deeply loved. We thank you Lord for the life you given us. No matter whatever it throws in our way, we will not give up. Our faith shall never fail. If God split the red sea for the children of Israel, fed them with manna in the wilderness, he will provide for us and lead us. Your word says, "Lift up your eyes to the heavens, and look at the earth below; for the heavens will vanish like smoke, the earth will wear out like a garment, and its people will die like gnats. But My salvation will last forever, and My righteousness will never fail." Your word says, " Nothing is impossible with God". "But in all these things, we more than conquer through the One having loved us". We shall never give up because your word says, "Behold I have given you the authority trample on serpents and scorpions, and over all the power of the enemy, and nothing by any means hurt you" Amen.


## The bible verses to study

Isaiah 51:6; Romans 8:37; Philippians 4:13; Luke 10:19: Romans 8:31; Psalms 91:7; Daniel 3:8-30

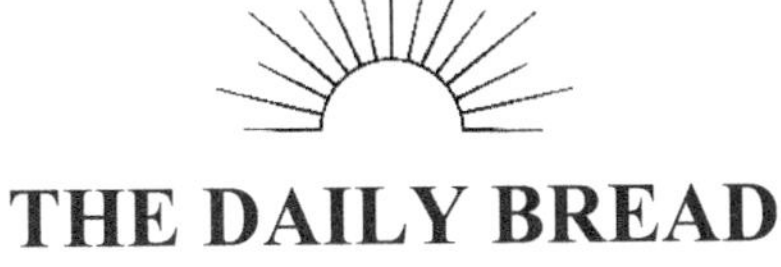

# THE DAILY BREAD

God has never doubted you. We should stop doubting ourselves. When we take a closer look into the word of God, we found out that Moses doubted himself. God told him to go and tell Pharaoh to let my people go, Moses questioned his speech. "Then Moses said to the LORD, "O my Lord, I am not eloquent, neither before nor since You have spoken to Your servant; but I am slow of speech and slow of tongue." So, the LORD said to him, "Who has made man's mouth? Or who makes the mute, the deaf, the seeing, or the blind? Have not I, the LORD?(Exodus 6:10-11) Moses doubted his abilities before he even tried. This morning do you doubt yourself that you will get employment, you will receive your healing, you will get married, your family can be saved, and God has called you in the ministry? Doubt is stopping people to live a life in abundance and what God has purposed in their lives. Doubt is those negative thoughts, that dis empowers you and you will end up believing in those negative thoughts and become your lifestyle. God loves you and He will always make a way for you. Like what he said to Joshua, God is saying go and take the land and wherever your feet steps on, it shall be yours. If you are doubting this morning, I say wake up before it's too late. Do not be hesitant, be courageous and act upon your faith. "And without faith it is impossible to please Him, for the one who comes to God must believe that He exists, and that He proves to be One who rewards those who seek Him." (Hebrews 11:6) The word of God says the just shall leave by faith. See those giants which are against you in your life as grasshoppers. "What, then, shall we say in response to these things? "If God is for us, who can be against us?"(Romans 8:31) Gideon was hiding in a cave because he doubted himself. "And the Angel of the LORD appeared to him, and said to him, "The LORD is with you, you mighty man of valour!" (Judges 6:12) . Looking at our capabilities and not focusing on God makes us to doubt ourselves. We should never remove our eyes from God. The word of God says, "Trust in the LORD with all your heart, And lean not on your own understanding;" ( Proverbs 3:5) . God bless you.

## Prayer

We pray that O Lord no matter what happen in our lives, we should never doubt ourselves as your word says, "Trust in the LORD with all your heart, And lean not on your own understanding;" It's not by strength, nor by mighty but by my Spirit says the Lord the Host. Your word says, "My grace is sufficient for you, for My strength is made perfect in weakness." Therefore, most gladly I will rather boast in my infirmities, that the power of Christ may rest upon me" . You are our refugee and our strong tower. We pray that we never entertain negative thoughts but cast them away. We pray that we will not look at our situations, but we will put my focus on you. We shall put our trust in you God to change our situation. Your word says, "For God has not given us a spirit of fear, but of power and of love and of a sound mind." Amen

## The bible verses to study

Exodus 6:10-11; Hebrews 11:6; Romans 8:31; Judges 6:12; Proverbs 3:5; John 14:27; Romans 8:15; Zechariah 4:6

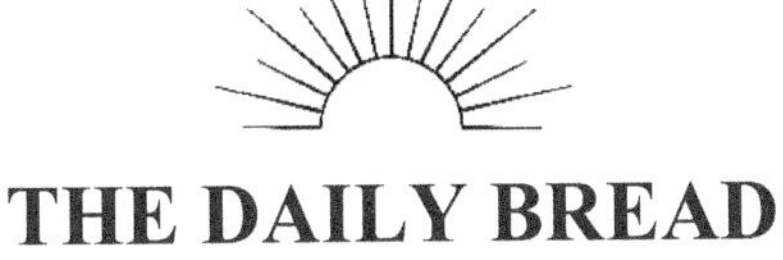

# THE DAILY BREAD

Decision making. Every day we make decisions one way or the other or even some people they make decisions for you. You may ask yourself how come I am in this position? It might be a successful position or less successful position. It's us who make decision to get married, to divorce, start a business, to choose our way of living and to be involved in crime. I am not sure what kind of decisions you are making today because they have a bearing on your future. It's important for us to pray every day in the morning asking for God to guide us and help us making decisions. "There is a way that appears to be right, but in the end, it leads to death." (Proverbs 14:12) They are a lot of people who influence us in making decisions but today when you look back do you not regret. "Trust in the LORD with all thine heart; and lean not unto thine own understanding." (Proverbs 3:5). For you to make a proper decision, you need to know all the facts. The answer to us is we do not know all the facts, but God does. Titanic, British luxury passenger liner that sank on April 15, 1912, en route to New York from Southampton, England, on its maiden voyage. The largest and most luxurious ship afloat, the *Titanic* had a double-bottomed hull divided into 16 watertight compartments. Because four of these could be flooded without endangering its buoyancy, it was considered unsinkable. Shortly before midnight on April 14, it collided with an iceberg southeast of Cape Race, Newfoundland; five compartments ruptured, and the ship sank. Some 1,500 of its 2,200 passengers died. As people we think we know everything but sometimes our decisions can be found wanting. They said the Titanic is unsinkable but still it sank. I urge you to be filled with the Holy Spirit so that you will be able make right decisions. Thereby live a prayerful life and you will see things at their value. Some geniuses have failed in life with all their knowledge. The word of God is saying, "For as the heavens are higher than the earth, So are My ways higher than your ways, And My thoughts than your thoughts." ( Isaiah 55:9) The decisions you are making today, will affect you, your family and the future generations. "This day I call the heavens and the earth as witnesses against you that I have set before you life and death, blessings and curses. Now choose life, so that you and your children may live" (Deuteronomy 30:19) I choose life today. The best decision I have made in my life is to accept Jesus Christ as my Lord and saviour.


**Prayer**

Your word says those who are led by the Spirit are the sons of God. We pray that we should walk by the spirit not by sight. You word says, " If any of you lacks wisdom, let him ask of God, who gives to all liberally and without reproach, and it will be given to him." We shall dwell in the secret place of the Most High and abide under the shadow on the Almighty. You are the Alpha and the Omega, the Author and the Finisher of our faith. We choose you Lord, we choose life. We pray that there is light at our workplaces, in our families, in our finances and in our health. We shall delight myself in you so that you can give me the desires of our heart. Amen


**The bible verses to study**

James 1:5; Proverbs 14:12; Proverbs 3:5; Isaiah 55:9; Deuteronomy 30:19; Daniel 2:21; James 3:17

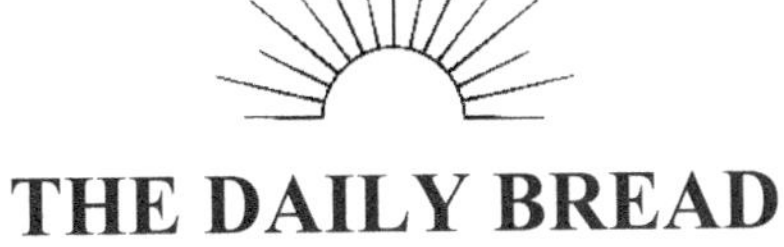

# THE DAILY BREAD

You are a steward of your destiny. They are 3 types of management styles (Leadership), autocratic, democratic and Laissez Faire. The autocratic is where the manager assumes all the powers, democratic is where the manager allow subordinates to make some decisions on their own whilst he monitors them and Laissez Faire is when the subordinates are left alone to make their own decisions without interference of the manger, and he does not control. Terribly some Christians have managed their life in Laissez Faire way. They sit back and relax and expect life to change on its own without them lift a finger. They want to be spiritual which is good but forget they operate here on the earth. But for a miracle to happen, it's not only the Holy Spirit who must do it alone, you must create an atmosphere for the miracle therefore action is required. Without sowing there is no reaping. God did not call us to be lazy and not to use our wisdom. You are already blessed, but your action is required. The children of Israel had to walk to the Promised Land to receive their blessing. The boy had to give his lunch of 2 fishes and 5 loaves to feed the 5000 men. The parable of talents shows us how dangerous it can be not to use our talents; they will be taken away and given to those who can use them. Faith without action is dead. This country is so blessed but if you find yourself living poor for the rest of your it's your own choice. Being born poor it's not your choice but staying poor it's your choice. Speaking in tongues will not pay your rent, you need to go work and earn a salary or sell goods to get money from your business. God need to do his own part and we do our own part. Life need to be balanced, there is time to pray and time to work. You don't build a house with bricks only, but you also need mortar. It's a brick-and-mortar combination. Also, in life its prayer and finances. You can't live on prayer only you need finances to survive. God gives us wisdom, but we need to actual apply the wisdom and create wealth. "Lazy hands make for poverty, but diligent hands bring wealth". (Proverbs 10:4). Diligent hands will rule, but laziness ends in forced labour. (Proverbs 12:24) When Jesus called his 12 disciples, he did not call people who were idle. The word of God says, the just shall live by faith. You need to apply the word of God to your situation. God bless you.

**Prayer**

We pray that, we shall never be lazy because poverty will creep in our lives. May you bless the works of our hands. We shall never be idle. As a man, husband, Father, we shall be a providers. We shall be faithful with what the talents you given us. We shall continue pursuing our dreams and we will never quit. Your word says, "Lazy hands make for poverty, but diligent hands bring wealth". Your word say, "Diligent hands will rule, but laziness ends in forced labour". Your word says faith without works is dead. And your word says the just shall live by faith, we shall apply your word faithful in our lives. Amen

**The bible verses to study.**

Proverbs 10:4; Proverbs 12:24; Romans 1:17; Genesis 2:15; Luke 16:10; Proverbs 10:5; Proverbs 12:11

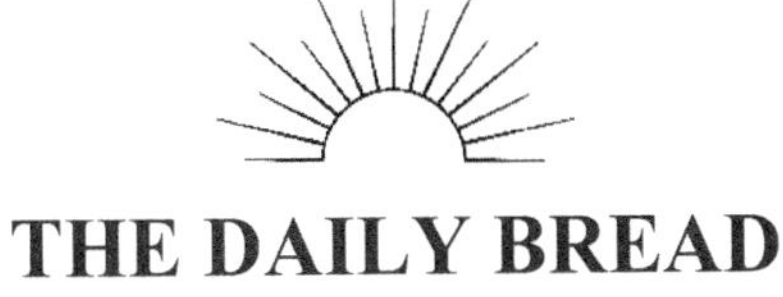

# THE DAILY BREAD

What would be your greatest regret in life? People have different regrets, I was supposed to be married with to this great man, I should have not sold my car, I should have studied further, I should have not lived in South Africa, and I should have gone overseas. This morning what is your greatest regret? My greatest regret would be if I miss my Calling. God called all of us to function in different ways in body of Christ. I pray that when God communicate with me through a burning bush, there is nothing distracting me, and I would be able to hear his voice. I pray that my job, my wife, my friends and family and my lifestyle will not make me miss my calling. When you are old, the greatest regret will not come from the things you tried and failed but from the things you never pursued. We always think we have time, but we don't. You keep on postponing until it's too late. My uncle always say if education is expensive try ignorance. We live life once. We should never fail to pursue our dreams . When you die you will be gone forever and never given a chance to come back gain. You are a world changer, and I am a world changer. They are so many things God deposited in us, but we need to do our part to reveal them to the world. "For the earnest: expectation of the creation eagerly waits for the revealing of the sons of God."( Romans 8:19). God will make a way for you. Be faithful to pursue your purpose and leave the rest to God. God bless you

**Prayer**

We cannot seize to thank you Lord. You have turned our mourning into dancing. You have exchanged our ashes for beauty. When you call us , we shall answer? Nothing can separate us from your Love, O God. You called us Lord from darkness into marvellous light for the purpose. We are yours, signed sealed and delivered. Help us O Lord to pursue our purpose as your word says, "For I know the thoughts that I think toward you, says the LORD, thoughts of peace and not of evil, to give you a future and a hope. Being confident of this, that he who began a good work in you will carry it on to completion until the day of Christ Jesus.


**The bible verses to study.**

Philippians 1:6; 1 John 2:15; Mathew 6:33; Romans 8:19; Philippians 4:13; John 9:4

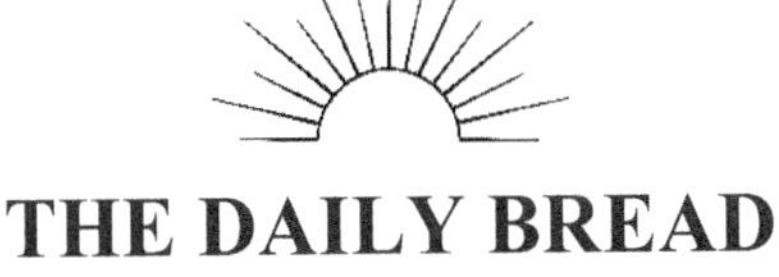

# THE DAILY BREAD

Take a leaf from Moses. His personal relationship with God was very immense. That made him to have that great conviction to go and face Pharaoh. Prior to the encounter with God, he was hopeless and unmotivated. His lived his life for his own. But because of the relationship which he had with God, there was a transformation, change and great improvement. If you want change to come in your life, have a relationship with God. Before you face the world, spend time with God, let him build you up. Moses threw the rod to the ground first in the wilderness before he threw it to the ground in the Palace of Pharaoh. Spend more time more time in presence of God, you will discover your purpose. Your focus will become broader, and you will be fearless. "I can do all things through Christ which strengthens me". (Philippians 4:13). God can bring a drastic change in your life; people who know you in your previous life will wonder is that you. It calls for us to bold, go out of our comfort zone. This will never happen if our relationship with God is non-existent. I pray for you this morning that you will have a deeper relationship with God, you will become world changers and God will use you to bring his will upon the earth. God will never give up hope on you. If God used a murderer Moses why not use, you. For us to be successful in pursuing our dreams it's not about the things we do in the public but in the private spaces. When you see the runner on the day of the race, you must know that they was a lot of sacrifice he /she put in preparing for the race. We should have disciplined prayer life. Moses faced his fear in Pharaoh. Moses had trust on God not his capabilities. Moses walked with God. God never gave him the whole story about what will happen in Egypt and how will he deliver the children of Israel. Moses just trusted God. God will never give you the whole picture its upon us to trust him like Moses and God will fulfil his promises. The word of God says, "One who watches the wind will not sow and one who looks at the clouds will not harvest." (Ecclesiastes 11:4). God bless you.


**Prayer**

We pray that we can build a relationship with you God. All we need is you. We believe in you and know that our future is blessed. We pray that we should not hold back in pursuing you God. As the deer pants for the water brooks, So pants my soul for You, O God. Create in me a clean heart, O God, And renew a steadfast spirit within me. As your word says, "One who watches the wind will not sow and one who looks at the clouds will not harvest," we shall not procrastinate in pursuing our dreams. Your word says, "I can do all things through Christ which strengthens me". Amen


**The bible verses to study.**

Philippians 4:13; Ecclesiastes 11:4;Jeremiah 29:11; Psalms 37:4-5; Ecclesiastes 9:5; Job 14:21; Acts 2:17

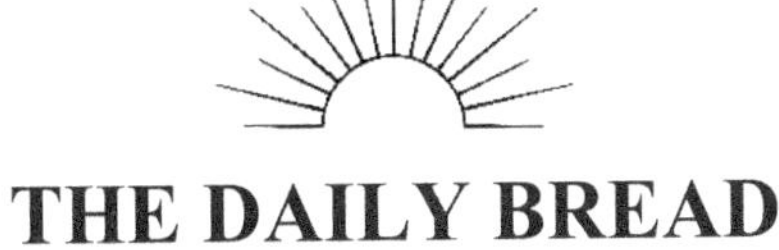

# THE DAILY BREAD

What influence do we have as a church to the world? The church has a role to play in the community especially as a source of leadership. The church has to influence the community one way or the other. The church needs to have more outreach programmes. Winning of souls and discipleship should be their priority. It must just find a way to be relevant to the community because the church serves that community. It must be able to gauge its influence through statistics. The success of a church must be gauged with its community. The quality of people's lives can be improved through the Church. The community must be able to see a change of behaviour and spiritual growth of the people. Christianity is not a religion but a way of life. God must touch the people through the church. Those who are hungry, homeless, sick and jobless must know the church is here for us. Those who are the members of the church must pay tithes so that in the house the God, there is no lack. As a church our priority is to be ambassadors of Jesus Christ and show the world that God is good through our actions. When the church sows in the community and definitely it will reap. "While the earth remains, Seedtime and harvest, Cold and heat, Winter and summer, And day and night Shall not cease. "Genesis 8:24) "For the earth shall be filled with the knowledge of the glory of the LORD, as the waters cover the sea." (Habakkuk 2:14) . I pray that God will raise those Joshuas and Calebs those who will be on fire for God and help the pastors to be effective in the community they live. Jesus said, "A new command I give you: Love one another. As I have loved you, so you must love one another." (John 13:34) The love we have for one another must attract people to Church. They must be no divisions in Church by serving one another and having one purpose. We as church we must present practical solutions to change our community. We must not lie to people and encourage laziness by telling them that they only need to give to God, and he will make them super rich. Instead, we must tell them that when they give to God, he removes a curse and bless them through the fruit of their labour. The church should encourage people to pursue their dreams and also a place to discover their talents. God bless you.

**Prayer**

We pray that as a church that we shall be relevant to our community. We shall be the eyes, hands and legs of the Lord to touch the people. We shall not grow weary in doing good because in due season we shall reap if we faint not. We shall be soul winners. Through our giving, the widows and orphans shall testify that there is a great God in heaven. We shall not condemn anyone, reject anyone one and throw stones against anyone but we shall bring them the Jesus. We shall be the light of the world and salt of the world. As a body of Christ, please God use us to edify the community and bear much fruit. We shall be the change we want to see in others. Amen

**The bible verses to study.**

Genesis 8:24; Habakkuk 2:14; John 13:34; Mathew 5:14-16

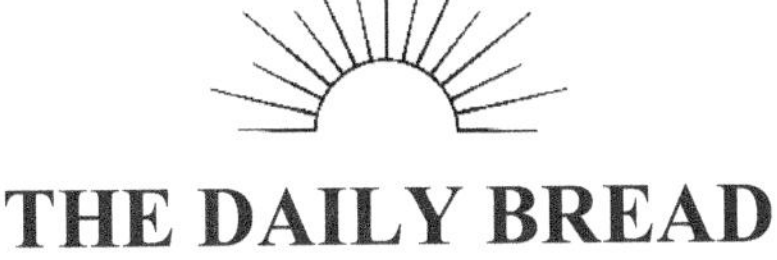

# THE DAILY BREAD

Deep. "When He had stopped speaking, He said to Simon," launch out into the deep and let down your nets for a catch." But Simon answered and said to Him, "Master, we have toiled all night and caught nothing; nevertheless, at your word I will let down the net." And when they had done this, they caught a great number of fishes, and their net was breaking ". (Luke 5:4-6) I am saying this morning how deep you can go, when the word of God has spoken upon your life. The word of God is giving you the perfect will of God upon your life that is to launch deep. Are you ready to let go your dependency on your knowledge, reasoning, strength and do what the word of God is saying? If you let it go, you will stop toiling. Launching deep requires faith, because at that time of the day you cannot catch fish by launching deep under the normal circumstances. Sometimes the things of God does not make sense. If it makes sense you will glorify on yourself but the reason why it does not make sense is that you know it's only God who did it. Do your own part and live the rest to God. You need to take action otherwise you will not catch fish. If God said it in your life, it shall come to pass, just put your trust on him. Launching to the deep requires obedience, time, dedication and commitment. You need also to have a boat and nets to use as tools to catch fish. Ministry need finances to enable it to win souls. It needs committed people who can move with the vision of the church. They are a lot of fish. They are more than you can contain. God promised that" However, as it is written: "What no eye has seen, what no ear has heard, and what no human mind has conceived" -- the things God has prepared for those who love him--" (1 Corinthians 2:9). That small project you are thinking of, that dream God has put in you yes it will shake the nations and win more souls, but you need to launch deep. Remember ".......Not by might, nor by power, but by my spirit, says the LORD of hosts"(Zechariah 4:6). It's not your business but God's business so he knows the end before you start so put trust in Him. God bless you.


**Prayer**

We shall launch to the deep as your word have commanded us and catch great fish that's wining more souls. We shall use our resources and time win more souls for you. Our Lord is ever shinning. You said in your word faith comes by hearing and by hearing the word of God. We shall hear more of the word of God so that we can have great faith. We shall not hold on to our past mistakes but look past our mistakes and have confidence that we will make it through by the grace of God. Your word says, "What no eye has seen, what no ear has heard, and what no human mind has conceived" -- the things God has prepared for those who love him--"


**The bible verses to study**

Luke 5:4-6; 1 Corinthians 2:9; Zechariah 4:6; Proverbs 11:30; John 15:16; 1 Corinthians 9:19-23; Mark 16:15

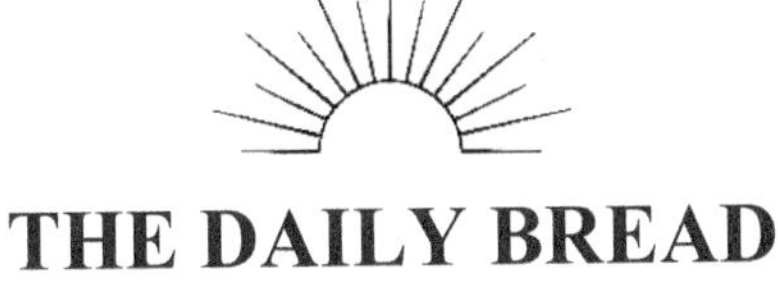

# THE DAILY BREAD

Comfortable. The questing you must ask yourself is have you became comfortable of your situation. Being comfortable it does not mean that your situation has changed but it means you have leant live with your predicament and accepted it. This means you will stop trying and give up. The beggar at the beautiful gate became comfortable in his situation. He could see himself begging only." The LORD our God said to us at Horeb, "You have stayed long enough at this mountain." (Deuteronomy 1:6). The children of Israel were now being comfortable, used to the life in the wilderness. Do you know that you have been broke for too long , you have been begging for too long , you have been crying for too long , you have been unemployed for too long and you have been sick for too long . The woman with an issue of blood tried everything and suffered in the hands of medical men but she touched the ham of Jesus's garment and got cured. Hannah was a wife without a child and year after year the other wife would provoke Hannah because the Lord did not give her any children. Hannah's husband did not understand why she was sad and continuously wept and would not eat. He believed that he was as valuable to her as ten sons. One day when Hannah could no longer bear the pain of her empty womb, she went to the temple to present her supplication to the Lord. She cried out to the Lord and wept bitterly. She was so upset that she made a promise to the Lord in her request for a son, she said: "LORD Almighty, if you will only look on your servant's misery and remember me, and not forget your servant but give her a son, then I will give him to the LORD for all the days of his life, and no razor will ever be used on his head." (1 Samuel 1:11) She was observed by the priest, Eli, who accused her of being a drunken woman. She explained that she had not had any wine nor strong drink and that instead she was deeply distressed and was praying to the Lord. Eli told her to go in peace and also asked that the

Lord would grant her request. After that Hannah was no longer sad and she no longer fasted. God remembered Hannah and she delivered a son. How dire is your situation, have you reached the boiling point where God is your last hope. If God did it for Hannah, God will do it for you. "Jesus Christ is the same yesterday and today and forever." (Hebrews 13:8) God bless you.

**Prayer**

We pray that we shall never lose our hope in you, if you did it for Hannah, you can still do it for us. Poverty is not our portion, unemployment is not our portion, sickness is not our portion, singleness is not our portion, bareness is not our portion, incarceration is not our portion because Jesus you came so that we can have life more abundantly. We shall seek you day and night. Our lives will not remain the same as your word says, "But if the Spirit of him that raised up Jesus from the dead dwell in you, he that raised up Christ from the dead shall also quicken your mortal bodies by his Spirit that dwells in you". We are a head not a tail and we are always above not beneath.

**The bible verses to study.**

1 Samuel 1:11; Deuteronomy 1:6; Ephesians 3:20; Luke 1:37; Mathew 19:26; Numbers 11:23

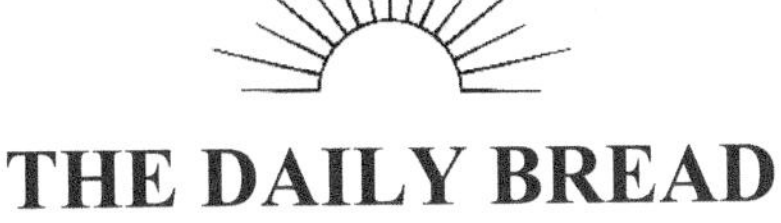

# THE DAILY BREAD

Living life for God. I have seen those who love soccer, they pay a fortune to watch it England, they fight for their team, in their house they have various items for their teams. They wear a printed t-shirt for their teams. Obvious they watch only soccer on TV like most of the times. They talk about soccer. When their team is playing, they sacrifice everything and make sure they watch it. They live for soccer. Liverpool supporters they sing more than people do in church for soccer. They cheer up their heroes but at the end they do not get anything out of it. The worst scenarios is having a bad mood when their team losses. Today I am asking you a question, who are you living for. Can you say my money belongs to God, car and house belong to God, my kids belong to God, my time belong to God and my wife belongs to God . What shows that you are living for God? Take an audit for your life and see what you are living for. Some people are living life for their marriages, what happens if your partner dies, some people are living life for their jobs but what happens if you get retrenched and some people live life their cars what happens if they got stolen. The word of God says, "but lay up for yourselves treasures in heaven, where neither moth nor rust destroys and where thieves do not break in and steal. For where your treasure is, there your heart will be also. ( Mathew 6:20-21) When you live for God , you must be in position to want to know more about God , stay in his presence every time , have your complete trust on God , let your life being centred on God and not to have other foreign gods . God must be always on your lips. People should see from your actions that you are sold out for God. Do you have any books for the word for God, what music are listening to and what are you watching on TV? What kind of friends do you have? Christianity is not a religion but a way of life. You cannot live the whole week as a devil and then on Sunday as a born-again Christian. We should not want God in our lives when it's convenient and using God as a 10111 call or crutches. The Psalmist said in (Psalms 91:1) He that dwells in the secret place of the most high shall abide under the shadow of the Almighty." Check the word dwell it does not mean pass by but living in. "For what is a man profited, if he shall gain the whole world, and lose his own soul? Or what shall a man give in exchange for his soul?" (Mathew 16:26) God bless you.

**Prayer**

We pray that we live for you like Paul and say, "I have been crucified with Christ; it is no longer I who live, but Christ lives in me; and the *life* which I now live in the flesh I live by faith in the Son of God, who loved me and gave Himself for me." We are sold out for you Lord. We live for you. All we need is in you Lord. We need your touch once again. Let us not trust on the physical things that are temporary but on you Lord. We give our life to you. Let us dwell in your presence. Let us meditate on your word day and night. Amen

**The bible verses to study.**

Galatians 2:20; Mathew 6:20-21; Psalms 91:1; 6:33; Job 19:25; Psalms 18:46; Romans 12:1

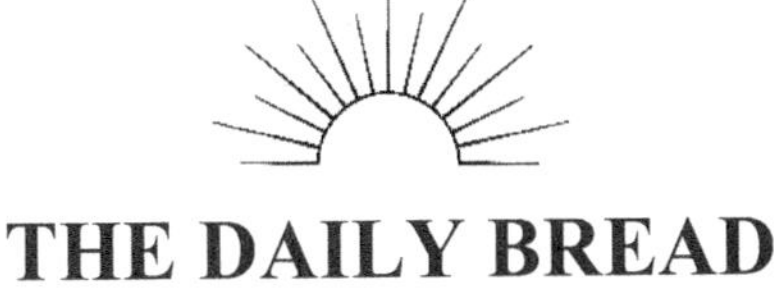

# THE DAILY BREAD

Who do you look like? When a child is born people always want to look and see who does the child looks like. You may be told you look like your uncle, mother, father and your grandmother. The word of God says you are created in the image of God after his likeness . I may look like my father here on earth, but I know my image is from God. "For if anyone is a hearer of the word and not a doer, he is like a man who looks at his natural face in a mirror; for once he has looked at himself and gone away, he has immediately forgotten what kind of person he was.... . (James 1:23-24). We are the image of the word of God. When we hear the word of God, it tells us who we are. The word of God that you hear that's who you are." In the beginning was the Word, and the Word was with God, and the Word was God." (John: 1:1) . The word is God. When I am reading the word, I am looking at myself in the mirror. So "Do not conform to the pattern of this world but be transformed by the renewing of your mind. Then you will be able to test and approve what God's will is--his good, pleasing and perfect will". (Romans 12:2)"If you belonged to the world, it would love you as its own. As it is, you do not belong to the world, but I have chosen you out of the world. That is why the world hates you." (John 15:19). God bless you.

**Prayer**

As your word says, we are created in the image of God after his likeness, we know that we are special . Thank you, Lord, for choosing us before the foundation of the world. We will praise You, for we are fearfully and wonderfully made; Marvelous are Your works, And that our soul knows very well. Your word says, "For we are His workmanship, created in Christ Jesus for good works, which God prepared beforehand that we should walk in them." Your word says, "For God so loved the world, that he gave his only begotten Son, that whosoever believes in him should not perish, but have everlasting life." Amen

**The bible verses to study.**

James 1:23-24; John: 1:1; Romans 12:2; John 15:19; John 3:16; Ephesians 2:10

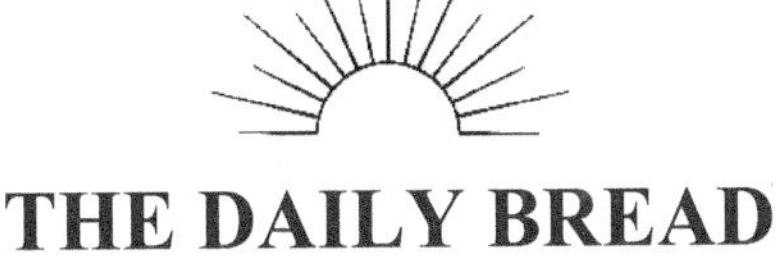

# THE DAILY BREAD

Compression is an increase in pressure of the charge in an engine or compressor obtained by reducing its volume. When you increase compression in the engine, you increase the power. Everyone has their different prayer lives. A person is made of 3 parts, these are the body, the soul and the Spirit. When we get born again our spirit is renewed but our body is not. And as we know that our body is a temple of the Holy Spirit. I know where my compression lies. When I stop to feed the flesh and feed the spirit through fasting and prayer, I increase my compression and thereby increase the power. Someone shared the word on what do you feed. If you feed your anger obvious you will be involved more fights, if you feed your lust it will manifest in your relationships, if you feed love, you will become a loving person. You are a product of what you feed. If you spend more time in the word, you will be different to a person who spends their time watching sopies. Jesus told his disciples to watch and pray so that they do not get into temptation. "But you will receive power when the Holy Spirit comes on you; and you will be my witnesses in Jerusalem, and in all Judea and Samaria, and to the ends of the earth." (Acts 1:8) Samson as long as he kept his hair, he had the power. For me my secret weapon to the devil is prayer and fasting, that is my secret, I will take the battle in the air where the snake is helpless without the stamina and power. When the people they look at me, they see this flesh then they say its George but it's not me, it's just my earthly suite to function on the earth. Me I am spirit amen just like my Father and one day I leave this world to be with Him in heaven. When I die and you look at my body it won't me, it's a just a suite I will be gone. Therefore, I do not work only for the flesh which is perishable but I also for my Spirit which will enjoy the everlasting life. God bless you.

**Prayer**

We thank you Lord Jesus for we have found grace in your eyes. Create hunger in us for your presence Almighty God. We are thirsty for you Lord. We need more of you in our lives. When Lord Jesus you found us, we found life. Thank you, Lord, for your love. We can't live without you. You are our everything Lord. We pray that we should live a life of prayer. Your word says, "Delight yourself also in the LORD, And He shall give you the desires of your heart." Amen.


**The bible verses to study**

Acts 1:8; Mathew 7:7; Job 22:26; Psalms 21:2; Psalms 81:10; Psalms 94:19; Job 27:10

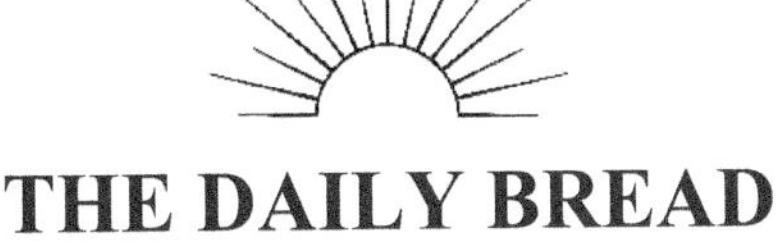

# THE DAILY BREAD

Please today I do not want to give you fish, but I want to teach you how to fish. First of all, I love you all and it's my wish that you excel in your calling and the love of God can expressed through you. I have written to you so many messages and God gives me the messages to write. I do not struggle to write. Because I have been faithfully and committed to write messages, God always give me more messages. God gives seed to the Sower. Did you notice that those who always receive money and do not give always remain poor and do not change? People next time when someone says I will pay for trip, and you can afford it refuse say I will pay for you instead. Do not let people steal your blessings. What I am saying do not be comfortable by just receiving but give too. Those who always gives, they always have something to give. Those who give their life will not remain the same. They continue to grow. They are principles here on earth that applies to everyone like gravity. If you give know that you shall receive. There is more joy in giving than receiving. That's why some people are miserable in their lives, they do not give. The word of God says "Give and it will be given to you. A good measure, pressed down, shaken together and running over, will be poured into your lap. For with the measure you use, it will be measured to you" (Luke 6:38). In an ecosystem there is interdependence. I want to teach you what I call eco finance. Your breakthrough is your seed in your hand. First of all, pay your tithes so that you do not get cursed by robbing God. Be faithfully in paying your tithes and giving. Do not just give, God loves a cheerfully giver. By myself writing messages faithfully, I have allowed myself to be connected to the power, (anointing) every time when I press the switch the light comes out. By you paying your tithes and giving faithfully, you have allowed yourself to be connected to heavenly finances. God will continue to give you because you will give to the ministry and to those who are in need and the praise will be given unto God. How can God continue to bless you when you say this is my money, I must eat it." The silver is mine and the gold is mine,' declares the LORD Almighty" (Haggai 2:8). When you receive and close your hand how can you receive again. You have broken the cycle that's explains my eco finances. God bless you.


**Prayer**

Thank you, Lord, for the life you have given us. Teach us to love because we cannot not love and fail to give. Create in us a giving heart so that we can live a blessed life. We are givers; we are donors by the grace of God. We shall not hold back our tithes and offering to you God, and God you will remove a curse from our finances. We pray that we shall sow our seeds than eating them. We pray that we become faithful in what you have deposited . We are blessed to be a blessing. Your word says, " Give and it will be given to you. A good measure, pressed down, shaken together and running over, will be poured into your lap. For with the measure you use, it will be measured to you" Amen.


**The bible verses to study**

Luke 6:38; Haggai 2:8; 2 Corinthians 9:7 Proverbs 11:25; Proverbs 3:9; 2 Corinthians 9:11; Malachi 3:10; Psalms 37:4

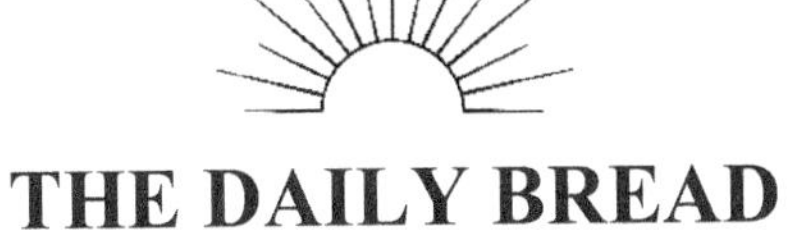

# THE DAILY BREAD

While the earth remains, seedtime and harvest, cold and heat, winter and summer and day and night shall not cease (Genesis 8:22). You cannot do away with seed time if you want to get a Harvest. There was a preacher who was invited to come and preach in the desert. His car broke down and he continued his journey on foot. The heat was so much but he persevered until he arrived at the meeting. He was so dehydrated, and he asked for the glass of water. He took a glass of water and he started to speak. "If I can drink this water in the glass I will live". He continued to say that until he fall down and died with the glass in his hand. The preacher knew that if he can drink the water in the glass, he will live but instead of drinking the water he continued talking. Now it's no longer time to continue talking about giving. Take a step of faith a sow a precious seed, give your best. No one can out give God. "The Queen of Sheba gave King Solomon, but she could not out give him." She gave to the King one hundred and twenty talents of gold, spices in great quantity and precious stones. There never again came such abundance of spices as queen of Sheba gave to King Solomon" (1 Kings 10:10). " Now king Solomon gave to queen of Sheba all she desired, whatever she asked, besides what Solomon had given her according to the royal generosity ......." (1 Kings 10: 13). If an earthly king Solomon could give whatever the queen of Sheba desires and whatever she asked, what will God give you when you give your best to Him? You cannot love without giving, I say no. God loved the world He, gave us his only begotten son, and he gained more sons. I am not sure what you believe God for today, it might be a house, car, job, wife, healing and breakthrough in your business and finances. It does not mean you must give money only, but I say go and give your best, something you value much. I want you to try God. I do not know who God gave me this word for? But you know your situation. "He that goes forth and weeps, bearing precious seed, shall doubtless come again with rejoicing, bringing his sheaves with him. (Psalms 126:6) God bless you.

**Prayer**

Thank you, God, for the glorious life you have given us. We stand on your word that says bring all the tithes and offering to the house of the Lord, try me and see if I cannot open up the windows of the heaven for you and pour out a blessing you cannot contain. Giving is our nature. We are fruitful. Is there anything too hard with God? You are a faithful God. We are blessed. Your word says, "He that goes forth and weeps, bearing precious seed, shall doubtless come again with rejoicing, bringing his sheaves with him". We shall sow precious seeds; we shall sow in the Kingdom of God, and we are sons in the house. Amen

**The bible verses to study**

Genesis 8:22; 1 Kings 10:10; 1 Kings 10: 13; Psalms 126:6; 2 Corinthians 9:6; John 3:16

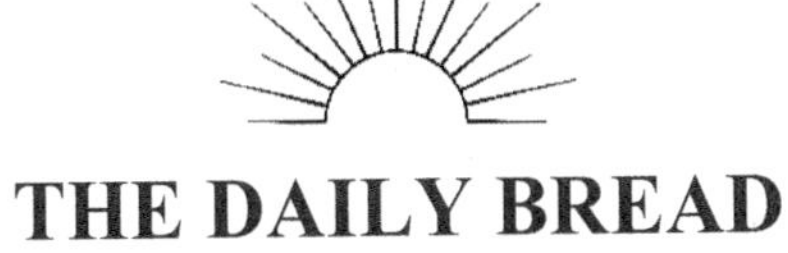

# THE DAILY BREAD

"At Caesarea there was a man named Cornelius, a centurion of what was known as the Italian Cohort, a devout man who feared God with his entire household, gave alms generously to the people, and prayed continually to God. About the ninth hour of the day, he saw clearly in a vision an angel of God come in and say to him, "Cornelius." And he stared at him in terror and said, "What is it, Lord?" And he said to him, "Your prayers and your alms have ascended as a memorial before God. "(Acts 10:1-4). Cornelius prayed and gave too. He gave to the poor people and to God. Cornelius was not a usual giver but a special giver because the word of God says he gave generously. When I was still baby in Christ, I used to treat God like He is a Homeless person, I will give the last note I have in church. I would treat the giving as a loss and do opportunity cost and say I could have bought a burger instead. My knowledge of God was shallow. I did not know that God did not need my money. But giving actually it was an opportunity for God to bless me more. "But the king replied to Araunah, "No, I insist on paying you for it. I will not sacrifice to the LORD my God burnt offerings that cost me nothing." So, David bought the threshing floor and the oxen and paid fifty shekels of silver for them." (2 Samuel 24:24). David knew God and did not want to give what cost him nothing. "And King Solomon offered a sacrifice of twenty-two thousand head of cattle and a hundred and twenty thousand sheep and goats. So, the king and all the people dedicated the temple of God." (2 Chronicles 7:5) . My prayer for you today is for you to understand that your breakthrough in your life is connected to your giving. "When I was a child, I spoke as a child, I understood as a child, I thought as a child: but when I became a man, I put away childish things" (1 Corinthians 13:11). I pray you grow, and God bless you that you can be a blessing to other people. No one can out give God. God bless you.

**Prayer**

Thank you, Lord, for teaching us on giving and now we live a life of overflow. You word says, "The just shall live by faith". Your word says delight yourself in the Lord, He shall give you the desires your of heart. Let us not miss the opportunity of getting blessed but not giving. We shall never lack any good thing in our lives because we are financing the house of God. Jesus you are our saviour. God you are our provider. The Lord is our Shepherd we shall not want. Give us this day our daily bread Lord . Let us not walk by sight but by the spirit. Help us Lord to understand our breakthrough in your life is connected to your giving. "Amen

**The bible verses to study**

Acts 10:1-4; 2 Samuel 24:24; 2 Chronicles 7:5; 1 Corinthians 13:11; Malachi 3:6-12

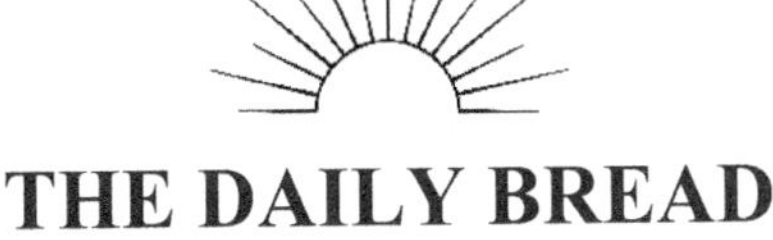

# THE DAILY BREAD

Lucky. It's no longer time for you to live by lucky. It's time you must live by faith. People know about faith, hear the word of God and confess it but actual do they live by faith. In most cases no. The word of God says the just shall live by faith. I cannot be like an agent who helps people to buy houses and I am a tenant. I want to practice what I preach. Some Christians they love God but as long as it does not involve their money. They do not have a full trust in God. When someone purchases a ticket of lotto, they hope that they can win lotto jackpot. Although they know that their chances are very slim they keep on playing. People trust lotto than God. It's easy in life to fast but worshiping God with your money it's difficult. If you trust God with your finances, you would have taken a giant step of faith. You can have peace of mind knowing that God is in charge of your finances. For where your treasure is, there will your heart be also. (Matthew 6:21). I know the times are hard; the devil is reminding you of your debts, the devil is telling you that you can do it next month. I encourage paying to start paying your tithes this month and sowing a seed in the ministry. By you not paying your tithes, have you got rich. In fact, you have cursed yourself. "Would anyone rob God? Yet you are robbing Me! But you say, 'How have we robbed You?' In tithes and offerings. You are cursed with a curse, For you have robbed Me, Even this whole nation. (Malachi 3:8-9) Even when you live 100 years not paying tithes, you will never get rich from that 10 percent you are robbing God. "But Samuel replied: "Does the LORD delight in burnt offerings and sacrifices as much as in obeying the LORD? To obey is better than sacrifice, and to heed is better than the fat of rams" (1 Samuel 15:22). Tithing its spiritual, if you use your reasoning, you will never tithe. Being black and grew up in so much poverty sometimes it's difficult, it needs a great change of mind-set. We were brought up with a dependency syndrome now we cannot give because the only thing we know is receiving. Today I encourage take that money, do not think about it, let it go and worship God. God bless you.

**Prayer**

We thank you Lord, that we no longer live by lucky but through faith. We thank you Lord for the blessings. Your word says, "Every good gift and every perfect gift is from above, and comes down from the Father of lights, with whom there is no variation or shadow of turning". We believe in you Lord that you are the one who reward those who seek you diligently. Let us not withhold anything from you. We shall worship you God with our finances. You're a faithful God. Your word says, "Delight yourself also in the LORD, And He shall give you the desires of your heart" Amen

**The bible verses to study.**

James 1:17; Psalms 37:4; Matthew 6:21; Malachi 3:8-9; 1 Samuel 15:22; Proverbs 3:5; Romans 1:17

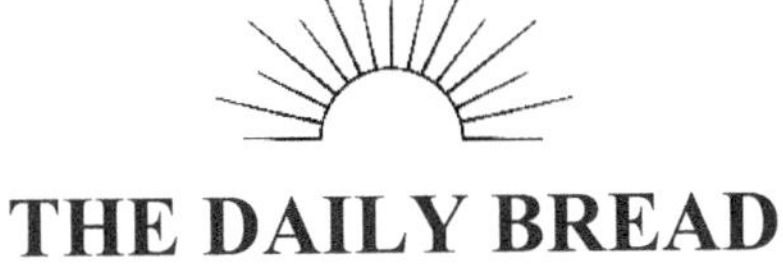

# THE DAILY BREAD

Have we become fruitless? "On the following day, when they came from Bethany, He was hungry. And seeing in the distance a fig tree in leaf, he went to see if he could find anything on it. When he came to it, he found nothing but leaves, for it was not the season for figs. And he said to it, "May no one ever eat fruit from you again." And his disciples heard it" (Mark 11:12-14). For example, if someone invest money in a bank, he expects it to earn interest. This fig tree had leaves on it which means that there was supposed to be fruits on the tree. So, when Jesus did not see those fruits on the fig tree, it was really improper. Why are we saved? Are we the salt of the earth? Are we the light of the world? Just take a stock take of your life since you have been a Christian has something changed in your life. Have you ever won even one soul, do your neighbors even know you are a Christian? Does your conduct able to turn people to God? Just go out there let the people see Jesus in you. Pray for those who are sick, give to the poor and love everyone with the love of God. What are you doing to further the kingdom of God? We cannot be like babies feed me. "1 Corinthians 12:7 says" But the manifestation of the Spirit is given to every man to profit withal". We need to grow and produce fruits. We cannot produce fruits if we are not in Christ. Today tell yourself that I am not going to be a hearer only but a doer too. May the word of God bring life to your bodies? Thank you. The word of God is saying, "You did not choose me, but I chose you and appointed you so that you might go and bear fruit—fruit that will last—and so that whatever you ask in my name the Father will give you." (John 15:16) God bless you.

**Prayer**

We shall never be fruitless because we are deep rooted in you Jesus Christ. Jesus you are our Alpha and the Omega. The author and the finisher of our faith. Let us run with your word. We are not only the hearers of the word but the doers too. Touch us once again. We are going to shine this light in us. We are blessed to be a blessing. Your word says, "But the manifestation of the Spirit is given to every man to profit withal". Create in us more hunger to win souls. Amen


**The bible verses to study.**

Jeremiah 17:7-8; John 15:16; Proverbs 18:21; Genesis 1:28; John 15:-1-2; Mark 11:12-14

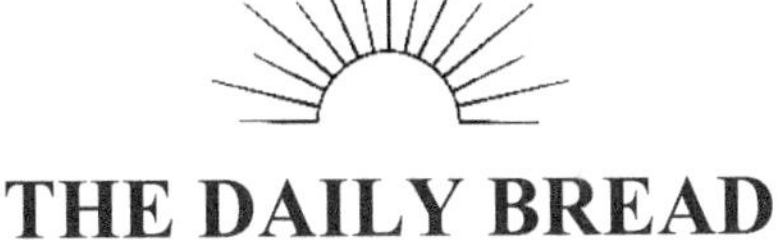

# THE DAILY BREAD

Look what you have become. When a child is born, the parents have high hopes for child. They think of good about you only. They will never picture their child as a prostitute, thief and a murderer. There is a story in the bible about a man who sowed seeds in his field but another one came and sowed weeds in the same field. He was surprised when he saw weeds springing up in his field. Yes, parents they do everything to bring their children upright but there is a devil waiting with a trap. His plan is to destroy, kill and steal. How many people who are sitting in prison regretting of the decisions they made. They are looking where they are now and would not have ever thought they will end up there. They believed lies from the devil. They served a wrong master. They were used by the devil. The prodigal son was a product of a good family. So, coming from a good family will not save you only Jesus can save you. You need the word of God to renew your mind so that you do not live an evil and destructive life. The first part of Psalms Chapter one says blessed is the man who walks not in the counsel of ungodly, nor stand in the paths of sinners nor sits in the seat of the scornful but his delight is in the law of the Lord and His law he meditates day and night. He shall be like a tree planted by the rivers of the water that brings forth its fruits in every season. There is no relationship between evil and good. Do not entertain evil in your life. Sin is what takes people out of Church. "Be sober, be vigilant; because your adversary the devil walks about like a roaring lion, seeking whom he may devour." (1 Peter 5:8)The devil will isolate you and devour you if you live a sinful life. Legion stayed by the graves because he was demon possessed. The demons isolated him and made him cut his body. When he was delivered, he begged to go with Jesus. The devil affects your mind and controls the way you're thinking. Only Jesus can save us from this destructive lifestyle of living by the graves. Let the word of God be the lamp upon your paths and the light on your way. Your parents still love you as imperfectly as you are. Come back home. God will never judge you. God is faithful. Every tree is known by its fruit. The reason why your life has turned that way is because you are abiding on a wrong tree. Your fruit can never be different from the tree. Jesus is a true vine; we need to abide in him then our lives will reflect Jesus Christ in our fruit. A Fruit will never fall far away from the tree. God bless you.

**Pray**

As your word says, "And do not be conformed to this world, but be transformed by the renewing of your mind, that you may prove what is that good and acceptable and perfect will of God," we shall study your word and renew our minds. We thank you Lord Jesus because you said you will never leave us nor forsake. Rejoice not against me my enemies, when I fall, I shall rise, when I sit in the darkness you are light upon me. Our faith shall never fail. You know the end from the beginning. We cannot seize to thank you Lord. Our hope is in you Lord and our trust is in you Lord. Your word says, "My grace is sufficient for you, for My strength is made perfect in weakness." Therefore, most gladly I will rather boast in my infirmities, that the power of Christ may rest upon me." Amen

**The bible verses to study**

2 Corinthians 12:9; Luke 15:11-32; Mathew 13:24-43; 1 Peter 5:8; John 10:10; Romans 12:2

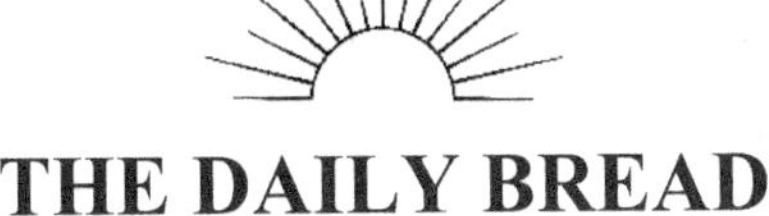

# THE DAILY BREAD

This morning I pray for you who are addicted to drug, gambling, sex and alcohol. I mean all those who have been made slaves by different substances and urges. The secret to break away from bondage is through prayer and fasting. "Then the disciples came to Jesus privately and said, "Why could we not drive it out?" And He said to them, "Because of the littleness of your faith; for truly I say to you, if you have faith the size of a mustard seed, you will say to this mountain, 'Move from here to there,' and it will move; and nothing will be impossible to you. "But this kind does not go out except by prayer and fasting."(Mathew 17:19-21) .The devil always hold people by addiction through lies like I am not hurting anyone ,one day I will stop, and I am in control . Addictions are killers of destiny and your purpose. The devil is very jealous. When you are addicted, you become a slave of the demons. You can't do anything in life except to please the demons. You become a dead person whilst you are living. If you are a gambler instead of serving God, you serve money. You can't study to improve your life, follow your career and start a business because your mind will be captured. You will live a miserable life of losing money thinking one day I will make it big. When you wake up you will think about money and when you go to sleep its money, but you are broke. Gambling makes you very selfish person because you will cut all meaningful relationships in life to serve the god of money. People do not realise what causes their urges. Behind every addiction there is a demonic spirit. Legion was demon possessed and they was no natural remedy for him. It was a spiritual thing. Jesus casted out the demons from Legion. Legion lost his mind because of demonic possession. People with addictions are self-destructive and their decision making is very flawed. Because of urges on their bodies and to feed their habit, some of them are involved in crime. Is there any area you are struggling with in your life? You have given yourself several deadlines. I will stop next year, but you always fall back to it. You cannot win this war alone. People like Whitney Houston fall in the trap and never got out. They went into rehab and thought they were getting better. With all the money she had, the drugs killed her. Allow Jesus to carry your burden. James 5:16 says" Therefore confesses your sins to each other and pray for each other so that you may be healed. The prayer of a righteous person is powerful and effective." The power of sin is in its secrecy. Let's expose it. You can be free. You must seek God and give Him the control of your life; the devil will flee. God bless you.


**Prayer**

We pray for those who are addicted to drug, gambling, sex and alcohol to be freed as your word says, "Therefore if the Son makes you free, you shall be free indeed". We pray for those who are going through stuff and lost everything for you God to restore them. We pray for those who are heart broken and hopeless for the good Lord touch them and heal them . In the name of Jesus every Spirit of additions must leave. Our bodies are temples of God. We pray for those who have given up hope to fight the addition, to those who are homeless, in prison and lost everything, may you God restore their mind and the zeal to fight for their lives. Your word says , You restore our souls. Please restore their souls. Let them know that nothing can separate them from you love. Amen.


**The bible verses to study. :**

Mathew 17:19-21; John 8:36; Mathew 11:28-29; Psalms 107:19-20; Jeremiah 17:14; 2 Corinthians 3:17; James 4:1

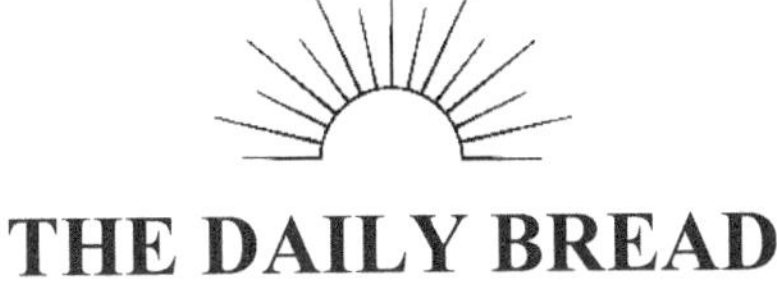

# THE DAILY BREAD

Where is my Rebecca? Isaac was mourning the death of his mother. When we look at how Rebecca came into Isaac's life, we understand that there was a hand of God. God chose the wife for Isaac. "Houses and riches are an inheritance from fathers, But a prudent wife is from the LORD." (Proverbs 19:14) When Isaac took Rebecca as his wife's he was comforted. I ask myself to say where my Rebecca is. Rebecca was given to Isaac. Now I ask myself am I Isaac. Isaac was a really faithful son. He was a Man of God. He was very obedient to his father. He was very loyal, and his father sought a wife for him. God has precious daughters to give but can he entrust you with one of them. A wife is a blessing from God. "He who finds a wife finds a good thing and obtains favour from the LORD". (Proverbs 18:22) They are some blessings we need to prepare ourselves so that we become ready for them. You cannot give a gun to a teenager it might be harmful to them than protect them. There is also a positional blessing where we need to move to certain position or area so that we can become entitled them. When we do not have certain things in life, we must pray so that God can reveal whether we are ready to receive them and show us which areas of our lives we need to work on. If the children of Israel had not moved from Egypt, they would not have enjoyed the benefits of the Promised Land. We must allow the Holy Spirit to teach us and train us so that we can be where God wants us to be. God is good. God bless you.

**Prayer**

I thank you Lord for the gift of a wife. You said that in your word it is not good for a man to be alone, please help me to find my helper. You said in your word whoever finds a wife has find a good thing and favor in God. Bless me O Lord. I know God when give, you give abundantly. Every perfect gift and without shadow of darkness comes from you. My days of being alone are over. Grace of God is sufficient for me. Amen.


**The bible verses to study.**

Proverbs 19:14; Proverbs 18:22; Genesis 24:1-67; Ephesians 5:25

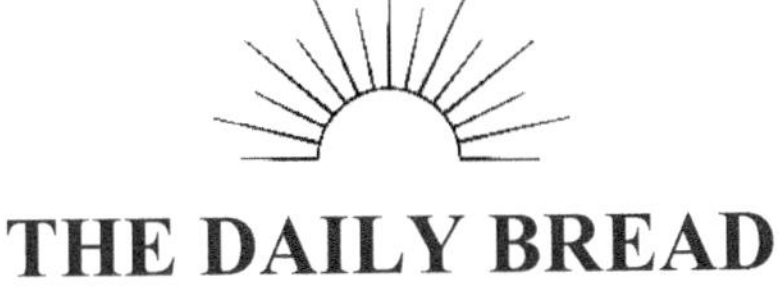

# THE DAILY BREAD

The church needs to kick out Lazarus spirit of poverty. Lazarus lived by the Richman. He made a living through begging. Lazarus focused his energy on wrong things that is begging. Begging needs a special skill that the person develops, why does a person use their creativity in other areas. I believe he never saw himself nothing else than a beggar. He lived a defeated life. A man has always been working since creation for example Adam in the Garden of Eden. People want to rely on the Government and other people to change their lives. Everyone was given the same hours in the day by the creator so it's up to individuals on how they spend those hours. If someone goes and come back in 10 years and found you on the same position in life, you have a problem. People shifts the blame to other people and their circumstances, my parents were not rich enough to send me to school but now you are a 40 years old , with my salary I can pay rent and food only and I will do it next year. The reason why most of the people cannot prosper in this country is that they work for alcohol. Large chunk of people's money is dedicated on alcohol. People are eating the eggs; they do not wait for them to hatch to produce chickens. No one wants to suffer but live luxurious. Most of the people are in debt because of expensive cars, and house and credit cards. How many people who have been blacklisted in this country because of lack of self-discipline? Let's be humble in life, God will lift us up. We must work hard and study. Let's pray to God for wisdom. We cannot keep holding on poverty it's not our portion. God does not promote laziness. If you continue to give excuses in life, your life will never change. It's a mental thing, we need to deal with poverty mentality. Its high time where you need to see that your destiny is in your hands and God is faithful to bless the works of your hands. Tell yourself that where you are today is not where you are going to be tomorrow. May God bless you that you will never lack any good thing in your life? God bless you.


**Prayer**

We thank you Lord Jesus because you were made poor so that we can be rich. You said on the cross it is finished and now we can never be poor anymore if we act on your word. We know the plans you have for us are to prosper us, to give us hope and to give us a future. Poverty is no longer our portion. We cannot live without you O Lord Jesus. Let us not put trust in ourselves but in you. Your word says, "But you are a chosen generation, a royal priesthood, a holy nation, His own special people, that you may proclaim the praises of Him who called you out of darkness into His marvellous light;" We are delighting ourselves in the Lord and He will give us all the desires of our heart. We shall not lack any good thing. Amen


**The bible verses to study.**

Luke 16:19-31; Proverbs 10:15; Proverbs 13:18; Proverbs 30:8; Proverbs 20:13; Proverbs 28:19

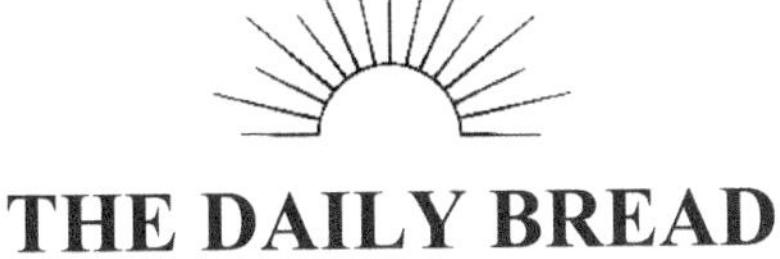

# THE DAILY BREAD

Beware of stagnation. "When we were at Mount Sinai, the LORD our God said to us, 'You have stayed at this mountain long enough. (Deuteronomy 1:6). Fear often paralyzes people, being scared of change and the fear of the unknown factor. Are they any mountains in our lives where we have stayed too long? It's high time to move forward and claim the promises of God's word in our lives. The Egyptians were history now, the Israelites were free people. God did not rescue them to stay at the mountain but Promised Land. You have stayed too long on the mountain of poverty, you have stayed too long on the mountain of unemployment, and you have stayed too long on the mountain of procrastination. It's easy to be comfortable and forget where you are going. Mediocre is an enemy to the life God has prepared for you. Don't settle too early. I am telling you today that you have stayed long in your mediocre life it's high time for you to get to your destiny. If you continue to be stagnant you will get contaminated. Anything that does not grow its dead. The promises were made to you by God. Do not limit yourself. You serve a great and mighty God. "Not that I have already obtained all this, or have already arrived at my goal, but I press on to take hold of that for which Christ Jesus took hold of me." (Philippians 3:12)" Sin is the number one reason why we become stagnant. You used to be hot for God and now who killed that fire. The devil has neutralised you and look at you now, you have stopped running your race. You are no longer pursing God and your dreams. Something has died inside of you. Its high time you must return the heart of worship and seek God through prayer, He will deliver you. The reason why you cannot leave this mountain of lack, mountain of poverty, mountain of unemployment and mountain of sickness it's the SIN in your life. You need to confront it head on. First thing for you to move away from this mountain is to deny yourself. You old self needs to die and then take on the new self. By the grace of God, you shall move away from this mountain and live fulfilled life. God bless you.

**Prayer**

We shall never be stagnant, but keep moving as your word says, "Not that I have already obtained all this, or have already arrived at my goal, but I press on to take hold of that for which Christ Jesus took hold of me." We thank you Lord because we are fearful and wonderful made. We are sitting together with Jesus in the Heavenly places. We refuse to live a sinful life and give up on our dreams. No matter how many times we have failed, we will keep going. We cannot disappoint you God, the trust you have given to us. We shall reach our destiny. Our faith shall never fail. The grace of God is sufficient for us, we are blessed. Amen.

**The bible verses to study.**

Deuteronomy 1:6; Philippians 3:12; Philippians 2:9; Romans 10:10: Zephaniah 1:12; Revelations 3:16

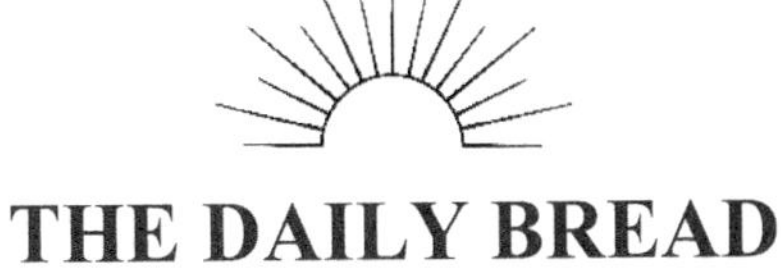

# THE DAILY BREAD

Personalize. People who buy cars they love to personalize especially their number plates. This morning I am looking at a deeper personalization. I want you to personalize the word of God, I mean to claim it and make it yours. The great man of God like David amen they grew in the spirit and were able to personalize. David confessed that the Lord is my Shepherd, and I shall not want. David had a relationship with God. People say God is good in my life, but how is God good in your life. Have you ever experienced His goodness, do you have a testimony where you can say the word become flesh and become part of my life? I mean the promises in the word of God get realized in your life. This calls for a closer personal relationship with God. Hannah was barren; she did not have her own children. People mocked her; people spoke about her like she is not there. One day she personalized, she could not take it anymore, her heart was broken, and she wept and prayed to God. She could not take the burden anymore and took it to God. She out poured herself to God. She did not care about anyone in the congregation. She totally surrendered to God. Come to God as you are, broken, venerable, weeping and do not hold anything back. People with nothing to lose have managed tap into the anointing and had their prayers answered. If you still have alternatives, you will be comfortable, but there comes a time when you know if God does not come for you, your life will be ruined or finished. I urge you this morning to live for God. Hannah gave birth to Samson, a powerful Man of God. There are so many barren women, but they are few like Hannah. Hannah had a personal testimony that being barren it does not mean you will never give birth to a child. Personalise your walk with God for a great testimony. God bless you.

**Prayer**

We pray to have a deeper personal relationship with you God. Help us O Lord to totally surrender our lives to you. We pray that we decrease so that you can increase in our lives . We pray that we can reach the same stage like Paul where he said I have been crucified with Christ, it's no longer I who lives but Jesus Christ living in me. We are the blessed because goodness and mercy is following us all the days in our lives. The grace of God is upon our lives. Touch us O Lord once again. Fill us up Lord until we overflow. Let us give all ourselves to you Lord and let us not hold back. We confess that our lives are blessed, our finances are blessed, and our health is blessed in the name of Jesus. Amen.


**The bible verses to study.**

Proverbs 8:17; Psalms 119:2; Mathew 6:33; James 4:8; Jeremiah 29:11; Psalms 63:1: Joshua 1:8; Hebrews 10:24-25

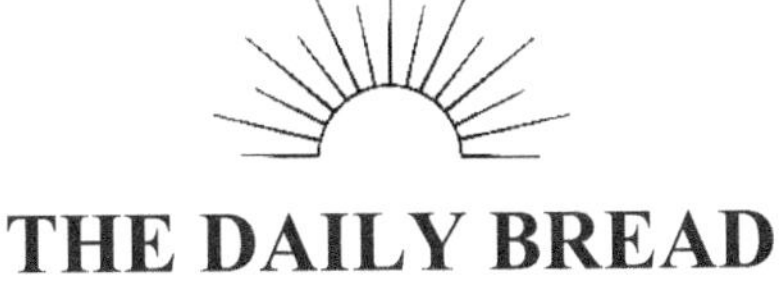

# THE DAILY BREAD

There are two ways of improving your situation. You can either change it or you can change the way you look at it. There are situations in your life that definitely need to change, but your participation is crucial. There are times when you are a victim of circumstances. In that case the world is most probably out to get you, but more often than not, you are part of the problem. You may think that you are the constant (which should not change) and everything else has to change to suit you. But Saul also believed that he was working for God. Yes you may be a child of God, but there are things you definitely have to change. You need to have an extraordinary encounter with Jesus that will reset your perceptions and make you see everything in a different light. You need an apocalyptic encounter that will make you fall to the ground. When Saul met Jesus, he fell down. He "got up from the ground, but when he opened his eyes, HE COULD SEE NOTHING...... For three days he was blind and did not eat or drink anything..." (Acts 9:8-9) During that time, God was resetting Saul's attitudes and perceptions. For you to be effective in your family, job, ministry, finances, you may need an attitude adjustment. You need to change the way you see everything. You need to be a new creation not just someone who holds on to things that are neither progressive nor holy. You are due for a life changing encounter with Jesus and what you eat, drink, see and think will be changed for good. God bless you.

**Prayer**

We pray that when we hear your word, we shall not harden our hearts. May we be able to hear the voice of the Holy Spirit and able to have a teachable spirit. Thank you, Lord Jesus, for the abundant life you have given us. We are blessed beyond measure. We glorify your name. Shine your light upon us Lord

Jesus . Let us be able to see your goodness in the land of the living. Open our eyes to see that those who are with us are more than against us. Your goodness and mercy is following us all the days in our lives. Your word says, " behold, I have done according to your words; see, I have given you a wise and understanding heart, so that there has not been anyone like you before you, nor shall any like you arise after you." Amen


**The bible verses to study.**

Acts 9:8-9; Luke 19:5; John 4:17-26; Mathew 4:18-20; Mathew 4:21-22; Acts 9:17-18; Mark 9:2-3; John 20:14-16

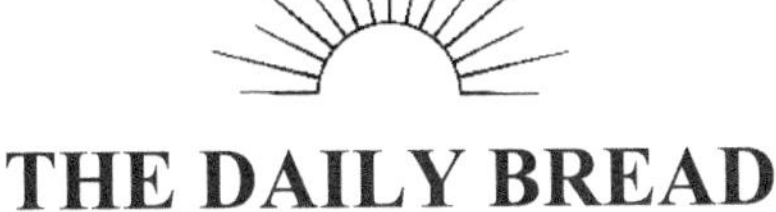

# THE DAILY BREAD

All the suffering and pain you are going through, the devil thinks that he got you and he is celebrating. He thinks you are going to turn away from God. Same devil who destroyed Job's life in terms of his possessions, family and health, he is still going after us. Look at Job, he refused to curse God but glorified God out of his predicament. The devil must have swallowed the words he spoke to God against Job. Job remained faithfully and God restored him more than double he was before. The more the Devil is attacking us; it brings us more close to God. When you are going through so much in life, your prayer life intensifies. Your relationship with God improves and your faith is strengthened. "Consider it pure joy, my brothers and sisters, whenever you face trials of many kinds, because you know that the testing of your faith produces perseverance."(James 1:2-3) When they tormented Christ on the way to the cross, the devil had no idea that he was unwrapping the power Jesus had inside Him. If Jesus didn't die and arose we would not have the Holy Spirit. The enemy paved the way. Daniel was taken into captivity because King Nebuchadnezzar had besieged Jerusalem ad requested young men in whom there were no blemish, but good looking, gifted in all wisdom and ability to work in the king's palace. God allowed this to happen so that he can fulfil his destiny. Daniel when he lived in the captivity, he told and interpreted the dreams of King Nebuchadnezzar which none could do. There was God's favour upon Daniel's life that he was promoted "Then the king placed Daniel in a high position and lavished many gifts on him. He made him ruler over the entire province of Babylon and placed him in charge of all its wise men" (Daniel 2:48) Just know the suffering we are going through now cannot be compared to the joy that is going to be revealed to us. Success comes when you are in an uncomfortable position. God bless you.

**Prayer**

Thank you, Lord, the suffering we are going through now cannot be compared to the joy that is going to be revealed to us. Weeping may endure overnight but joy comes in the morning. Our enemies do not rejoice again us, when we fall, we shall rise, when we sit in the darkness the Lord shall be light upon us. He who has begun a good work in us shall continue until the Lord Jesus comes. Your word says, "Consider it pure joy, my brothers and sisters, whenever you face trials of many kinds, because you know that the testing of your faith produces perseverance." We shall never give up as your word says, "Let us not become weary in doing good, for at the proper time we will reap a harvest if we do not give up". Amen

**The bible verses to study.**

Galatians 6:9; James 1:2-3; Daniel 2:48; Romans 5:3; James 5:11; James 1:12; 2 Peter 2:9

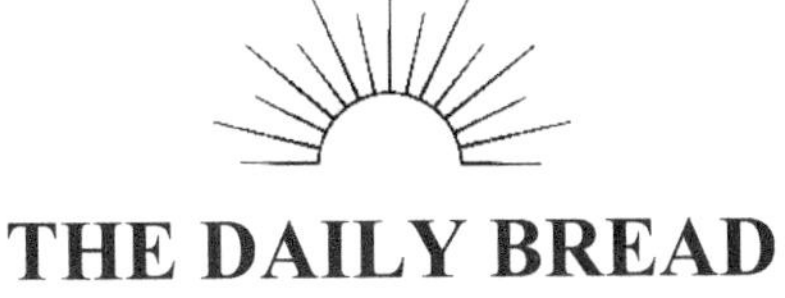

# THE DAILY BREAD

I have often heard some preachers saying, "Christianity is NOT a religion, but it is a WAY of life..." and I thought I understood what they meant. However, when I thought about it seriously, the statement gave me a new way of looking at my faith. Indeed, religion has to do with external rules and regulations that are scrupulously followed by people trying to be in tandem with what they believe. But when you are a REAL BELIEVER, all your words, desires and actions are directed in a different way. As the Bible says, "at Caesarea, there was a man named Cornelius, a centurion in what was known as the Italian regiment. He and ALL his family were devout and God fearing; he gave generously to those in need and prayed to God regularly. One day at about 3 in the afternoon.... He DISTINCTLY SAW an angel of God, who came to him...... "(Acts 10:1-3) Cornelius was a classic example of a believer whose faith was from inside and manifested on the outside. His unwavering faith touched the heart of God even though he was gentile. He didn't know much about Jesus (hence God had to send Peter to him), he didn't have Jewish blood, but he had the seed of faith within him. To Cornelius, righteousness was a way of life. It was not a learned routine and so should it be with you. It is time for you to make righteousness a part of your life. It is time you rethink your priorities. God wants to visit you in a special way, but only when you decide to make righteousness a way of life. God bless you.


**Prayer**

As your word says the just shall live by faith, we pray that we shall live through faith. Your word says, "But without faith it is impossible to please Him, for he who comes to God must believe that He is, and that He is a rewarder of those who diligently seek Him." We thank you God, we are alive. We are grateful to you Lord. All we need is you, Lord. Bless us O Lord, every day. We can't live without you. We want more of you Lord. Cover us Lord under your wings. God you are love, teach us how to love. Anoint us with oil O Lord, our cups are running over, we are blessed. Amen


**The bible verses to study.**

Acts 10:1-3; Galatians 2:20; Romans 12:2; Colossians 3:5-10; Ephesians 5:15-16; Proverbs 21:21

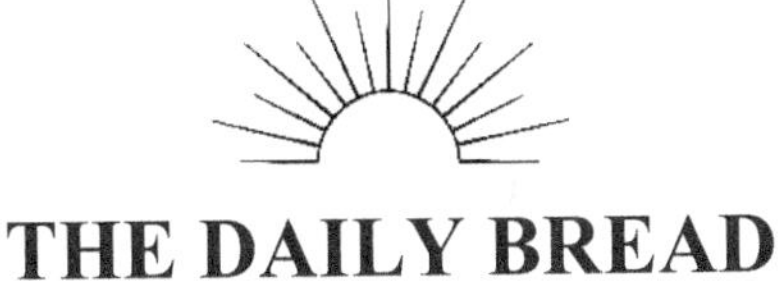

# THE DAILY BREAD

There comes time, when your situation has deteriorated to the point of dire desperation. You have lost hope and wish for a speedy death to spare you the misery. Even those closest to you, are convinced that your demise is imminent and are praying for a faster and less painful exit, just like Job's wife. And like Job, you may be saying "God has made me a byword of the people (the talk of the town), and I have become one in whose face men spit." (Job 17:6) People may be pointing at you as you walk as a pale shadow of your former self. People also thought Peter was a dead man. But when he showed up at Mary's door and Rhoda told the believers, "they wouldn't believe her ...... dismissing her report (saying) "You're crazy". They (even) said, 'It must be his angel'." (Acts 12:15) You are poised for a dramatic comeback that will shock even yourself. Your business, relationship, health, crisis or challenge is about to make an unexpected, but welcome change. Soon you are going to receive a call that will change your life forever. God bless you.


**Prayer**

Thank you, Lord, for loving us and preparing a table before us in the presence of our enemies. Your word says, "For a righteous man may fall seven times And rise again, But the wicked shall fall by calamity". " My enemies do not rejoice again me when I fall, I shall rise, when I sit in the darkness the Lord shall be the light upon me". Our faith shall never fail. God you are faithful. We will never give up because God you will never give up on us. Weeping may endure over night by joy comes in the morning. Your word says, " And we know that all things work together for good to those who love God, to those who are the called according to His purpose." Amen

**The bible verses to study.**

Acts 12:15; Johua 8:1-29; Proverbs 24:16; Psalms 37:24; Psalms 145:14; Micah 7:8; Psalms 20:8; 2 Corinthians 4:8-9

# THE DAILY BREAD

There is something off about loving the world. Do you love the world? The word of God says those who love the world and everything in it have no love for God. The perfect example of the world is Sodom and Gomorrah. There was so much evil. If you look at the way of their life, they lived to fulfil their lust. There was no fear of God in them. If we look at the world of today, is there any difference to the way of life lived in Sodom and Gomorrah. God destroyed Sodom and Gomorrah. God rescued Lot's family. Lot's wife left Sodom and Gomorrah, but her heart was still in Sodom and Gomorrah. She really loved the place. God said they must not look back. But perhaps Lot's wife said let me do it one more time and she lost her life. Are there Christians who still love things of the world? The Children of Israel in the Wilderness told God that it was better in Egypt because they had pots of meat and garlic. Egypt is another perfect example of the world. We are born in the world, and we get used to world system. When we become saved amen, we still look back. We admire our past life. There was nothing good about it. It's a lie which the devil places in our hearts. Christianity is not boring and is not for people who are weak. The devil is a liar from the beginning thus why they call him the father of lies .The word of God says you must know the truth and then only the truth will set you free (John 8:32) .God is spirit so we must worship him in truth and in spirit . Only dogs are the one that returns and eat their vomit. Remember how miserable you were before Jesus Christ came into your life. We were lost sheep without a shepherd. We were without hope. We were walking in darkness. We were dead in sin. Now we are sitting together in Christ in heavenly places. "But you are a chosen people, a royal priesthood, a holy nation, God's special possession, that you may declare the praises of him who called you out of darkness into his wonderful light." (1 Peter 2:9) God bless you.

**Prayer**

Thank you, Lord, for choosing us, we were of the world now we belong to you. We do not have confidence in the flesh. What does it benefit us to gain this world and lose our souls? We refuse to be conformed to the pattern of this world but be renewed by reading the word of God. We are in this world but not of this world. Today Lord, we will make a choice to choose light and to choose life. There is no darkness in our finances, in our families and at our workplaces. Thank you, Lord, for saving our souls. Thank you for blessing us. Amen

**The bible verses.**

1 John 2:15-17; James 4:4; Mathew 6:24; 1 John 3:13; John 15:18-21; Mathew 7:13; 1 Tomothy 6:10; 2 Corinthians 4:4

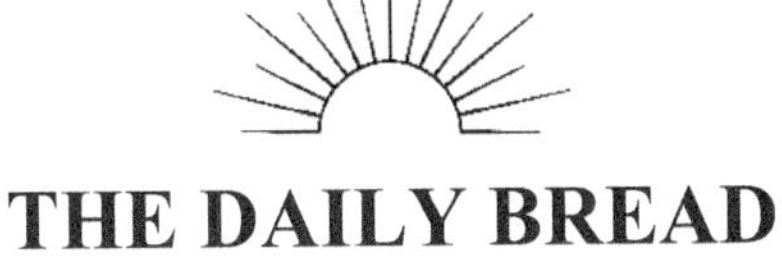

# THE DAILY BREAD

Do not miss your blessings. "And the servant ran to meet her, and said, let me, I pray thee, drink a little water of thy pitcher. And she said, Drink, my lord: and she hasted, and let down her pitcher upon her hand, and gave him drink. And when she had done giving him drink, she said, I will draw water for thy camels also, until they have done drinking. And she hasted, and emptied her pitcher into the trough, and ran again unto the well to draw water, and drew for all his camels. And the man wondering at her held his peace, to wit whether the LORD had made his journey prosperous or not". And it came to pass, as the camels had done drinking, that the man took a golden earring of half a shekel weight, and two bracelets for her hands of ten shekels weight of gold" (Genesis 24:17-22) Water the camels. Most people they miss it. They want the crown without the cross. Why should I do it for him or her? Am I the only one? I have a life to live. This morning I urge go an extra mile. Do not be limited. I do not need anyone. We miss our blessings by not going out of our way, by not having a serving heart, by being busy and selfishness. It's not always about making profit or reasoning Jesu said, "But he who is greatest among you shall be your servant. Whoever exalts himself shall be humbled, and whoever humbles himself shall be exalted. " (Mathew 23:11-12) . It might not make sense now, but God will make a way in your life. The word of God says, "For whoever desires to save his life will lose it, but whoever loses his life for My sake and the gospel's will save it."(Mark 8:35) You reap what you sow. God is love. Look at the people the way how God will look at them. If you can love the unlovable you will be maturing in Christ. Do not live life for your own. Do acts of kindness. The word of God says, "But this I say: He who sows sparingly will also reap sparingly, and he who sows bountifully will also reap bountifully." (2 Corinthians 9:6) . Why don't you expect God to go extra mile for you whilst you don't go extra mile for anybody, and you don't serve in Church. It's always about me and no one else. We need to come down our high horses and have a servant heart. Easy come and easy go. We need to roll our sleeves and get the work done. When we take care of God's house, he will take care of our homes. God bless you.


**Prayer**

Thank you, Lord, for blessing us, when the Kairos moment comes let us not miss it. When you bless others don't forget to pass by us too. Each day we live Lord it's a testimony of your goodness. We pray that when we hear the word, we shall not harden our hearts. Let your word be thy light upon our path, and thy lamp upon thy feet. As your word says, "But he who is greatest among you shall be your servant," we pray that we should have a servant heart. We shall never grow weary of doing good because in due season we shall be blessed if we faint not. Amen.


**The bible verses to study.**

Genesis 24:17-22; Mathew 23:11-12; Mark 8:35; 2 Corinthians 9:6; Mark 9:35; Luke 22:26

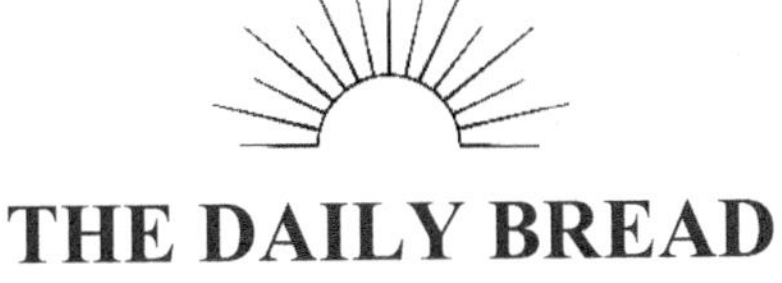

# THE DAILY BREAD

Don't Let Bar-Jesus Spoil Your Plans ......You may be a prudent Christian, Bible believing and tongue speaking, and you cannot be easily waylaid by demons, but there is a Bar-Jesus (bad habit) who has wormed his way into your life without you noticing it. You don't compromise on ANY of your principles, and you are resolute when it comes to righteousness, but there is this sinister habit that is threatening your integrity. The Bible says at Paphos, there was "a Jewish wizard who had WORKED himself into the CONFIDENCE of the governor, Sergius Paulus, AN INTELLIGENT MAN not easily taken in (SWINDLED) by charlatans. The wizard's name was Bar-Jesus. He was as crooked as a corkscrew. (He is) trying to divert (you) from (realising that you are losing (the plot)." (Acts 13:10-9) You obviously have not realised how this dark cloud has crept into your life, but it has. You are now quick to offer bribes, commit adultery, steal, lie, gossip, hate or speak obscenities. You are slowly adopting an evil demeanour that is spoiling your potential! But it is time you wake up and stop this Bar-Jesus from spoiling your future . It is not the water outside the boat that sinks the boat, but the water that is allowed inside the boat. The word of God says, Therefore, since we are surrounded by such a great cloud of witnesses, let us throw off everything that hinders and the sin that so easily entangles. And let us run with perseverance the race marked out for us, "(Hebrew 12:1) God bless you.

**Prayer**

Deliver us from evil O Lord. Cover us with your blood of Jesus O Lord . Your word says, He who dwells in the secret place of the Most High Shall abide under the shadow of the Almighty. I will say of the LORD, "He is my refuge and my fortress; My God, in Him I will trust." Surely, He shall deliver me from the snare of the fowler And from the perilous pestilence." We pray that we shall never lower our standards. We pray that your book shall not depart from our mouths, and we shall meditate on it day and night so then we will live a blessed life. We shall not be conformed to the pattern of the world, but we will be renewed by your word to prove the pleasing, perfect will of God. The devil does not have power over us, we are more than a conquerors through him who gives us strength. Amen


**The bible verses to study.**

Acts 13:10-9; Psalms 91:1-2; Hebrews 12:1; Romans 13:12; 1 Corinthians 9:24; Ephesians 4:22; Ephesians 4:25

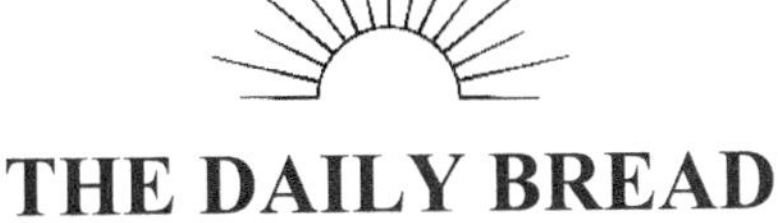

# THE DAILY BREAD

What happens when your name is mentioned? (Job 1:1) says "There was a man in the land of Uz, whose name was Job; and that man was blameless and upright, and one who feared God and shunned evil" The word gives us a summary of who was Job. When we say your name to people who you live with what will they say, when we say your name to your wife and kids what will they say; when we say your name to your employer and work colleagues what will they say and when we say your name to your parents what will they say . Job was upright; He feared God and shunned evil. There was a testimony written about him. The bible mentioned the area where he stayed. Are you faithfully in the area which God has put you? Those people who you meet and live with must have a testimony about you. When we ask them, what will they say? It's high time we should become the light of the world, the salt of world. Another Man of God with a TV ministry said our ministry is not in church but it's out there. In church we come together, to be filled and taught. When we go out there and practice what we have been taught in church that's where our ministry is. We really need to be faithfully in the place where God puts us that is out there. At funeral people they always speak positive about the person who died because we live in a lie. We do not want the truth. But the testimony written about Job challenges me. He was born with flesh like me. But he was known of his righteousness. You are a Christian but out there what does the people say about you. Do you know God? Do you live for God. The reason why people's lives does not change is because they do not know God. Because when you have an encounter with God, you will never remain the same. Saul changed to Paul because he met Jesus, and his life was never the same. What legacy are you leaving when you die. Christianity is not a religion by a way of life. Our lives should preach more than our words. The God we live is more powerful to people than the God we preach. The word of God says, "For as the body without the spirit is dead, so faith without works is dead also." ( James 2:26). God bless you.

## Prayer

As your word says, " so faith without works is dead," we shall practise what we preach. Help us to shun away evil like Job. Thank you for saving our lives Lord Jesus, we were dead in our sins. We were condemned without future then Lord Jesus, you died for us. Your blood Lord Jesus, it speaks better than the blood of the goats, than the blood of Abel. Your grace is sufficient for us . Whilst were sinners Jesus Christ you died for us. Thank you for dying for us because you gave life and hope. The life we are living now is not our own but it's because you died for us. We cannot seize to thank you Lord. Amen

## The bible verses.

Job 1:1; James 2:26; James 5:11; Genesis 6:19; Genesis 17:1; Job 1:8; Proverbs 21:21; Romans 2:6; Mathew 6:22; Psalms 37:5-6

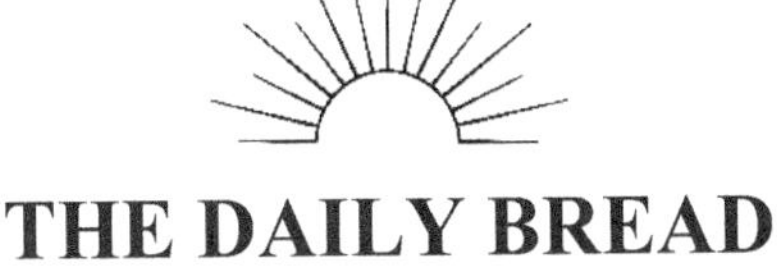

# THE DAILY BREAD

It is inadvisable to remove the foot from the pedal in our Christianity way. We should continue to be hungry for things of God and keep pursuing him because there is no ceiling. The beloved, we need to press on like Paul, do not let anything or anyone come between us and God. The moment you remove your eyes on God, you may regress and fall back into sin. Paul said "Not that I have already obtained all this, or have already arrived at my goal, but I press on to take hold of that for which Christ Jesus took hold of me. Brothers and sisters, I do not consider myself yet to have taken hold of it. But one thing I do: Forgetting what is behind and straining toward what is ahead, I press on toward the goal to win the prize for which God has called me heavenward in Christ Jesus."( Philippians 3:12-14) We are in a spiritual welfare. Thus, why Paul said put on the full armour of God. The devil is roaring like a lion seeking whom he might devour. But our weapons are not carnal but mighty to pull down the strongholds. An idle mind is a devil's playground. David was a man after God's heart. He was a powerful man of God. As usually he was supposed to go to war amen, but he did not. He was resting. We all know that David when he was idle, he committed adultery and killed Uriah the husband of the Bathsheba. The word of God says neither give the place to the devil (Ephesians 4:27). When we think we have done so much for God and want to take a break that's when the devil strikes. They were certain times I took off days in the spirit, I paid dearly, and I had to lose something. Stay in Goshen, out there, there is destruction. I now know how it is important to stay in the presence of God always. The way we learn in life is through our mistakes. But as long as we allow a lot of off days in the spirit, we will make a lot of mistakes. We will pay dearly for those. We need God to lead us and guide us. God told Joshua not let the book of law depart from his mouth and meditate on it day and night and He will make his ways prosperous. God created the heavens and earth. He is the Alpha and Omega. We need to totally surrender our lives to God and live for God. God is faithfully. God bless you.

**Prayer**

Thank you, Lord, for the gift of life. We pray that we shall be full of the Holy Spirit rather than wine. We will offer our bodies as a living sacrifice, Holy and acceptable to God that's a reasonable service. Your word says, "Unless the Lord builds a house those who builds it labours in vain, unless the Lord watched over the city, those who watches over it watches in vain." In everything we do O Lord, Let us start with you Lord and end with you. You are the Alpha and the Omega, the author and the finisher of our faith. Let us live for you Lord and forsake all the ways of darkness. You anoint our heads with oil, our cups are running over and surely goodness and mercy shall follow us all the days of our lives. We shall never give a place to the devil in our lives. Amen

**The bible verses to study**

Philippians 3:12-14; Proverbs 8:17; Hebrews 11:6; 1 Chronicles 16:11; 2 Chronicles 15:2: Amos 5:4-5; Psalms 37:4; Psalms 34:4

# THE DAILY BREAD

I choose glorify God. There is no use to complain, just to wake up every morning it's a miracle. Do you know what will be happening when you are sleeping? The children of Israel complained and cried to God every time when they faced a challenge on their way to the Promised Land. What do you do when you face a disappointment, what will you do if you lose your job, what will you do if you fall sick and what will you do if you go to prison? Will you still praise God when you know you do not have money to pay rent, will you still praise God when the doctors tell you have cancer, do you still praise God when do not have food to eat. When the children of Israel faced the Red sea, they complained and cried to God, when they arrived in Marah where there is bitter water they complained and cried to God. They complained and cried to God because they were too fleshy and did not have faith in God. They did not know God. Job when he lost everything, he tore his robe and worshiped God. Even his wife said curse God and die. Are you facing a challenge amen, do not complain keeping praising God? If complaining is the way you face challenges in life, you need the Holy Spirit to work on you. Do not become a victim of circumstances. Joseph was tried and tested he never complained to God. He was sold by his own brothers to slavery and as his life was prospering, he was accused of rape. Joseph did not change his attitude and joy of life. His circumstances never made him bitter. God is good no matter where you are in life. Keep praising God, God is faithfully, nothing is too hard with God. God said I will never leave you nor forsake you. No matter what comes my way, I will keep praising God. It's your choice to be bitter or have joy in your life. There is no way a Holy Spirit filled Christian who lives a grumpy life, if you live a grumpy life go and get filled again with the Spirit. " Then he said to them, "Go your way, eat the fat, drink the sweet, and send portions to those for whom nothing is prepared; for this day is holy to our Lord. Do not sorrow, for the joy of the LORD is your strength." (Nehemiah 8:10) . Pure joy does not come from things outside you but come from things inside of you. Jesus managed to sleep in storm because what was inside him. Jesus said, "Peace I leave with you; my peace I give you. I do not give to you as the world gives. Do not let your hearts be troubled and do not be afraid." (John 14:27) God bless you.


**Prayer**

We glorify you God today; you are the Alpha and the Omega. Without you Lord, nothing was made. You are high and lifted up. There is no one like you Lord Jesus. Before this world was made, you were there. Everything in this world was created by you. Lord, you make the sun to come out and set the sun. Lord you are the one who brings early rain and latter rain. You are a wonder working God, you are a miracle making God and a great God. You are Jehovah Jireh, you are Jehovah Al Shaddai, you are Jehovah Nissi, you are Jehovah Shalom. You are all powerful and is there anything too difficult with you Lord. You are ever shinning my Lord. Amen.


**The bible verses to study**

Nehemiah 8:10; John 14:27; 1 Corinthians 6:19-20; Genesis 37; Job 1; 2 Samuel 12:19-2

# THE DAILY BREAD

Its high time. No more procrastinating, like I will give my life to Jesus completely when I get a job, when I am married, when I finish school, when my finances are fine and next year." Then He said to another, follow me." But he said," lord let me first go and bury my father ". Jesus said to him "Let the dead bury their own dead, but you go and preach the kingdom" (Luke 9:59-60) Do you know the devil is robbing you your youthful years to serve God. The devil is happy as long as we are prayerless Christians, powerless Christians and no growth in our lives. God is spirit, and his worshipers must worship in the Spirit and in truth. "So, we are lying if we say we have fellowship with God but go on living in spiritual darkness; we are not practicing the truth. (1John 1:6) So many Christians have become like movie actors, there is no reality in their lives. When they came to church, they will be acting. They have become used things of God. We need to pray familiarity spirit out of the Church. They are like whitewashed tombs stones inside them have skeletons. People treat church like to getting high because they do not change their lives. Time is going and you are still at one place. People in the world are laughing at us and say look at them if this is how it means to be a Christian, I will never aspire to be one. Jesus told the woman caught in adultery to say go and do not sin anymore. "When the unclean spirit has gone out of a person, it passes through waterless places seeking rest, and finding none it says, 'I will return to my house from which I came.' And when it comes, it finds the house swept and put in order. Then it goes and brings seven other spirits eviller than itself, and they enter and dwell there. And the last state of that person is worse than the first." (Luke 11:24-26). Do not be an empty house. Let Jesus be the owner house (body and soul). "See then that you walk circumspectly, not as fools redeeming the time, because the days are evil. Therefore, do not be unwise, but understand what the will of the Lord is " (Ephesians 5:15-17). How many times have we lived in our own, trusting on our flesh but we got burned? Today let God be the Lord of your life. Do not resist let it go. You will have peace and joy in your life. Its high time you must be serious about things of God and live a life of prayer. Its either you serve God or the god of this world. Its either you are in the things of God, or you are not. No one can serve two masters. God bless you.


## Prayer

Today we pray that we let God be God in our lives. Let us not procrastinate in giving our lives completely to you God. We pray that we give away our lives to you so that we can gain them. You said in your word if we are willing and obedient, we shall eat the good of the land. Let us forsake the worldly life and pursue after the life of righteousness . We shall never serve two masters; we shall serve only the Living God. Let us be able to dedicate our lives to you. We shall empty ourselves so that you can fill us with you. You are our everything Lord. We have decided to follow Jesus no turning back. Your Lord says, "Delight yourself also in the LORD, And He shall give you the desires of your heart." Amen


## The bible verses to study

Luke 9:59-60; 1 John 1:6; Luke 11:24-26; Ephesians 5:15-17; Mathew 6:33: Mathew 13:44-46, Mathew 3:2

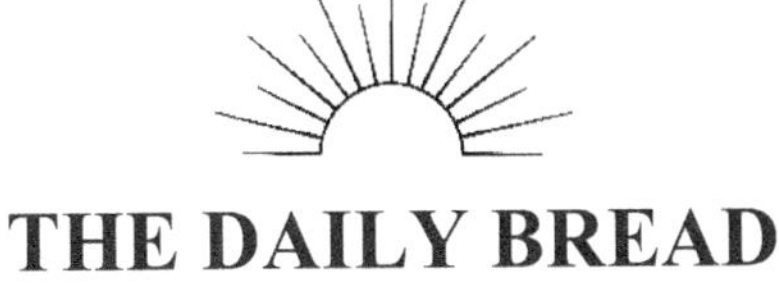

# THE DAILY BREAD

Avoid Having a Demon as an Amour Bearer.........Not all publicity is good publicity. Do not allow yourself to be constantly introduced by a demon. Indeed, demons know you and your capabilities, but their intentions for giving you a resounding introduction are so that you develop pride. A demon will tell people about you and your strength more than the God you represent. The Bible says Paul was annoyed by such a demon when they" .... were met by a female slave who had a spirit by which she predicted the future.... fortune-telling...She followed Paul .... shouting, "These men are servants of the Highest God..." (Acts 16:16-18) Do not give demons a microphone to speak. Yes, they may be telling the truth at that time, but they are interested in making mileage using you. If you entertain them, you are tacitly endorsing them by allowing them to speak in your support and ultimately giving you glory instead of God. The cheering of demons' sows' seeds of pride in you, so avoid making a demon your amour bearer. God bless you.

**Prayer**

Blessed is the man who walks not in the counsel of ungodly, nor walk in the paths of the unrighteous, nor sit in the seat of the unrighteous. He delights himself in the law of the Lord and in his law, he meditates day and night. He shall be like a tree planted by the rivers of the water. That brings forth its fruit in its season and whose leaves shall not wither and whatever he does shall prosper. The ungodly are not so, they are like the chaff which the wind drives away therefore the ungodly shall not stand in the judgment day nor sinners in the congregations of the righteous. Amen

**The bible verses to study.**

Acts 16:16-18; Mark 1:25;26;34; Acts 3:6; Ephesians 4:27; Psalms 1; James 4:7

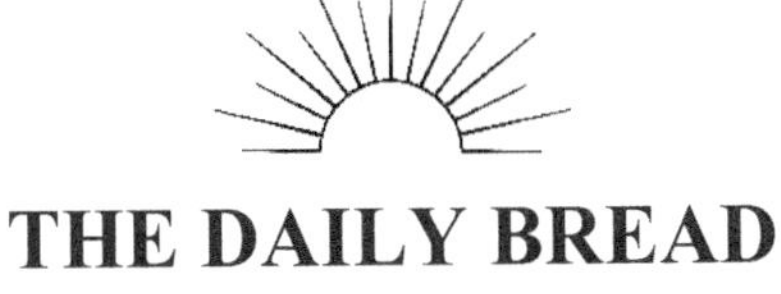

# THE DAILY BREAD

The Other Prisoners Are listening.... Have you ever considered the impact that your words have on the lives of other people? You may not appreciate it, but there are people who are oppressed and are looking up to you as a person of faith. They look at you as a role model, expecting to be encouraged. Yes, you may be in a precarious and painful position, you may think you are at your lowest, but you are still a role model. God designed you to be a beacon of hope and a city built on a hill. Your faith is supposed to help uplift not only you, but also a lot of other people who are in bondage. Be strong, for yourself as well as for those who look up to you. The Bible says, ".... at midnight Paul and Silas were Praying and SINGING HYMNS to God, and THE PRISONERS were LISTENING to them." (Acts 16:25) Many people are in spiritual, physical, emotional, financial or health related bondage and you may seem to be in the same predicament with them, but you are exceptional. You are beyond ordinary. It is time for you to stop feeling sorry for yourself and be a pillar of strength for someone else. Arise, sing hymns, worship God, and pray. God bless you.


**Prayer**

We pray that we live a life that points out that there is a God in heaven. Let us be a living epistle, a living bible that others can read and find Jesus in their lives. We will not be conformed to the pattern of this world but be renewed by the word of God to prove what is pleasing, perfect, good will of God. You make us walk in the path of righteousness for your name sake. Yea, though we walk through the valley of the shadow of death, we will fear no evil; For You are with us. The joy of the Lord is our strength. We shall bring light to those who are still sitting in the darkness because we are the light. Your grace is sufficient for us. Amen.

**The bible verses to study.**

Acts 16:25; Ephesians 5:20; 2 Corinthians 4:8-9; Psalms 34; Psalms 57:5; John 16:32-33: Romans 8:28

# THE DAILY BREAD

God is love. Sometimes the gospel we preach to you its solid stuff. We know most the people who come to church are broken hearted; they really need God in their life. They are dealing with stuff. Paul said, when I was child I spoke like a child, understood like a child, I thought like a child; but when I became a man, I put away childish things. (1 Corinthians 13:11) I pray that you grow from childish to be a man. And Jesus grew in wisdom and stature, and in favour with God and man. (Luke 2:52). As long as you are attending church do not lose hope. Keeping coming, God wants you as you are. Do your part and leave the rest to God. I pray that when you come to church, you meet the Jesus the Messiah. The presence of God will change you. The Holy Spirit is already working in you. You might not see the change but being confident of this, that he who began a good work in you will carry it on to completion until the day of Christ Jesus.( Philippians 1:6) Do not mind about the disappointments, as long as you do not look down, you keep your focus on Jesus you will never sink . It's a journey, the Holy Spirit will teach you and comfort you. Develop a hunger for God. Press on. But without faith it is impossible to please him: for he that comes to God must believe that he is, and that he is a rewarder of them that diligently seek him. (Hebrews 11:6) The body of Christ does not condemn people; the grace of our Lord Jesus Christ is sufficient. God loves you. Nothing can separate you from the love God. You are precious to God. This morning just develop the love for God. "And we know that all things work together for good to them that love God, to them who are the called according to his purpose". (Romans 8:28) God bless you.

**Prayer**

Thank you, O God, for saving us. God you are love. Help us grow to become a man and leave away all my childish ways. We shall dwell in the house of the Lord forever. The Holy Spirit is teaching and changing us. The same Spirit that raised Jesus Christ from the dead, dwells in us and it shall quicken our mortal bodies. You said in your word the just shall live by faith. We shall live a life full of faith. Nothing will ever separate us from the love of God. Our faith shall never fail. God you are faithful. Before we were formed in our mothers' wombs you knew us, you set us apart and called us to be your prophets. If God is for us, who can be against us. All things are working together for the good for us. Amen

**The bible verses to study.**

1 Corinthians 13:11; Luke 2:52; John3:16; 1 Samual 3:7; 1 Corinthians 13:10; 1 Corinthians 3:1;2 Ecclesiastes 11:10.

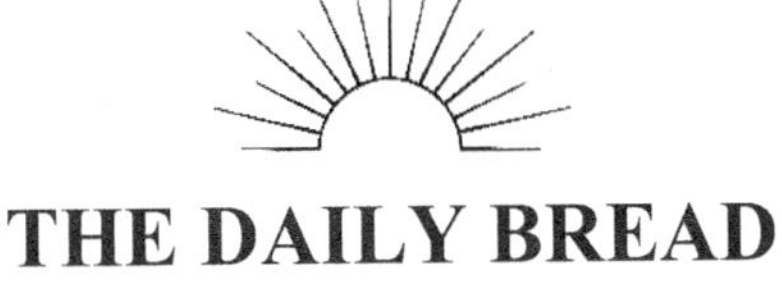

# THE DAILY BREAD

Stay in the presence of God. When I was standing in the park when the word was being preached on Monday, it started to rain. I went under an umbrella. God gave me a word that He is my umbrella. He is covering me like the umbrella. The moment I steps out, I will get rained. Psalms 91:1 says He that dwells in the secret place of the Most high shall abide under the shadow of the almighty. Psalms 91:4 says, "He shall cover me with His feathers and under His wings shall I trust .........." We are like fish in water. God is the one who sustains our lives so as the water to the fish. When you take the fish out of the water it dies. In the absence of God's presence, we suffer a spiritual death. The moment we move away from God, we will be in want like the prodigal son. We become like pigs and eat pig's food. Sin takes us away from fellowship from God. We must strive to live a righteous life. The word of God in Philippians 2:12 says" Therefore, my dear friends, as you have always obeyed--not only in my presence, but now much more in my absence--continue to work out your salvation with fear and trembling," David knew how it means to be in the presence of God when he said in (Psalms 51:11) Cast me not away from thy presence; and take not thy holy spirit from me. David said the Lord is my Shepherd and I shall not want, who is your Shepherd this morning. This morning pray that you will always stay in the presence of God. God bless you.


**Prayer**

Thank you, Lord, for this great life you have given us. . No matter what happens Lord, please do not ever take your presence away from us. If you do not go with us Lord, do not let us go. Your word says, " For a day in thy courts is better than a thousand. I had rather be a doorkeeper in the house of my God, than to dwell in tents of the wicked." Your word says, " The Lord is my Shepherd, I shall not want". In your presence there is healing Lord, there is joy, there is fulfilment, there are breakthroughs and there are miracles. Thank you, Lord, for your presence in our lives. Your word says, " . Unless the LORD builds the house, They labour in vain who build it; Unless the LORD guards the city, The watchman stays awake in vain." In your presence, we are content . Amen

**The bible verses to study**

Psalms 127:1; Philippians 2:12; Psalms 91:1; Psalms 97:4; Psalms 95:2; Exodus 33:14-15; Isaiah 41:10; Psalms 23:4

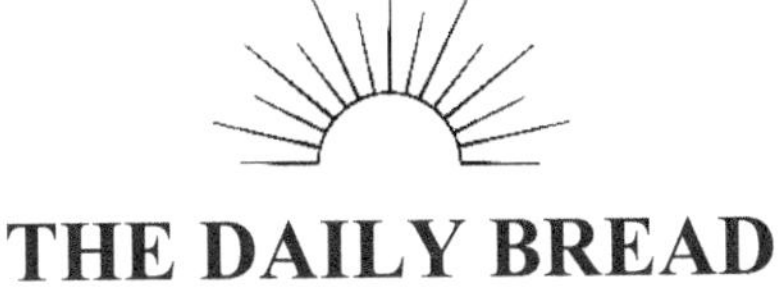

# THE DAILY BREAD

Flash back. I have so many times which God touched my life. This testimony still really challenges me. I was going to college. I was attending lectures in the evening (doing part time). I wanted to look for an attachment, but the predicament was that at lunch time I was supposed to pick a child from school. I was going to Anglican Church those days. I was having my powerful quiet times with God. I could share a word to people who I met in streets. My relationship with God was really great. The Holy Spirit was working so much in my life. I prayed to God and asked to let my sister to say I must not go and pick him up. The child could come back alone. I fasted for one day. If I had asked my sister, I know maybe she might say no. But that day when I was fasting, when my sister came and sat in the sitting room and said I will not be going to pick the child anymore. I did not speak to her about that, but it was God who made her to say that. God came through for me even before I finished fasting. God is faithfully. Have faith. Have a relationship with God. The reason why my brother or a friend can ask me for money is that we have a relationship. Because of the relationship we can do anything for those who we love. Jesus loved Lazarus and he raised him from the dead. God loves us you. You need to have a fellowship with him. "Take a delight in the things of God, He will give you the desires of your heart" (Psalms 37:4). The next day, I went and prepared my CV. I got the internship I was looking for the same day. God is faithful. God bless you.

**Prayer**

Thank you, Lord, for giving us the best life. They were times when we were down but Lord, you picked us up, they are time when we had lost everything but Lord, you restored us, they were times when we could not see but you opened our eyes Lord, they were times when we were broken but Lord you restored our souls and they were times when we fell but Lord, you lifted us up . They are times when people had thrown stones against us and also they were times when people had buried us but God, you gave us a second chance. You heard our prayers in the bell of the fish like Jonah. God, you have not given up hope on us. Thank you, Lord, for giving us million chances. Lord, you took away our shame and clothed us with glory. Praise God, you are faithful Lord Jesus. Amen


**The bible verses.**

Psalms 37:4; Galatians 6:9; Revelations 12:11;Psalms 66:16; 2 Tomothy 1:8; Revelation 6:9; John 8:17-18; 2 Timothy 1:8; 1 John 5:11

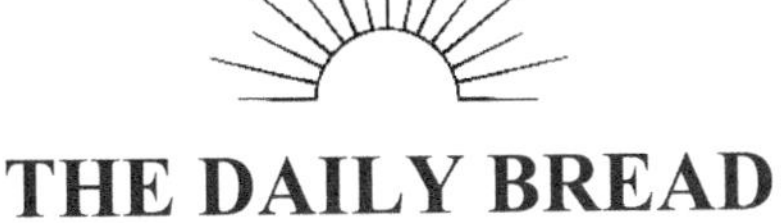

# THE DAILY BREAD

Have You Received the Holy Spirit Since You Believed....Have you ever gone to school and studied, but did not get a certificate to prove that you have gone to school? The certificate is the seal of your education and the solid proof that you have been trained. You may be confident in your training, but the certificate gives you power to claim that you know. Whilst in Ephesus Paul asked some DISCIPLES, "Did you receive the Holy Spirit when you believed?" So, they said to him, "We have not so much as heard whether there is a Holy Spirit." (Acts 19:2 NKJV) Maybe you have believed for real, but you are like a graduate without a certificate. You are tossed about by the devil as if you are a non-believer. You may be wondering what you are doing wrong because you have tried to be as upright as any Saint could be. But your answer may be simple. As Jesus said, "... you shall receive POWER when the Holy Spirit has come upon you." (Acts 1:8 NKJV) Indeed, a believer without the Holy Spirit is like a graduate without a certificate, a gun without bullets! So, have you received the Holy Spirit since you believed? God bless you.

**Prayer**

Thank you, Lord, for the gift of the Holy Spirit. Holy Spirt prays for us with groaning when we cannot even pray for ourselves. The Holy Spirt you are our comforter, our teacher and our Leader. The same Spirit that raised Jesus Christ from the dead dwells in us and it shall quicken our mortal bodies. Fill us up O Lord with your Spirit until we overflow, we want to run over. Your words says, "Those who are led by the Spirit of God Lord, are the children of God." We shall never be filled by the wine to the excess but by the Holy Spirit. Sprit of God lead us to a place where my trust is without borders. Amen.

**The bible verses to study.**

Acts 19:2; Acts 1:8; Ephesians 5:18; Acts 2:4; Acts 4:31; Acts 4:8; John 6:63; 1 Corinthians 6:19; 1 Thessalonians 5:19

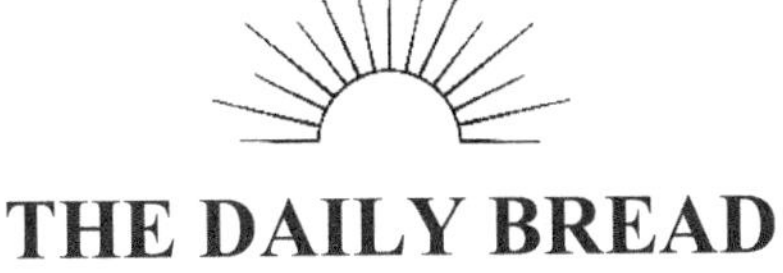

# THE DAILY BREAD

Who is chasing after you? The children of Israel lived in bondage; God hit the Egyptians with plagues. Finally, Pharaoh agreed to let them go. When they were facing the red sea, the Egyptian came against them with a great army with horses and chariots. The Egyptians had sophisticated weapons, highly trained and horses. On other side the Israel had God. Through the natural eyes, they were like the grasshoppers, light weights but in the spirit, they were very powerful because God was with them. Maybe the situations and circumstances have stolen much from you but after you have received your victory, the enemy is still chasing after you. There is no need for you to weep and be in fear, call upon the name of the Lord. The enemy is reminding you how sick, poor and how useless you are. "Therefore, if any man be in Christ, he is a new creature: old things are passed away; behold, all things are become new". (2 Corinthians 5:17). The Egyptians perished in the red sea, but the Israelites walked on the dry land. "That at the name of Jesus every knee should bow, of things in heaven, and things in earth, and things under the earth ". (Philippians 2:10). I urge you not to look at what you have, education and where you come from, with God nothing is impossible. Stop confessing how big your problems are, start telling your problems how big your God is. There is a favour of God upon your life. You are guaranteed for success. Do not concentrate on what is the enemy doing but focus on God. God bless you.


**Prayer**

Thank you, Lord, let us focus on you alone not the chaos around us. It may rain today but the sunshine will come tomorrow. We pray against all the negative spirits in our lives, we pray against the spirit of giving up, we pray against the spirit of poverty, and we pray against the spirit of death. A thief comes not unless it is to steal, kill and destroy but you Lord, you came to give us life more abundantly. We pray that the devil will give us back all what he has stolen from us. The Lord will restore to us according to prophet Joel, all the years the locust has eaten, the cankerworm, and the caterpillar, and the palmerworm, your great army which is among us. The favour of God is in our lives. We are blessed. The grace of God is upon our life. God you are faithful. Amen.

**The bible verses to study.**

Exodus 14:13; 2 Corinthians 5:17; Philippians 2:10; Romans 8:37; 1 Corinthians 15:57; 2 Chronicles 20:25-27

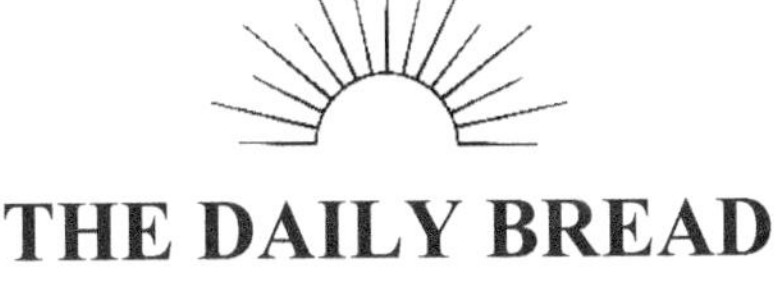

# THE DAILY BREAD

Step up. This morning I am speaking to you all who have been called by God that it's high time you must step up. The first thing we must do is not to fear suffering. Jesus left the throne when he knew definitely, he was going to suffer many things, and people were going to reject him, accuse him and crucify him. Jesus stepped up. If you humble yourself, God will lift you up. What is holding you back to walk with God? People do not want to suffer. Jesus spent 40 days and 40 nights fasting in the wilderness before he started his ministry. The four lepers who were not permitted to enter in into the city because of their sickness they had nothing to lose. "If we say, we will enter into the city, then the famine is in the city, and we shall die there: and if we sit still here, we die also. Now therefore come and let us fall unto the host of the Syrians: if they save us alive, we shall live; and if they kill us, we shall but die." (2 Kings 7:4). They entered into the city against all odds. They went into the camp of the Syrians, and no one was there. God made the sound of the four walking lepers to be of a great army. When they entered into the uttermost of the camp, they ate, drink and they was gold raiment, and they went and hid it. The lepers were not afraid of death. If you want to be successful amen, if you are working you need to study. For a woman to have a child, she needs to have nine months of pregnancy. For you to harvest you need to sow first. When God give you a dream, he will provide for it. Do not be comfortable with where you are. Take a giant leap of faith. Everyone have a potential to be successful before you die. All what you need God have already given to you. Are you ready to step out of you boat? God shows up when we are in an uncomfortable position. I know you can make it because with God nothing is impossible. God bless you.

**Prayer**

Thank you, Lord, for calling us from darkness into marvellous light. We shall never be comfortable with mediocre life as your word says, "So then, because you are lukewarm, and neither cold nor hot, I will vomit you out of My mouth. Give us strength Lord that we do not follow the world way of doing things, we do not take short cuts, we shall wait on you Lord. Your word says, "Those whose wait on the Lord will renew their strength. They will soar their on wings like eagles, they will run and not grow weary, they will walk and faint not." We know that Lord you have prepared for us, what has not entered in the heart of a man, what the eyes have never seen and what the ears have never heard. Thank you, Lord, for all the blessings. Praise God. Amen

**The bible verses to study.**

2 Kings 7:4; 2 Corinthians 5:7; Proverbs 3:5-6; Ephesians 6:1-24; Psalms 107:26; Proverbs 15:24; Luke 14:10; Isaiah 60:1;

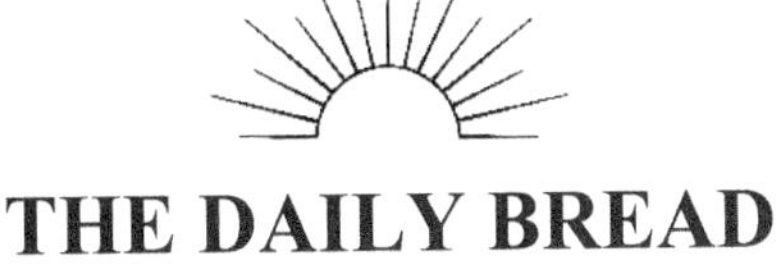

# THE DAILY BREAD

Don't Hold Back What God Has Given You......The greatest evil that has befallen the church is that of great men of God who have personalised the gospel and have convinced themselves that there is no life after them. When God has anointed you or given you a gift, it is for the perfecting of the saints and for the work of the ministry. Like Elijah, you should train an Elisha and like Paul, you should train a myriad of leaders as great as or even greater than you. Like Paul be able to say "You know that from day one of my arrival.... I was with you TOTALLY—laying my life on the line.... I didn't skimp or trim (THE WORD) in any way. Every TRUTH and encouragement that could have MADE A DIFFERENCE to you, you got. I taught you out in public and I taught you in your homes, urging Jews and Greeks alike to a radical life-change before God and an equally radical trust in our Master Jesus." (Acts 20:18-21) How many times have you held back because you want to be remembered as the best there ever will be. Play your part but be FRUITFUL by training others. You are a SEED that should give rise to more of your kind. Don't hold back what God has given you. God bless you.

**Prayer**

Thank you, O Lord, for the life you have given us, we are blessed to be a blessing. Use us O Lord to bring light to those sitting in darkness. Let us not hold back in doing good for in the due season we shall reap the reward if we faint not. We pray that we shall make a disciples of all the nations. Let us continue to abide in you so that we can be fruitful. Open our eyes to see the people as you O Lord. Teach us how to love. Amen

**The bible verses to study**

Acts 20:18-21; John 3:16; Mathew 28:19; 1 Timothy 4:14; Mathew 10:1; Philippians 2:3; Luke 22:26

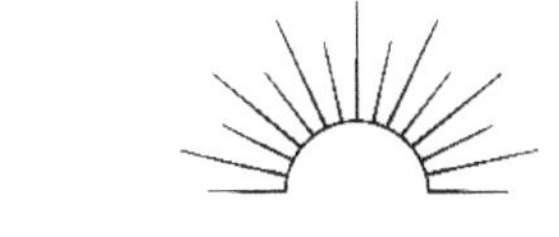

# THE DAILY BREAD

Who is taking away your joy for God? A lot of people have suffered so much due to self-condemnation. The devil has taken your joy. They are treating God as schoolteacher. They are like people walking on a thin ice. The word of God in Ephesians 2:8 says, "For by grace you are saved through faith; and that not of yourselves: it is the gift of God". The devil is an accuser of man, we know him from the days of Job. "If we claim to be without sin, we deceive ourselves and the truth is not in us". (1 John 1:8). We still have Christians living like they are during the old covenant (Old Testament). They are rendering the death of Jesus in vain. The reason why you are still alive, having a job and having a good health is also by the grace of God. They are churches who have chased people away, punished and exposed people (mentioning their names in church for the sin they committed) as sinful people. As the body of Christ, we are there to love, cover and give light so that people so that they can move away from darkness. God is love. Nothing can separate you from the love of God. But God commends his love toward us, in that, while we were yet sinners, Christ died for us. (Romans 5:8). The grace of God will not give you ammunition to sin but strength to not want to sin. Please do not run away from God, come to God and confess your sins and repent. When the devil accuses you, tell him you have been defeated at the cross and the grace of God is sufficient for me. If we fall in sin, we need to quickly repent and confess our sins. Confess your trespasses to one another, and pray for one another, that you may be healed. The effective, fervent prayer of a righteous man avails much. (James 5:16) . If you are struggling with sin do not ran away from Church. Jesus is saying, "Come unto me, all you that labour and are heavy laden, and I will give you rest." ( Mathew 11:28) The devil want to isolate and make you feel condemned. Do not let disappointments drive you out of CHURCH. Like what God told

Zerubbabel "Not by might nor by power, but by my Spirit,' says the LORD Almighty." (Zechariah 4:6). God bless you.


**Prayer**

Thank you, Lord, because whilst we were sinners Christ you died for us. Your grace is sufficient for us. "The Lord is my Shepherd; I shall not want. He makes to lie down on greener pastures and lead me beside still waters. He restores my soul. He leads me in the paths for righteousness for His name sake." Let us shun away evil ways. Nothing can separate us from the love of God . We defeat the devil by the blood of the lamb and the word of our testimony. We shall testify that greater is He that is in us than he than he is in the world, we are blessed, the way we are looking today is not the way we are going to look tomorrow. Your grace is sufficient for us Almighty God. Your word says, "being confident of this very thing, that He who has begun a good work in you will complete it until the day of Jesus Christ;" Amen


**The bible verses to study**

Ephesians 2:8; 1 John 1:8; James 5:16; Mathew 11:28; John 4:10; Acts 15:11; Hebrews 6:4; Jeremiah 31:25; Isaiah 42:22-25

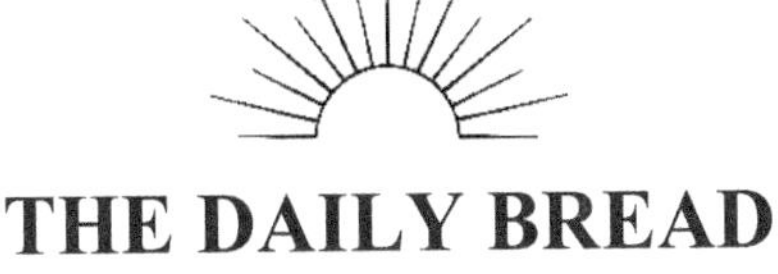

# THE DAILY BREAD

We are in a winning team. When you watch soccer amen, there is a referee. He needs to blow a whistle to end the match. There is always frustration, people wanting for the referee to blow the final whistle and end the match. The game of soccer has 90 minutes and then extra time normally due to injuries and substitutes .During this extra time, you always want the referee to blow the whistle and end the match if you are in a winning team. As the children of God, we have the victory already. The devil was defeated on the cross. Although God has given us the victory, we are still waiting receive some of things promised in the word of God. In the waiting period people get frustrated. We always want everything now. But we do not have the whistle. God has the whistle. He will blow the final whistle when he wants. What we know is that for sure the match is going to end and there is only one result that is a win. For all the promises of God are "Yes" in Christ. And so, through Him, our "Amen" is spoken to the glory of God. (2 Corinthians 1:20) God answers our prayers, and every good gift comes from God. If you are believing God for a marriage, job, car, house, healing and finances and wondering why I have not received yet, my answer is you now nearer than before, you are in extra time and very soon the whistle will be blown, and you will get the result which you want . Isaiah 40:31 says, "But they that wait upon the LORD shall renew their strength; they shall mount up with wings as eagles; they shall run, and not be weary; and they shall walk, and not faint". A tree that takes times to grow bears much fruits. But seek you first the kingdom of God, and his righteousness; and all these things shall be added unto you. (Mathew 6:33) Waiting on Lord involves you actively pursuing God and you walking with God. The word of God says, "The steps of a good man are ordered by the LORD, And He delights in his way". David understood this when He said, The Lord is my shepherd I shall

not want". If God is leading you, you shall never wait in vain."
And we know that all things work together for good to those who
love God, to those who are the called according to His purpose."(
Romans 8:28) God bless you.

**Prayer**

We are more than a conquerors through him who gives us
strength. Christ in us is the hope of glory. The devil was defeated
on the cross. We have power and authority over the enemy. No
weapon formed and fashioned against us shall prosper. Thank
you, Lord, for every good gift and perfect without any shadow
comes from you. Our enemies do not rejoice against us. When
we fall, we shall rise, when we sit in the darkness the Lord shall
be a light upon me. The grace of God is sufficient for us. Your
word says, "But they that wait upon the LORD shall renew their
strength; they shall mount up with wings as eagles; they shall
run, and not be weary; and they shall walk, and not faint" Amen.

**The bible verses to study**

2 Corinthians 1:20; Isaiah 40:31; Mathew 6:33; Romans 8:28;
Philippians 4:13; Deuteronomy 20:4; John 6:33

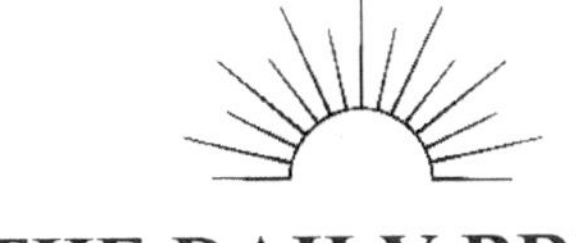

# THE DAILY BREAD

Who you are inside of you can have far reaching on the quality of life you are living? Lot when he was asked to choose where to go, he judged the book by its covers. "And Lot lifted up his eyes, and beheld all the plain of Jordan, that it was well watered everywhere, before the LORD destroyed Sodom and Gomorrah, even as the garden of the LORD, like the land of Egypt, as thou comes unto Zoar."(Genesis13:10) Lot never prayed and consulted with God and even Abraham. The choices people doing alone are making them miss on God's best in their lives. Prayerless life leads to faithless life. People want to be comfortable; they make obvious choices. I challenge you go out of comfort zone. Be obedient to the Holy Spirit. Do not be like a grasshopper by fighting against God's will and lose your legs. Enquire with God who to do business with, who to marry and every life changing decision you need to make. "Trust in the LORD with all thine heart; and lean not unto thine own understanding" (Proverbs 3:5). The steps of a good man are ordered by the LORD, And He delights in his way. God want to direct our footsteps. A committed prayer life helps you not to make decisions that inspired by God. That's why it's necessary to spend more time in the presence of God. If you spend more time in the presence of God, you will not be led by your flesh but by the spirit. The word of God says, "For to be carnally minded is death, but to be spiritually minded is life and peace." (Romans 8:6) . "For as many as are led by the Spirit of God, they are the sons of God." (Romans 8:14) . "For we walk by faith, not by sight."(2 Corinthians 5:7) The life you are living now it's a picture of your faith. God leads us to make informed decisions. It may not look popular now but in future when you look back you can say praise God, I dodged a bullet. The word of God says," There is a way which seems right to a person, But its end is the way of death."(Proverbs 14:12) . The word of God says, "Enter by the narrow gate; for wide is the gate and broad is the way that leads to destruction, and there are many who go in by it." (Mathew 7:13). We do know what will happen in future when making decision that's why we need God's help. Jesus said, "Can the blind lead the blind? Will they not both fall into the ditch?"(Luke 6:39) . As people we are limited, we need God who know everything, the Alpha and the Omega to assist us in making decisions. God bless you.

**Prayer**

We pray that we do not walk by sight but being led by the Holy Spirit. Let us yield to the voice of the Holy Spirit. We know that there is a way that looks right to men but at the end it leads to death. Give us the wisdom Lord to distinguish between evil and good. We pray that Lord, you make your word be thy lamp upon thy feet and be thy light upon thy path. We need your presence God, if you do not go with us, do not let us go. Deliver us O Lord from the evil one. The joy of the Lord is our strength. In our weakness you are strong. Thank you, Lord. Your word says, "Enter by the narrow gate; for wide is the gate and broad is the way that leads to destruction, and there are many who go in by it." Amen

**The bible verses to study.**

Genesis13:10; Proverbs 3:5; Romans 8:6; Romans 8:14; 2 Corinthians 5:7; Proverbs 14:12; Mathew 7:13; Luke 6:39; Proverbs 8:15; Psalms 25:4; Proverbs 4:5

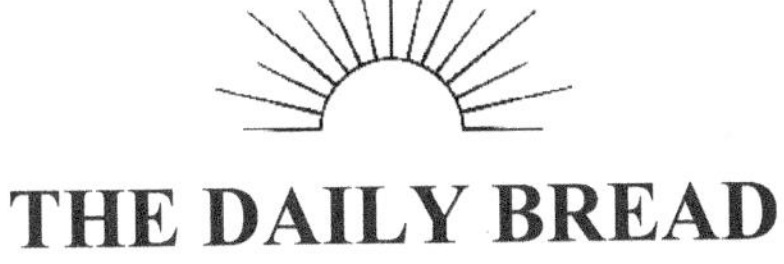

# THE DAILY BREAD

A mountain in your life. "You have made your way around this hill country long enough; now turn north" (Deuteronomy2:3). Is there a mountain in your life? Something you have gone around and around but you seem not to find a solution. You have been around this mountain long enough. Sometimes you can stay too long. Sometimes you can wait too long. Sometimes you can procrastinate too long. Sometimes you can put off doing what you are supposed to do too long. Sometimes you can ignore a situation too long. Sometimes you can hold a grudge too long. Sometimes you can pretend not to see what you know you see too long. Sometimes you can stay stuck too long. Sometimes you can wait, and life gives you a window. God is good but He gives you window that will eventually close. The Bible says for everything there is a season. Seasons do come back around. God will give you another chance, but it may be years before that chance comes again. You can be staying at a house too long because you don't want to move. You can stay on a job too long. You better go when it is time to go. You better move when it is time to move. God said that you have been around this mountain too long. As a result, you have been stagnant. Sometimes you have to press forward regardless. When your disappointment becomes your dwelling place, your heartache becomes your home, your setback becomes your excuse, your detour becomes your destiny, and your place of rest to take a break becomes your permanent dwelling place, you have been around that mountain too long. There comes a point where you need to lift up your head, stop complaining, and trust God. For instance, a woman will blame her weight gain on having a baby, but the baby is 21-year-old. That excuse is old now. She has been around that mountain too long. Your fortune is in the hand of God. He has the whole world in His hands. You can always make excuses. Can you name your own mountain?

Your mountain is the thing you keep circling around and coming back to. Moses told the people that their disobedience had held them back, but God had still been merciful towards them. Even in your mess, God can still be good to you. You are comfortable but you are lost. You are safe but you are not at home. We belong at the Promise Land not at Mount Horeb. God bless you.


**Prayer**

Thank you, Lord, for the grace you have given us. We refuse to be poor, to be sick, to be unemployed, to be without a car or house, to be not married and to be uneducated. The way we are today is not the way we are going to be tomorrow. Jesus Christ, you were made poor so that I can be rich. Poverty, sickness and bareness were defeated on the cross. The hand of the Lord is strong in our lives. We are walking in power; we are walking in miracles, and we live a life of favour. He who has begun a good work in us shall continue until Lord Jesus comes. We are blessed and we will no longer settle for less. We shall fight a good fight of faith and complete our race. Amen


**The bible verses to study.**

Deuteronomy2:3; John 5:1-18; Numbers 20:15; Joshua 24:7; Hosea 3:3

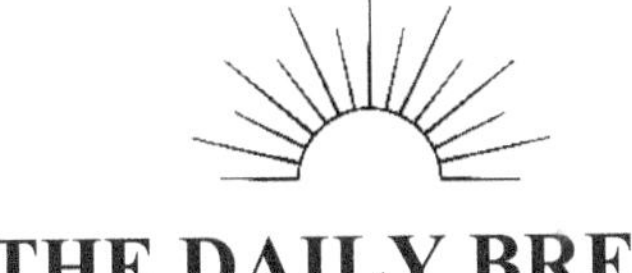

# THE DAILY BREAD

The world is full but foolish. "Because, although they did not glorify Him as God, nor were thankful, but became futile in their thoughts and their foolish hearts were darkened. Professing to be wise, they become fools and changed the glory of the incorruptible God into an image made like corruptible man-birds and four-footed animals and creeping things. Therefore, God also gave them up to uncleanness, in the lusts of their hearts, to dishonour their bodies among themselves, who changed the truth of God for a lie, and worshiped and served the creature rather than the Creator, who is blessed forever. Amen." ( Romans 1:21-25) I remember on Friday brother Olwen said "God said let there be light and saw that the light was good. God separated the light from darkness. There was a separation of light and darkness. "If we claim to have fellowship with him and yet walk in the darkness, we lie and do not live out the truth". (1 Joh 1:6) In your life there must be a total separation. Abraham was separated by God, he left his land of birth, Joseph was sold by his bothers, he was separated too. If there is no separation in your life, the world will corrupt you and influence you. There must be a total separation amen. 1 John 2:15 says "Do not love the world or anything in the world. If anyone loves the world, love for the Father is not in them". "What is more, I consider everything a loss because of the surpassing worth of knowing Christ Jesus my Lord, for whose sake I have lost all things. I consider them garbage, that I may gain Christ" (Philippians 3:8). The word of God furthers says, "No one can serve two masters. Either you will hate the one and love the other, or you will be devoted to the one and despise the other. You cannot serve both God and money."(Luke 16:13) God bless you.

**Prayer**

Thank you, Lord, for blessing our lives with a new life . We were lost and now we are found. Whilst we were still a sinners Jesus Christ died for us. You called us from darkness into marvellous light for your greatness. We were dead now we are alive in Christ Jesus . You gave us a life; you gave us a future. Thank you, Lord Jesus, for dying for us. You came so that we can have life more abundantly. All we have is because of you Lord. You are the one who raises the poor from dust and sit them with the Kings. Your grace is sufficient for us. We are blessed to be a blessing. We shall never have fellowship with unfruitful works of darkness. Amen

**The bible verses to study**

Romans 1:21-25; 1 Joh 1:6; 1 John 2:15; Philippians 3:8; Luke 16:13; John 17:15-18; John 19:19; Deuteronomy 14:2; Hebrews 7:26

# THE DAILY BREAD

The Holy Spirit is our teacher. Jesus said, "But the Helper, the Holy Spirit, whom the Father will send in My name, He will teach you all things, and bring to your remembrance all that I said to you."( John 14:26) We do not stop to learn in life. Why do we need to be taught? We need to be taught to gain knowledge. Knowledge is power. The word of God says, " My people are destroyed for lack of knowledge. Because you have rejected knowledge, I also will reject you from being priest for Me; Because you have forgotten the law of your God, I also will forget your children."(Hosea 4:6) If someone told you one plus one is four. If you are mathematically challenged, you will believe that person. You can go telling people who do not know the wrong answer. But when you, really know that one plus one is two nothing will change your mind. What is the Holy Spirit teaching us? The Holy Spirit is teaching us the truth. The word of God says you shall know the truth and only the truth shall set you free. What is the truth? Christ is the truth. Jesus said I am the way the truth and life. The Holy Spirit reveals Christ. Paul was given this revelation. " By which, when you read, you may understand knowledge in the mystery of Christ, which in other ages was made known to the sons of men, as it has now been revealed by the Spirit of God to His holy apostles and prophets "(Ephesians 3:4-5). When we read the word of God, we get revelation of the word through the Holy Spirit. Christ is the word. In the beginning was the word and the word was God, and the word was with God. Christ is the word. When we are out there doing the will of the father, we need the Holy Spirit to lead and guide us. "But you will receive power when the Holy Spirit comes on you; and you will be my witnesses in Jerusalem, and in all Judea and Samaria, and to the ends of the earth." (Acts 1:8) The Holy Spirit gives us revelation of the word of God. We get understanding of the word of God through the Holy Spirit.

It's important that we are filled with the Holy Spirit, and we shall live the life that is pleasing in the eyes of God. God bless you.


**Prayer**

Thank you, Lord, for the gift of the Holy Spirit. Help us Holy Spirit to reveal the hidden treasure in the word of God. Holy Spirit you are our comforter and our teacher. Please Lord, open the eyes of our understanding so that we can know the hope of our calling. Let us meditate on your word day and night so that we can live a blessed life. Renew our minds Heavenly Father through your word. Give us a new heart O Lord that is after you. Deliver us from the evil one O Lord. Let us walk in the paths of righteous because you said in your word if you are willing and obedient, you shall eat the good of the land. Amen.


**The bible verses to study**

John 14:26; Nehemiah 9:20; Mathew 10:19-20; Mark 13:11; Luke 12:12; 1 John 2:27

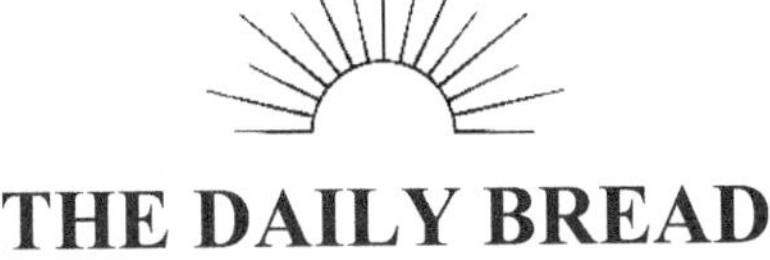

# THE DAILY BREAD

Relationship. We were created to have close relationship with God. Look in the Garden of Eden, Adam had a close relationship with God. The great Man of God like Abraham, Isaac and Jacob they dwelled in the presence of God. I have stayed out of presence and in the presence of God. I know how it feels to be in the presence of God and not. The Holy Spirit always makes us feel His presence upon our life. I feel joy in the spirit sometimes. After helping with the training at Church, I came home singing with joy that day so many people were delivered. When I entered the house, I was singing. To be filled with the Spirit "speaking to one another in psalms and hymns and spiritual songs, singing and making melody in your heart to the Lord ". (Ephesians 5:19) God is not silent. When you have done very wonderful God makes you feel it. When Jesus was baptized, the heavens opened to Him, and He saw the Spirit of God discerning like a dove and alighting upon Him. And suddenly a voice came from heaven, saying, this is my beloved Son, in whom I am pleased. You might not hear the voice in loud; the Holy Spirit inside you will make you know it. When the Seventy returned with joy and gave a good report to Jesus, in that hour Jesus rejoiced in the Spirit. Sometimes there is joy in my spirit, I speak in tongues and sing. When the spirit of God is present, I have noticed that some preachers they become one with the word they preach. You cannot separate them from the word. The word just flows. When this happens, I feel joy in my spirit. When this word is delivered and register in the Spirit in me there is joy, I feel like I want to leap in joy. The preacher will be having the Holy Spirit in him which is also in me. So, there is communication between the Holy Spirit in me and the preacher. Mary visited Elizabeth during their pregnancy. "And it happened, when Elizabeth heard the greeting of Mary, that the babe leaped in her womb; and Elizabeth was filled with the Holy spirit". (Luke 1:41) Mary and

Elizabeth were pregnant and their pregnancy was filled with the Holy Spirit. There was communication between babies and another baby leaped with joy. We have the same Spirit of God. The relationship we have with God need to be kept burning. It should not be one sided amen both parties must do something. You cannot say you love God, but your actions are contrary. You need to sacrifice your time, resources, lifestyle and raise the bar high. This morning I challenge you to have an existent relationship with God not just talking. God bless you.


**Prayers**

Thank you, Lord, for your presence in our lives . Your presence is like a heaven to us. In your presence there is healing, fulfilment, peace, prosperity and miracles. Like David whatever I do O Lord, do not take your presence away from me. Let us put my trust and hope in you so that we do not lean on my understanding. We need your touch O Lord once again. Fill us up again with your Holy Spirit. We need your presence Almighty God, in your presence there is fulness of joy. Amen


**The bible verses to study.**

Ephesians 5:19; Mather 3-13-17; Luke 1:41; Psalms 97:5; Psalms 95:2; Exodus 33:14-15; Psalms 23:4

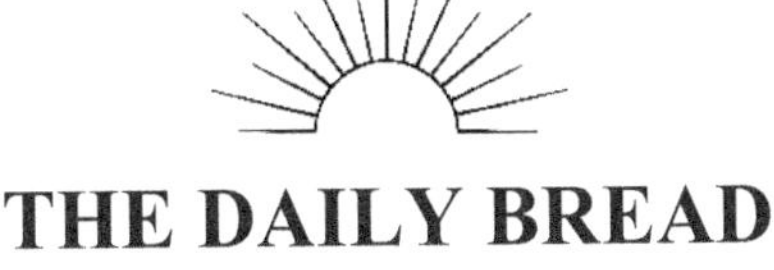

# THE DAILY BREAD

For I am not ashamed of the gospel of Christ: for it is the power of God unto salvation to everyone that believeth; to the Jew first, and also to the Greek. (Romains 1:16). For whosoever shall be ashamed of me and of my words, of him shall the Son of man be ashamed, when he shall come in his own glory, and in his Father's, and of the holy angels. (Luke 9:26) Christians are even ashamed to carry a bible and they do not stand when their faith is being attacked. Brother Olwen, I thank you for highlighting on the issue of negative humility, sometimes we let things slide away, we shy away and think we are being humble. We need to be bold amen, people will take you to a topless bar and you can just go because you are thinking I am showing them respect. Tell the people that it's against what I belief and the people will respect you for what you believe. We cannot be like dead fish which goes where the river flows. Start telling people this is not for me, what does the word of God says. You cannot stop the birds to fly over you, but you can stop them from creating a nest on top of your head. Whatever we compromise for in life, we will lose it . Value your salvation, work on it with fear and trembling. Let's stand for what we believe, and the world will respect us. God bless you.

**Prayer**

Thank you, Lord, for all the blessings, for we are not ashamed of the gospel of Christ, for it is the power of God of salvation to everyone who believes. Jesus you are our everything, You promised us not to leave us nor forsake us. We shall never seize to give praise to you God. Shine your light on us God and open our eyes to see that those who are with us are more than those against us. The grace of our Lord Jesus Christ is upon my life. We shall stand upon the word of truth and shine away evil. We shall never be conformed to the standards of this world, but be transformed by the renewing of our minds, that we may prove what is that good and acceptable and perfect will of God. Amen


**The bible verses to study.**

Romains 1:16: Luke 9:26; Mark 8:38; Romans 2:9; 1 Corinthians 1:18; 2 Timothy 1:8 Psalms 40:9-10;

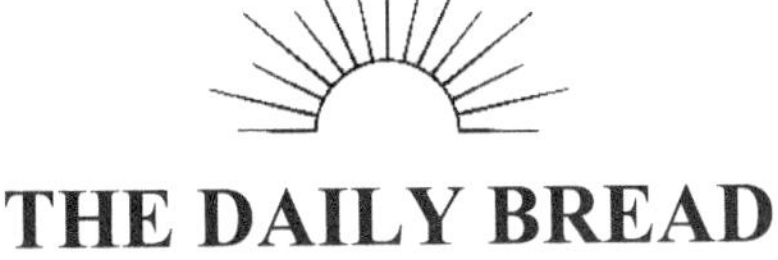

# THE DAILY BREAD

It is wonderful to receive gifts. All of us appreciate gifts especially when we really need them. But many times, we fail to realise that for us to receive, someone should have given. The most appreciated gift is an undeserved gift. It is a gift that comes straight from the heart. Just like, "God so loved the world that He GAVE His ONLY begotten son......" (John 3:16) We didn't deserve it, but we got it all the same. If we didn't deserve what we got from God (grace - unmerited favour), why then would we want to give what we have only to those who deserve? God gave His son Jesus and now He is harvesting sons. Give someone something important and undeserved today and you would have sown something you will always harvest from in future. God bless you.

**Prayer**

Thank you, Lord, for loving us, whilst we were sinners Jesus Christ died for me. We did not deserve it; we did not qualify but Jesus, you qualified us. God you are love. Help us O Lord to live a life of love. Lord, you gave us your Son to die of us, we are forever very grateful and teach us to give the best. We pray that we shall never break the chain, whatever we receive, we shall also freely give. Let us be able to sow in someone else life. Your grace is sufficient for us. We are blessed to be a blessing. We shall never overcome evil with evil but evil with good. In Jesus name, Amen.

**The bible verses to study**

John 3:16; Proverbs 13:4; James 1:17; 2 Corinthians 9:11-13; Acts :1-8; 2 Corinthians 9:7; Acts 20:35; Proverbs 11:25; Luke 6:38

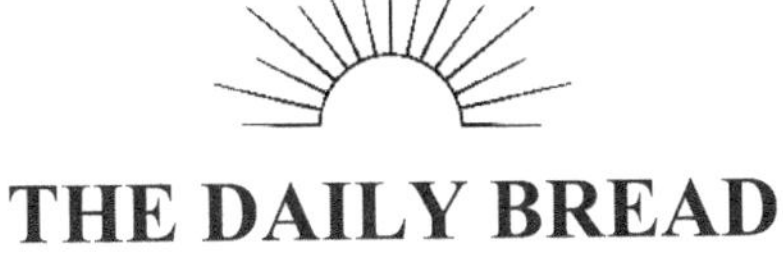

# THE DAILY BREAD

Do not sit on your past victories. I know you achieved so much last year in your spiritual growth and life itself. But this does not call for a time to relax. Challenge yourself this year to do more. On the plans you are making for yourself this year also make some spiritual targets, like if you were not serving in church say I will start serving, if you were serving aspire to be a leader, if you were not fasting make it your priority that you will fast, also if you were not paying tithes let it be your year for you to start paying tithes . Everyone knows their weakness and where the area they need to grow. Step out of boat, out of you comfort zone and experience the miracles of God. Let us not be quantity Christians that we are just numbers but rather be quality Christians who have power to affect our environment. I know with Christ in you, you can bring the light to the world. Step up, rise up and be obedient to voice of the Holy Spirit . You can't live on yesterday's manna; you need fresh anointing that's why Jesus taught us to pray to say give us this day our daily bread. The word of God warned us that, "Be sober, be vigilant; because your adversary the devil walks about like a roaring lion, seeking whom he may devour." ( 1 Peter 5:8) . When we stop to aspire to grow and challenge ourselves further, we become stagnant and backslide. Seeking God should be a daily thing that's why the word of God speaks about carrying the cross daily. We have to grow, anything that does not grow is dead. We need to have more hunger to do great exploits for God. The children of Israel almost settled at a mountain not the promised land. They had victory when God freed them bondage in Egypt, but God did not promise them the mountain but the promised land. The word of God says, "But as it is written: "Eye has not seen, nor ear heard, Nor have entered into the heart of man The things which God has prepared for those who love Him."( 1 Corinthians 2:9). God bless you.

**Prayer**

Thank you, Lord ,for telling us that we have stayed too long in poverty, we have stayed too long unemployed, we have stayed too long sick, and we have stayed too long single now its high time we should move to the life you have promised us. As we are more that conquerors through Jesus who gives us strength, we shall never settle for less. We shall never settle for the past victories. We will never give up on ourselves because God you will never give up on us. We shall continue to fight the good fight of faith and lay hold of the life you promised us. Your word says, "And we know that all things work together for good to those who love God, to those who are the called according to His purpose." Amen

**The bible verses to study.**

Psalms 139:16-17; Jeremiah 29:11-13; Mathew 6:33; 1 Chronicles 16:11; Hebrew 11:6

# THE DAILY BREAD

A letter to the broken heart. Dear broken heart, you have been cheated by, lied to, abused and robbed. "The LORD is near to those who have a broken heart And saves such as have a contrite spirit."(Psalms 34:18) . Just remember that "The thief comes only to steal and kill and destroy; I have come that they may have life and have it to the full." (John10:10). Let this not be an excuse for you not to love again trust again and try again. The world might have shortchanged you. Let not the ugly of the world turn you into a beast. Neither give a place to the devil. (Ephesians 4:27) Never live a bitter life. "But I tell you who hear me: Love your enemies, do good to those who hate you, bless those who curse you, pray for those who mistreat you". (Luke 6:27-28) Please forgive those who trespassed against you because your father in heaven has forgiven your trespasses. There is a song that says, "cast your burdens unto Jesus for He cares for you". All those people who left you amen served for a certain purpose in your life and they were not worth your future. If you lost a source of income amen just know a better one is coming. "But seek first His kingdom and His righteousness, and all these things will be added to you". Therefore, do not worry about tomorrow, for tomorrow will worry about itself. Each day has enough trouble of its own. (Mathew 6:33-34). Being a Christian does not guarantee that you will not face challenges in life. The word of God says, "My brethren, count it all joy when you fall into various trials, knowing that the testing of your faith produces patience."(James 1:2-3) God said I will never leave you nor forsake you. I pray against the spirit of depression and suicide. "Rejoice not against me, O mine enemy: when I fall, I shall arise; when I sit in darkness, the LORD [shall be] a light unto me."(Micah 7:8) And we know that all things work together for good to them that love God, to them who are the called according to his purpose. (Roman 8:28). May God restore you according to Prophet Joel, "So I will restore to you the years that the swarming locust has eaten, The crawling locust, The consuming locust, And the chewing locust, My great army which I sent among you."(Joel 2:25) Weeping may endure overnight by joy comes in the morning. God will exchange your ashes for beauty. God bless you.


**Prayer**

Thank you, Lord, for healing our broken hearts. We know that Lord you always there for us. Despite our hurts, our pains, we find comfort in you. Your word says, "Come to Me, all you who labour and are heavy laden, and I will give you rest." Teach us to love the unlovable. We shall never keep a grudge against anyone. Thank you, Lord, for giving us the power to forgive. All those who have hurt us, we have forgiven them because we were forgiven too. Love keeps no record of evil. We shall not return evil with evil but evil with good. Amen


**The bible verses to study**

Psalms 34:18; John10:10; Ephesians 4:27; Luke 6:27-28; Mathew6:33-34; James 1:2-3; Micah 7:8; Joel 2:25

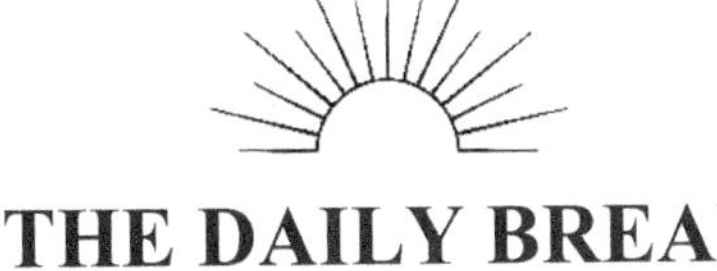

# THE DAILY BREAD

Failure. Do not take your failure as a reason to quit but a setback. When you fall rise up and dust yourself and go. Failure is not a problem but giving up is a problem. But he said to me, "My grace is sufficient for you, for my power is made perfect in weakness." Therefore, I will boast all the more gladly of my weaknesses, so that the power of Christ may rest upon me. For the sake of Christ, then, I am content with weaknesses, insults, hardships, persecutions, and calamities. For when I am weak, then I am strong". (2 Corinthians 12:9-10). Everybody fails from time to time. No one you know is perfect, and almost everyone can outline at least a few failures. God understands and prepares us for it in Proverbs 24:16. We are not perfect, even in our faith, and God wants us to understand and accept that. God knows we're going to fail every once in a while. It preordained before the foundation of the world that the lamb will be sacrificed. Yet, He also stands by us and helps us get back on our feet. Is it easy to accept failure? No. Can it make us depressed and feel down? Yes. Yet, God is there to help us work through our anger and disappointment. - "and pulled me from a lonely pit full of mud and mire. You let me stand on a rock with my feet firm, and you gave me a new song, a song of praise to you. Many will see this, and they will honour and trust you, the LORD God" (Psalm 40:2-3 )When we allow ourselves to quit and stop trying amen, we are also failing other people. Our success is not for us only but for other people including our families. We must not give up; they are so many people looking for help from us. Do not give up, God has shown favour upon your life, your faith shall never fail. God bless you.

**Prayer**

Your word says, " Do not rejoice over me, my enemy; When I fall, I will arise; When I sit in darkness, The LORD will be a light to me." When we fall, we shall never remain down as your word says, "For a righteous man may fall seven times And rise again, But the wicked shall fall by calamity." Thank you, O Lord, for the gift of life. Our hope and trust is in you Lord. All things are working together for good for us. The grace of God is sufficient for us. If God is for us who can be against us. The pain we are going through now cannot be compared to the glory that will be revealed to us. Our enemies do not rejoice against us, when we fall, we shall rise and when we sit in the darkness the Lord shall be light upon us. Amen.


**The bible verses to study.**

2 Corinthians 12:9-10; Proverbs 24:16; Psalm 40:2-3; Micah 7:8; Psalms 127:1; Psalms 37:24

# THE DAILY BREAD

Your life has never been lived by anyone and your dreams have never been dreamed by anyone else. Your fingerprints are unique, and no one have the same like yours. You are the only one in town. "For we are God's handiwork, created in Christ Jesus to do good works, which God prepared in advance for us to do" (Ephesians 2:10).But as it is written, Eye has not seen, nor ear heard, neither have entered into the heart of man, the things which God hath prepared for them that love him.( 1 Corinthians 2:9) . God paid the highest price for you, to live your life to the fullest. You have a paint brush in your hand, what are you painting. You have creative powers like your father in heaven. Go for it, God is with you. "For he whom God has sent speaks the words of God: for God gives not the Spirit by measure unto him ". (John 3:34) "And the angel of the LORD appeared unto him, and said unto him, The LORD is with thee, thou mighty man of valour". (Judges 6:12) Do not just live life without a purpose and faith. You are righteousness of God, rise up and claim your rightfully position in this life. The word of God says "For you created my inmost being you knit me together in my mother's womb. I praise you because I am fearfully and wonderfully made; your works are wonderful; I know that full well." (Psalms 139:13-15) For we are His workmanship, created in Christ Jesus for good works, which God prepared beforehand that we should walk in them. (Ephesians 2:20) . You are clothed with glory, "But one testified in a certain place, saying: "What is man that You are mindful of him, Or the son of man that You take care of him? You have made him a little lower than the angels; You have crowned him with glory and honour, And set him over the works of Your hands. You have put all things in subjection under his feet." For in that He put all in subjection under him, He left nothing that is not put under him. But now we do not yet see all things put under him."(Hebrews 2:6-8). God has already blessed you, " Then God blessed them, and God said to them, "Be fruitful and multiply; fill the earth and subdue it; have dominion over the fish of the sea, over the birds of the air, and over every living thing that moves on the earth." (Genesis 1:28) God bless you.


**Prayer**

Thank you, Lord Jesus, for the life you have given us. For you have given us life in abundance. You have set a table before us in the presence of our enemies. You have made us to lie down on greener pastures and our cups are running over. We serve a very big God, and we will not settle for less. We are a head not a tail and we are always above not beneath. The same Spirit that raised Jesus Christ from the dead dwells in us. The earnest expectation of the world is the manifestation of the children of God. Whatever is born by God shall overcome the world. Amen


**The bible verses to study.**

Ephesians 2:10; 1 Corinthians 2:9; John 3:34; Judges 6:12; Psalms 139:13-15; Ephesians 2:20; Hebrews 2:6-8; Genesis 1:28

# THE DAILY BREAD

The Beloved of God let your light shine." If we claim to have fellowship with him and yet walk in the darkness, we lie and do not live out the truth". (1 John 1:16). Jesus is the true Light, which lights every man that comes into the world. And the light shines in darkness; and the darkness comprehended it not. (John 1:5). Where there is light amen, there is power. It shows you are connected to the source. Where there is light, there is freedom. The light is good. God saw that the light is good and separated it from the darkness. Therefore, when your light is on amen, you are separated from the darkness. How can we sustain our light? The Holy Spirit in us is the one who keeps the lights on. In the parable of 10 virgins waiting for the bridegroom, 5 were foolish and 5 were wise. The 5 wise virgins took jars with oil and the 5 foolish did not. The word of God says, " But while the bridegroom was delayed, they all slumbered and slept. "And at midnight a cry was heard: 'Behold, the bridegroom is coming; go out to meet him!' Then all those virgins arose and trimmed their lamps. And the foolish said to the wise, 'Give us some of your oil, for our lamps are going out.' But the wise answered, saying, 'No, lest there should not be enough for us and you; but go rather to those who sell, and buy for yourselves.' And while they went to buy, the bridegroom came, and those who were ready went in with him to the wedding; and the door was shut. "Afterward the other virgins came also, saying, 'Lord, Lord, open to us!' But he answered and said, 'Assuredly, I say to you, I do not know you.' "Watch therefore, for you know neither the day nor the hour in which the Son of Man is coming." Mathew 25 :5-13). We should not run out of oil otherwise our lights with go off and walk in darkness. "This is the message we have heard from him and proclaim to you, that God is light, and in him is no darkness at all. If we say that we have fellowship with Him, and walk in darkness, we lie and do not practice the truth." 1 John 1:5-6) The word of God says, " Do not quench the Spirit.(1 Thessalonians 5:19) . The Holy Spirt is the source of our light. "But you will receive power when the Holy Spirit comes on you; and you will be my witnesses in Jerusalem, and in all Judea and Samaria, and to the ends of the earth" (Acts 1:8). When we have the power, our lights they shine so brighter, and we become witness of Jesus the true light. Paul pointed out that we must be filled with the Spirit, let your light shine today. God bless you.

**Prayer**

Thank you, Lord for calling us from the darkness into the marvelous light. You are the true LIGHT. We believe in you, our Lord. No matter how dark it is our Lord we shall continue to shine our lights. Weeping may endure overnight but joy comes in the morning. Help us O Lord to be a true light bringing light to those still in the darkness. We are the light of the world and the salt of the earth. We are blessed to be a blessing. We have forsaken the works of darkness to follow you. We pray that there is no darkness in our finances, in our workplaces, in our health and our families. We refuse to complain and murmur but we choose to praise God. We shall never quench the Holy Spirit. Amen

**The bible verses to stud**

Mathew 5:16; Isaiah 60:1; Daniel 12:3; 2 Corinthians 4:6; John 8:12; Mathew 5:14; 1 Peter 2:9; Psalms 119:105; Proverbs 4:18; 1 John 1:5; Mathew 5:1-13

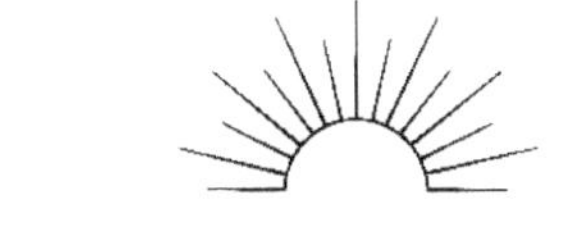

# THE DAILY BREAD

Do not lose hope. "For we do not wrestle against flesh and blood, but against principalities, against powers, against the rulers of the darkness of this age, against spiritual hosts of wickedness in heavenly places" (Ephesians 6:12). When you were saved, you had issues, things you were subject to. You gave yourself deadlines and I am going to stop this next year. But next year became next year. There might be something which the devil is still holding on your life. Paul confessed this, "For we know that the law is spiritual, but I am carnal, sold under sin. For what I am doing, I do not understand. For what I will to do, that I do not practice; but what I hate, that I do. If, then, I do what I will not to do, I agree with the law that it is good. But now, it is no longer I who do it, but sin that dwells in me. For I know that in me (that is, in my flesh) nothing good dwells; for to will is present with me, but how to perform what is good I do not find. For the good that I will to do, I do not do; but the evil I will not to do, that I practice. Now if I do what I will not to do, it is no longer I who do it, but sin that dwells in me."(Romans 7:14-21) Paul fought his battles of flesh and won through Jesus Christ. What's important is that you gave your life to Jesus, and you also prayed about it. It might look like it still have power over you but by the grace of God you will overcome it. The Holy Spirit will continue to work in your life until you are free from whatever is holding you back. "For whatsoever is born of God overcomes the world: and this is the victory that overcomes the world, even our faith. (1 John 5:4). It's not about your effort. You tried on your own, but you failed but when the grace of God kicked in you managed to overcome it. It's only by the grace of God. One day you will wonder why you do not have those cravings. The devil was defeated on the cross; we are coming from the position of victory. God has already answered your prayers. You might not see the change now. "Be anxious for nothing, but in everything by prayer and supplication, with thanksgiving, let your requests be made known to God"; (Philippians 4:6). It might not be easy to let go other habits you practiced for so many years, but do not lose hope. Because God called you from darkness into light amen it will be over before you know it. "If the Son therefore shall make you free, ye shall be free indeed". (John 8:36). The word of God is saying, "But he said to me, "My grace is sufficient for you, for my power is made perfect in weakness." Therefore, I will boast all the more gladly about my weaknesses, so that Christ's power may rest on me." ( 2 Corinthians 12:9) God bless you.


**Prayer**

We thank you Lord for calling us from the darkness into the marvellous light. You said in your word come unto me all that weary and heavy burdened and I will give you rest. You have turned our mourning into dancing and exchanged our ashes for beauty. You always give us another change O Lord . Your word says, "My grace is sufficient for you, for my power is made perfect in weakness." Order my footsteps, God because you said in your word the footsteps of the righteous man are ordered by God. We pray that out of your glorious riches you may strengthen us with power through your Spirit in our inner being, so that Christ may dwell in our hearts through faith. And we pray that we, deep rooted and established in love in Christ Jesus. Amen


**Bible Verses to study**

Proverbs 23:18; Psalms 25:3; Psalms 25:5; Psalms 33:22; Romans 8:24-25; Romans 7:14-21

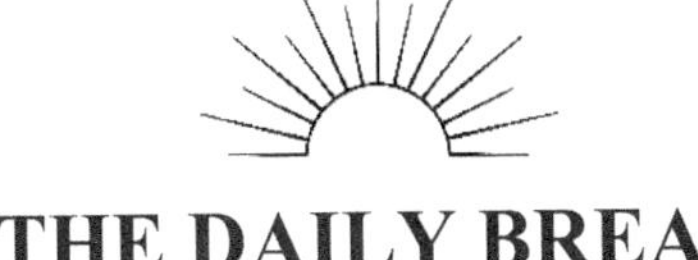

# THE DAILY BREAD

Today I want to share this word to people who are closed up. They are people who their youthful years suffered a lot. Although they have grown up, their plight has changed. Because they were not raised in love, they have a difficult in expressing love. They have built walls around themselves. They live a broken social life. They never experienced family love. That's why some people are leaving isolated lives. They are comfortable in their own environment. The devil robed you love. God is love. God will restore you and heal you. Jesus said "Come to me, all you who are weary and burdened, and I will give you rest. (Mathew 11:28). The Holy Spirit will comfort you and teach you how to love. You cannot give something you do not have. God is love. It's the nature of God to love and when God give, He gives in abundance. God will give you more love amen. When you are in Christ your world will open up. Something that was dead in you will live again. Everyone who met Christ, their lives never remained the same Jesus said "A new command I give you: Love one another. As I have loved you, so you must love one another (John 13:34)." I will refresh the weary and satisfy the faint." (Jeremiah 31:25). You need to give love so that you can get love. Get yourself involved with the activities that reach out to those who are in need, and you will see how blessed you are. This will give you a great motivation to love and opportunity to receive love. I pray that God will heal you, restore you and be able love yourself and your neighbour. May you be deep rooted in love. God is love. Whoever lives in love lives in God, and God in them. This is how love is made complete among us so that we will have confidence on the day of judgment: In this world we are like Jesus. There is no fear in love. But perfect love drives out fear, because fear has to do with punishment. The one who fears is not made perfect in love. We love because he first loved us. Whoever claims to love God yet hates a brother or sister is a liar. For whoever does not love their brother and sister, whom they have seen, cannot love God, whom they have not seen. And he has given us this command: Anyone who loves God must also love their brother and sister. (1 John 4:16-21) God bless you.

**Prayer**

We pray to you Father of Glory, that you shall give us more love. God you are love , teach us how to love. May you restore our souls and heal our broken hearts. Your word says, "For God has not given us a spirit of fear, but of power and of love and of a sound mind." Jesus, you taught us to love by saying , "I am giving you a new commandment, that you love one another; just as I have loved you, that you also love one another." We shall never give a place to the devil and keep fighting the good fight of faith. Amen

**Bible Verses to study**

1 Corinthians 13:7; 1 Peter 5:7; 2 Corinthians 12:9; 1 Saiah 6:1; Isaiah 41:10; Isaiah 57:15; John 14:1; Mathew 11:28

# THE DAILY BREAD

The voice of flesh. We are surrounded, internally and externally, with flesh voices. And the external corrupting voices are often - just an extension of our own flesh. "For the time will come when they will not endure sound doctrine. But, wishing to have their ears tickled, they will accumulate teachers according to their own desire and will turn aside their ears from the truth and turn aside to myths" (2Timothy 4:3-4). People like voices that resonate with their own. Deception is a factor. Do not assume I consider myself immune. Concerning the flesh, Paul said, "I know that nothing good dwells in me, that is, in my flesh ..." (Romans 7:18). We are also told, "there is a way that seems right to a man, but its end is the way of death" (Proverbs 14:12). In our natural state, we are described as "alienated and hostile in mind" (Colossians 1:21) This I say then, walk in the Spirit, and you shall not fulfil the lust of the flesh. For the flesh lusts against the Spirit, and the Spirit against the flesh: and these are contrary the one to the other: so that you cannot do the things that you would. But if you be led of the Spirit, you are not under the law. Now the works of the flesh are manifest, which are these; Adultery, fornication, uncleanness, lasciviousness, Idolatry, witchcraft, hatred, variance, emulations, wrath, strife, seditions, heresies, Envying, murders, drunkenness, revelling's, and such like: of the which I tell you before , as I have also told you in time past , that they which do such things shall not inherit the kingdom of God. But the fruit of the Spirit is love, joy, peace, longsuffering, gentleness, goodness, faith, Meekness, temperance: against such there is no law. And they that are Christ's have crucified the flesh with the affections and lusts. If we live in the Spirit, let us also walk in the Spirit (Galatians 5:16-25) . God bless you.

**Prayer**

God help us O Lord to do away with lustful thoughts and ungodly feelings coming from our flesh. Give us the strength to say no to my evil desires and say yes to living a righteous life. We will say like Paul, we have been crucified with Jesus Christ, it's no longer us leaving but Jesus Christ living through us. Thank you, Lord, for calling us from darkness into the greater light for your purpose. Sin shall not reign in our mortal bodies and shall not have power over us anymore, the grace of God is sufficient for us. Goodness and mercy shall follow us all the days of our lives and we shall dwell in the house of the Lord forever. Amen


**Bible Verses to study.**

Galatians 5:24; Galatians 5:16:25; Ephesians 2:3; Romans 13:14; Galatians 6:12-13; Romans 7:5; 2Timothy 4:3-4

# THE DAILY BREAD

Before some farmers sow some seeds, they make sure that the land is protected from goats, donkeys and other animals by erecting a fence. Before they put seeds in the soil, they break the ground. They put the seeds on the ground and cover it with soil protecting them from the sun and birds. Some farmers buy expensive equipment to irrigate their crop. When the crop germinates the farmer has joy. He enjoys seeing the fruit of his labour. When the farmer looks at the crop; he can identify himself with the crop. He is connected to it. He will make sure that it's well watered and it will never wither. He can even buy fertilizer to increase its growth. If a man can do all this for a crop what more has Jesus done us? Jesus Christ left his thrown in heaven and died a very painful and humiliating death on the cross for you and me so that when we believe in him, we shall not perish but have an everlasting life. The blood of Jesus bought us. Jesus, he has prepared future for us and it's not to harm us but to prosper us. We are created in his image after his likeness. When Jesus looks at us, He is full joy. He is connected to us. He can identify himself with us. Jesus has so much expectation on us. He is protective and provides. He gave us life in abundance. Jesus cares for us. God clothed us with glory. "But one testified in a certain place, saying: "What is man that You are mindful of him, Or the son of man that You take care of him? You have made him a little lower than the angels; You have crowned him with glory and honour, And set him over the works of Your hands. You have put all things in subjection under his feet." For in that He put all in subjection under him, He left nothing that is not put under him. But now we do not yet see all things put under him".( Hebrews 2:6-8). "Yet I tell you that not even Solomon in all his splendour was dressed like one of these. If that is how God clothes the grass of the field, which is here today and tomorrow is thrown into the fire, will he not much more clothe you—you of little faith? So do not worry, saying, 'What shall we eat?' or 'What shall we drink?' or 'What shall we wear?' For the pagans run after all these things, and your heavenly Father knows that you need them. But seek first his kingdom and his righteousness, and all these things will be given to you as well. Therefore, do not worry about tomorrow, for tomorrow will worry about itself. Each day has enough trouble of its own. (Mathew 6:30-34). God bless you.


## Prayer

Thank you, O Lord Jesus, for the life you have given us. We have failed you many times, but you have never given up on us. You said in your word, you shall never leave us nor forsaken us. Your word says, "Yet I tell you that not even Solomon in all his splendour was dressed like one of these. If that is how God clothes the grass of the field, which is here today and tomorrow is thrown into the fire, will he not much more clothe you—you of little faith? So do not worry, saying, 'What shall we eat?' or 'What shall we drink?' or 'What shall we wear?' For the pagans run after all these things, and your heavenly Father knows that you need them." " And my God shall supply all your need according to His riches in glory by Christ Jesus." Amen


## Bible Verses

Psalms 23:1; 2 Corinthians 9:8; Philippians 4:7; Mathew 6:30-34; Hebrews 2:6-8

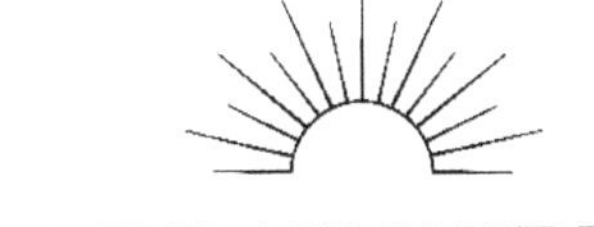

# THE DAILY BREAD

The cross. Thousands wear crosses of gold and silver. Many beautifully decorated with even diamonds. One can wear a cross, completely unaware of the meaning of the true cross, the cross of Jesus. The cross can so easily become just another item of jewellery and decoration. Only a symbol, a trademark, of the Christian faith, and nothing more. It can be a trademark of Christianity, without any bearing on its true meaning in the hearts of those who wear and use it. The cross of Jesus has immeasurable power and immense promise. Because of the cross of Christ, we can have hope, faith, love and salvation. Because of the cross of Christ, we receive forgiveness. Because of the cross of Christ, our lives find purpose and meaning. Because of the cross of Christ, we are made whole. In the cross we find healing and freedom. The cross of Christ has power. As Isaiah said centuries earlier: "Surely our grief's He Himself bore, and our sorrows He carried; Yet we ourselves esteemed Him stricken, smitten of God, and afflicted. But He was pierced through for our transgressions, He was crushed for our iniquities; The chastening for our well-being fell upon Him, and by His scourging we are healed." (Isaiah 53:4-5)Paul said: "God was in Christ reconciling the world to Him." The cross of Jesus should make a radical, reconciling, redeeming difference in your life. Jesus came to die on the cross, that we may have life. Jesus suffered on the cross, because he loves us with divine love. Jesus suffered on the cross, because it was God's salvation plan for us. The cross shows us the love of God. It assures us that God is on our side. Because of the cross, we can believe that we are saved and eternally protected by our Lord. The cross teaches us how to live! Jesus not only died to carry the punishment for our sins, but to show us that the old, sinful person must die too. Without dying we are not raised to new life for the Lord. The cross teaches us to die daily to our selfishness and greed, our own desires and impurities –and to start living for God. The cross is much more than a decoration or a symbol of our faith. The cross, an instrument of death, is our way of life. It is our priority. It is our motive to give Christ precedence, always. God bless you.

**Prayer**

Thank you, Lord Jesus, for dying for our sins. When we look at the cross, we know that our old self need to die so that we can be alive in you. We believe that you died and resurrected, and you are sitting together with the Father on the right hand. We are a living testimony of you grace. There is power in the blood of Jesus. We thank you Lord Jesus Christ for your love because whilst we were a sinners Jesus you died for us . Your word says, "But God, who is rich in mercy, because of His great love with which He loved us, even when we were dead in trespasses, made us alive together with Christ (by grace you have been saved), and raised us up   together,   and   made us sit   together   in   the heavenly places in Christ Jesus, that in the ages to come He might show the exceeding riches of His grace in His kindness toward us in Christ Jesus." Amen

**Bible Verses**

Mathew 10:38; Mathew 16:24; Mathew 27:32-35; John 19:18; Isaiah 53:4-5;Philippians 3:18; 1 Corinthians 1:18; Galatians 6:14; John 19:17; Mathew 27:32

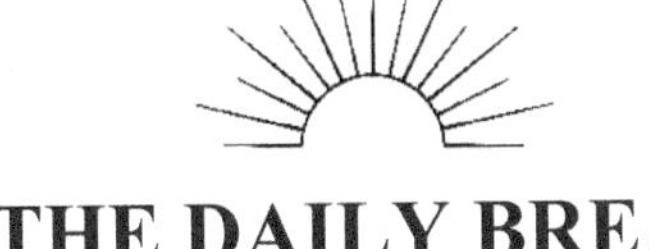

# THE DAILY BREAD

Growth. It's hard for a mother to wean her child that is to stop breast feeding. The child may cry the whole night and it might be painful for the mother, but the child has to grow. The growing part needs the child to eat solid food. The question I am asking you, are you growing. When I joined Acts Bible School 3 years ago, I was very shy to pray for people and share the word. After the first year of my studies something changed in me. My first step was to begin a prayer group at work, and we are still praying every day. I was using a minibus to work and saw an opportunity to minister and started a taxi Ministry. It was not easy to start praying in the minibus. I used to pray in a minibus every day on my way to work. People did not know my name they used to call me pastor. I left the taxi ministry now I am involved in the park ministry. We meet as Christians every day during the week to minister in the park at lunch time. God has always opened opportunities for me in my life. It's not easy grow, the responsibility, the time you spend and spiritually welfare that you go through. I discovered that I needed to grow. You cannot grow unless you practise. You can start but affecting your environment maybe at work or at home. Take responsibility and become a Cell leader or any leadership in any of small groups. This will challenge you to grow. People love to be spoon fed but as individuals who have been called by God we need to rise up. We are the light of the world and the salt of the earth. The messages I write every morning it's the grace God. With the grace of God, I wish to continue to grow so that I can feed many sheep. Challenge yourself and grow. Paul knew when he said, "Not that I have already obtained all this, or have already arrived at my goal, but I press on to take hold of that for which Christ Jesus took hold of me". (Philippians 3:12). We are in journey and our journey will end one day. If God will ask you, what you did with your life here on earth, what you will say. We need to be involved, faith without action is dead. This is my year to grow, and I know God has prepared so much for me and you. "Arise, shine, for your light has come, and the glory of the LORD rises upon you". (Isaiah 60:1). Pray and ask God to show you the opportunities suitable for you to be involved. It's not easy to grow. God bless you.

**Prayer**

We pray that Lord you will put our feet grounded on the ground. We pray that we will be humble and pray against the Spirit of being pompous. We pray that we will not settle for less, we shall continue to grow until we attain it what you have set before for us. Give us more strength O lord so that we do not become weary in doing good. Our faith shall never fail. Greater is He that is in us than he that is in the world. The grace of God is sufficient for us. Your word says, "Arise, shine, for your light has come, and the glory of the LORD rises upon you". Amen

**Bible Verses to study.**

1 Samuel 2:26; 1 Peter 3:18; Hebrews 6:1; Jeremiah 12:2; Philippians 3:12; Isaiah 60:1; 1 Corinthians 3:2

# THE DAILY BREAD

Obedience Amen....obedience is better than sacrifice. You must be aligned to the word of God entirely not some of it. That way you will stand in the light. You cannot stand in light and darkness at the same time. Do not have double standards in your life. Anything not aligned to the word of God must smell to you like some rotten eggs. You can write a book, build jails, or give a murder sentence but it will not stop people from stealing, killing, committing adultery, and drinking alcohol. They are people who believed that they could get married to unbelievers and bring them to church. But they did not know what they were getting themselves into deeper trouble. You cannot change a person no! only the Holy Spirit can, unless you change your name to the Holy Spirit. The Holy Spirit is the only one who can change a person and not jails and death sentences. But let me warn you not to be an example of living an adulterous life by dying with AIDS, example of stealing by being caught and going to jail and example of consuming alcohol by destroying your family and other families. The Holy Spirit is the only one that can change a person. Another pastor said I invited an alcoholic to church. He did not say to him alcohol is bad amen but the more he came to church one day he told the pastor that alcohol smells bad to me now, I have stopped drinking. Something happened amen. The Holy Spirit touched this man. It might be hard to convince someone to pay tithes, give offering in church but when the Holy spirit reveals it to them, and they will become faithfully. The Holy Spirit in the comforter and a teacher too. The receiving of the Holy Spirit is very important. I encourage you this morning to be obedient to the word of God. Saul disobeyed God. The word of God says, " And he sent you on a mission, saying, 'Go and completely destroy those wicked people, the Amalekites; wage war against them until you have wiped them out.' Why did you not obey the LORD? Why did you pounce on the plunder and do evil in the eyes of the LORD?" "But I did obey the LORD," Saul said. "I went on the mission the LORD assigned me. I completely destroyed the Amalekites and brought back Agag their king. The soldiers took sheep and cattle from the plunder, the best of what was devoted to God, in order to sacrifice them to the LORD your God at Gilgal." But Samuel replied: "Does the LORD delight in burnt offerings and sacrifices as much as in obeying the LORD? To obey is better than sacrifice, and to heed is better than the fat of rams." (1 Samuel 15:18-22). Saul was supposed to destroyed everything of the Amalekites, but he brought back King Agag , sheep and cattle against the will of God. God rejected Saul as a King of the children of Israel because of disobedience. Through disobedience we delay God's plan over our lives and also be cut out of God's plans. When we compromise with the word of God, we lose everything. God told Joshua, " This Book of the Law shall not depart from your mouth, but you shall meditate on it day and night, so that you may be careful to do according to all that is written in it; for then you will make your way prosperous, and then you will achieve success." (Joshua 1:8) God bless you.


**Prayer**

As your word says obedience is better than sacrifice, we pray that we shall not disobey your word. Help us O Lord to put trust in you not to lean on our understanding. Lead us O Lord to live a life pleasant in your sight not to live a life disobedience. You lead us in your path your righteousness for your name sake. We are the children of God; we were bought by the precious blood of Jesus. Your word says, "For what will it profit a man if he gains the whole world, and loses his own soul? You said in your word, "My grace is sufficient for you, for My strength is made perfect in weakness." Therefore, most gladly I will rather boast in my infirmities, that the power of Christ may rest upon me." Amen

**Bible Verses to study**

John 14:23; Deuteronomy 11:1; Romans 5:1; Ephesians 6:1-3; John 14; 1 Peter 1:14; Isaiah 1:19;

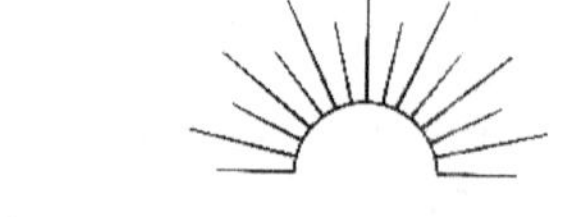

# THE DAILY BREAD

Packaging is materials used to wrap or protect goods. Packaging itself is done to protect the goods physically, sometimes as barrier from oxygen and moisture. All this done to make sure that product is not contaminated and when it reaches the intended consumer it will be in the same state. As a believer," ……you were sealed with that Holy Spirit of promise. (Ephesians 1:13) "And do not grieve the Holy Spirit of God, by whom you were sealed for the day of redemption" (Ephesians 4:30). "If the Spirit of him who raised Jesus from the dead dwells in you, he who raised Christ Jesus from the dead will also give life to your mortal bodies through his Spirit who dwells in you." (Romans 8:11). "Or do you not know that your body is a temple of the Holy Spirit within you, whom you have from God? You are not your own," (1 Corinthians 6:19). The value of the packaging determines the value of goods. If something is very expensive, the packaging must be very special. Tell yourself that this morning; I am very special because the Holy Spirit dwells in me. Your body it's just a package so you need to protect what is inside of you. It should not be contaminated with your way of life, no more living like the way you used to. The lack of knowledge is making us to grieve the Holy Spirit. Where is your hope? Where do you belong? Who are you afraid of, your situation or God. Where is your faith? Does your life point out to who you believe? You cannot stop birds flying over your head, but you can stop them from laying eggs over your head. You cannot be ignorant but let you be knowledgeable of the word God and apply it so that you do not walk as a fool but redeeming the time, because the days are evil. "For we are His workmanship, created in Christ Jesus for good works, which God prepared beforehand that we should walk in them." (Ephesians 2:10) God bless you.

**Prayer**

Thank you, Lord, for the gift of life. The life we are living is not of our own but it's from Christ Jesus who gave his life for us. We were bought through the precious blood of our Lord Jesus Christ. May God give us wisdom to walk wisely not as fools because the days are evil. Fill us up with your Spirit O Lord. If we can remember what the Lord has done for us, we will never go back again. We are the light world and the salt of the earth. We are a living epistle that everyone can read. Thank you for choosing us. Amen

**Bible Verses to study**

Ephesians 1:13; Ephesians 4:30; Romans 8:11; 1 Corinthians 6:19; Ephesians 2:10; Romans 15:13; John 14:26

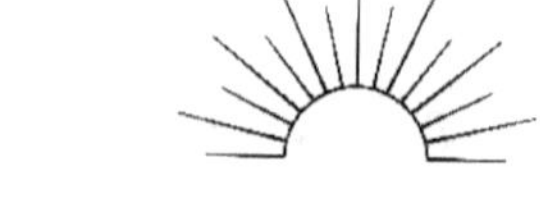

# THE DAILY BREAD

Righteousness – I can define it as being right with God. When you see your marriage is broken, your finances are broken, your family relationship is broken, your body is broken, your company is broken and your dreams are broken, why do you not make it right with God? When your relationship with God is broken, it affects all other relationships you enter in. If you take a stock take of your life this morning, will you say your relationship with God is right. Paul begged us "Therefore, I urge you, brothers and sisters, in view of God's mercy, to offer your bodies as a living sacrifice, holy and pleasing to God--this is your true and proper worship'. (Romans 12:1). If you know that, God is giving you good health every day, putting food on your table, giving you a gift of life every day, giving you angels to be in charge over you, so why don't you make your relationship with God right. "In the land of Uz there lived a man whose name was Job. This man was blameless and upright; he feared God and shunned evil." (Job 1:1). Grace does not give us license to sin, but it makes us not want to sin "For we wrestle not against flesh and blood, but against principalities, against powers, against the rulers of the darkness of this world, against spiritual wickedness in high *places*."(Ephesians 6:12). We do not need you to be Lukewarm. "So , because you are lukewarm neither hot nor cold...I am about to spit you out of my mouth" (Revelation 3:15) The devil has been robbing you from day one now it's time to show him the sign sold, I belong to Jesus who paid the highest price for me . "A thief comes only to steal and to kill and to destroy. I have come so that they may have life and have it in abundance." (John 10:10). Please just remember whatever you compromise for, you will lose it. God bless you.

## Prayer

We pray that we live a life that is pleasing to God so that we can have a right relationship with him. We need you God in our lives, finances, marriages, and Jobs. We pray that we shall offer our bodies as a living sacrifice, holy and pleasing to God--this is my true and proper worship. May we live our lives like Job who was blameless and upright; he feared God and shunned away evil. May we delight myself in you O Lord so that you can give us the desires of our hearts. We pray that we shall never give the place to the devil. May thy world be thy lamp up thy feet and thy light upon thy path. Thank you, Lord. Amen.


## Bible Verses to study

Mathew 6:33; Romans 12:1; Job 1:1; Proverbs 21:21; Romans 2:6; 1 Timothy 6:11; Psalms 37:28; Proverbs 21:3; Galatians 6:9; Philippians 4:8; Psalms 1:1